Pro HTML5
Programming

Second Edition

PETER LUBBERS
BRIAN ALBERS
FRANK SALIM

Apress®

Pro HTML5 Programming, Second Edition

ISBN-13 (pbk): 978-1-4302-3864-5

ISBN-13 (electronic): 978-1-4302-3865-2

Trademarked names, logos, and images may appear in this book. Rather than use a trademark symbol with every occurrence of a trademarked name, logo, or image we use the names, logos, and images only in an editorial fashion and to the benefit of the trademark owner, with no intention of infringement of the trademark.

The use in this publication of trade names, trademarks, service marks, and similar terms, even if they are not identified as such, is not to be taken as an expression of opinion as to whether or not they are subject to proprietary rights.

President and Publisher: Paul Manning
Lead Editor: Ben Renow-Clarke
Technical Reviewer: Tony Pye
Editorial Board: Steve Anglin, Mark Beckner, Ewan Buckingham, Gary Cornell, Morgan Ertel, Jonathan Gennick, Jonathan Hassell, Robert Hutchinson, Michelle Lowman, James Markham, Matthew Moodie, Jeff Olson, Jeffrey Pepper, Douglas Pundick, Ben Renow-Clarke, Dominic Shakeshaft, Gwenan Spearing, Matt Wade, Tom Welsh
Coordinating Editors: Debra Kelly and Jennifer L. Blackwell
Copy Editors: Heather Lang, Andy Rosenthal, and Nancy Sixsmith
Compositor: Bytheway Publishing Services
Indexer: SPI Global
Artist: SPI Global
Illustrations by: Peter Cohen
Cover Designer: Anna Ishchenko

Distributed to the book trade worldwide by Springer Science+Business Media, LLC., 233 Spring Street, 6th Floor, New York, NY 10013. Phone 1-800-SPRINGER, fax (201) 348-4505, e-mail orders-ny@springer-sbm.com, or visit www.springeronline.com.

For information on translations, please e-mail rights@apress.com, or visit www.apress.com.

Apress and friends of ED books may be purchased in bulk for academic, corporate, or promotional use. eBook versions and licenses are also available for most titles. For more information, reference our Special Bulk Sales–eBook Licensing web page at www.apress.com/bulk-sales.

The information in this book is distributed on an "as is" basis, without warranty. Although every precaution has been taken in the preparation of this work, neither the author(s) nor Apress shall have any liability to any person or entity with respect to any loss or damage caused or alleged to be caused directly or indirectly by the information contained in this work.

Any source code or other supplementary materials referenced by the author in this text is available to readers at www.apress.com. For detailed information about how to locate your book's source code, go to www.apress.com/source-code/.

For my beautiful wife, Vittoria,

and for my sons, Sean and Rocky. I am so proud of you!
And to our cat—Cornelius—may you rest (and hunt) in peace.

—Peter Lubbers

For John. You make it all worthwhile.

—Brian Albers

For people who still read books.

—Frank Salim

Contents at a Glance

Contents

Foreword

In June 2004, representatives from the semantic web community, major browser vendors, and the W3C met in San Jose, California to discuss the standards body's response to the rise of web applications. At the end of the second day, a vote was held to decide whether the W3C should augment HTML and the DOM to address the new requirements of web applications. Minutes from the event record the anonymous and curious result, "8 for, 14 against."

This schism lead to a divergence in effort: two days later, the WHATWG was formed from the major browser vendors to solve emerging issues. Meanwhile, the W3C pushed forward with the XHTML2 specification, only to drop it five years later to focus on an aligned HTML5 effort with the WHATWG.

Now, seven years since, we stand to benefit greatly from the passionate minds that have designed HTML5. The features both codify de facto standards that have been in use for years and lay the groundwork for next-generation web applications. Putting them to use means a more engaging and responsive web experience for your users and, oftentimes, far less code for you.

In this book, you'll find a well-designed learning curve bringing you up to speed on the features within HTML5 and its associated specifications. You'll learn best practices of feature detection, appropriate use cases, and a lot of the whys that you won't find in the specifications. The code examples are not plain, trivial uses of each API but instead lead you through building actual web applications. I hope this book is able to serve you well, and I hope you'll be as excited about the next generation of the web as I am.

Paul Irish
Google Chrome Developer Advocate,
Modernizr & HTML5 Boilerplate Developer

About the Authors

■ **Peter Lubbers** is the senior director of technical communication at Kaazing. An HTML5 and WebSockets enthusiast, Peter is a frequent speaker at international events and teaches HTML5 training courses worldwide. Prior to joining Kaazing, Peter worked for almost ten years as an information architect at Oracle, where he wrote award-winning books and developed patent-pending software solutions. A native of the Netherlands, Peter served as a Special Forces commando in the Royal Dutch Green Berets. Peter lives on the edge of the Tahoe National Forest in California, and in his spare time, he bungee jumps and runs ultramarathons. And, yes, he owns the original HTML5 license plate. You can follow Peter on Twitter (@peterlubbers).

■ **Brian Albers** is the vice president of research and development at Kaazing. His career in web development spans a decade and a half, including his most recent position as a senior development manager at Oracle. Brian is a regular speaker at conferences, such as Web 2.0 Expo, AJAXWorld Expo, and JavaOne, where he focuses on Web and user interface technologies. A native Texan and current California resident, Brian spends as much time as possible escaping to Hawaii. When he cannot relax on the beach, Brian can be found frequenting a variety of virtual worlds in his spare time.

■ **Frank Salim** is one of the original engineers at Kaazing who helped craft the WebSockets gateway and client strategy. Frank is a San Diego native currently residing in Mountain View, California. He holds a degree in computer science from Pomona College. When he is not programming, Frank enjoys reading, painting, and inline skating.

About the Technical Reviewer

 **Tony Pye** has a background in software consultancy, web development, and engineering. However, instead of taking his technical expertise into manufacturing, he took the path to geekdom and in 2003 became a partner and Head of Development at INK Digital Agency, one of the UK's top 100 creative agencies*

As well as having an extensive knowledge of current software and coding standards, Tony keeps a sharp eye to the future, watching for emerging technologies, thus ensuring his development team remains at the forefront of an ever-changing digital landscape. Although businesses face many challenges, Tony has the underpinning knowledge and experience to define their technical problems and produce innovative digital solutions for a range of commercial environments. While he is particularly proud of his mobile application development and a self-service touchscreen kiosk web application, which was a first for the fitness industry, he is very coy when it comes to talking about his development work on multi-million pound e-commerce web sites. Generally, though, Tony is a "thoroughly good egg," and for anyone that has a digital dilemma he is the man that can find a solution. If you'd like to talk to Tony about digital development or anything else for that matter; drop him a line: tony@inkdigitalagency.com.

*Recognized by the 2010 Recommended Agencies Register survey

Acknowledgments

I'd like to thank my wife, Vittoria, for her love and patience, and my talented sons, Sean and Rocky—reach for the stars, boys!

Thanks to my parents, Herman and Elisabeth, my sister, Alice, and my brother, David, for always believing in me, and to my late grandmother Gebbechien whose courageous acts during the Nazi occupation of Holland were a great lesson to our family.

To my coauthors, the never-tiring Brian and the code-generating human Frank, it has been an honor to work with both of you.

Thanks also to Clay at Apress for all your support, and, finally, thanks to Jonas and John at Kaazing for pushing us to write a "real" book—an "unofficial e-book" would still be just a figment of our imagination, I am sure!

—Peter Lubbers

To my parents, Ken and Patty Albers, I offer my deepest love and appreciation for the sacrifices you made to bring me so many opportunities. Without your encouragement and the values you instilled in me, I would never have completed this or any other major life journey. You've been guiding me every step of the way.

To John, my deepest thanks for your patience every time that extra hour of work stretched to two, three, or more. You amaze and inspire me.

To Pitch, Bonnie, and Penelope, a scritch on the chin and a promise that dinner won't be so late any more. To the cats who came before, your purrs stay with me.

To my coworkers at Kaazing, much appreciation for the chance to work with the best and the brightest.

And a special thanks to the editorial staff at Apress for first believing that the time was right for an HTML5 book and then for having patience with us while we attempted to document a rapidly moving target.

—Brian Albers

I'd like to thank my parents, Mary and Sabri, who are responsible for my existence and without whom this book would literally not be possible.

—Frank Salim

Introduction

HTML5 is brand new. Indeed, it isn't even completely finished yet. And if you listen to some ornery pundits, they'll tell you that HTML5 won't be ready for ten years or more!

Why, then, would anyone think that now's the time for a book called *Pro HTML5 Programming*? That's easy. Because for anyone who's looking for an extra edge to make your web application stand above the rest, the time for HTML5 is right now. The authors of this book have been working with, developing, and teaching HTML5 technologies for more than two years now and can claim with certainty that adoption of the new standards is accelerating at dizzying speeds. Even over the course of writing this book, we've been forced to continually update chapters and reevaluate our assumptions about what is ready to use.

Most users don't really understand the power that's available in the browsers they are now using. Yes, they might notice some minor interface enhancement after their favorite browser has automatically updated. But they might have no idea that this new browser version just introduced a free-form drawing canvas or real-time network communication, or any number of other potential upgrades.

With this book, we aim to help you unlock the power HTML5.

Who This Book Is For

The content in this book is intended for the experienced web application developer who is familiar with JavaScript programming. In other words, we won't be covering the basics of web development in this text. There are many existing resources to get you up to speed in the fundamentals of web programming. That said, if you see yourself in any of the following bullets, this book will likely provide you with useful insight and information you are looking for:

- You sometimes find yourself thinking, "If only my browser could. . ."

- You find yourself using page source and developer tools to dissect a particularly impressive website.

- You enjoy reading the release notes of the latest browser updates to find out what's new.

- You are looking for ways to optimize or streamline your applications.

- You are willing to tailor your website to provide the best possible experience for users on relatively recent browsers.

If any of these apply to you, this book may be a good fit with your interests.

While we take care to point out the limitations of browser support where appropriate, our aim is not to give you elaborate workarounds to make your HTML5 application run seamlessly on a ten-year-old browser. Experience has shown that the workarounds and baseline browser support are evolving so rapidly that a book like this is not the best vehicle for such information. Instead, we will focus on the specification of HTML5 and how to use it. Detailed workarounds can be found on the Internet and will become less necessary over time.

An Overview of This Book

The thirteen chapters of this book cover a selection of popular, useful, and powerful HTML5 APIs. In some cases, we have built on the capabilities introduced in earlier chapters to provide you with richer demonstrations.

Chapter 1, "Introduction to HTML5," starts off with the background of past and current versions of the HTML specification. The new high-level semantic tags are presented, along with basic changes and the rationale behind all the recent developments in HTML5. It's good to know this terrain.

Chapter 2, "Using the Canvas API", Chapter 3, "Working with SVG," and Chapter 4, "Working with Audio and Video," describe the new visual and media elements. In these chapters, the focus is on finding simpler ways to spruce up your user interface without plugins or server-side interaction.

Chapter 5, "Using the Geolocation API," introduces a truly new feature that was not easily emulated before now—the ability for an application to identify the user's current location and use that to customize the experience. Privacy is important here, so we cover some of the caveats, as well.

The next two chapters, "Using the Communication APIs" and "Using the WebSocket API," present increasingly powerful ways that HTML5 lets you communicate with other websites and stream real-time data to an application with both simplicity and minimal overhead. The techniques in these chapters will enable you to simplify the many overly complex architectures deployed on the Web today.

Chapter 8, "Using the Forms API," presents you with minimal tweaks you can make to your desktop or mobile web applications today to increase usability, as well as more fundamental changes you can make to detect page entry errors in very common usage scenarios. Chapter 9, "Using the Drag and Drop API," elaborates on the new Drag and Drop API features and shows how you can use them.

Chapters 10, 11, and 12—"Using the Web Workers API," "Using the Storage API," and "Creating Offline Web Applications"—deal with the internal plumbing of your applications. Here, you will find ways to optimize the existing functionality to obtain better performance and better data management.

Finally, Chapter 13, "The Future of HTML5," will give you a tasty preview of what's still to come.

Example Code and Companion Web Site

The code for the examples shown in this book is available online in the Source Code section of the Apress web site. Visit www.apress.com, click Source Code, and look for this book's title. You can download the source code from this book's home page. In addition, we are hosting a companion site for the book at www.prohtml5.com, from which you can also download the sample code and some practical extras.

Contacting the Authors

Thank you for buying this book. We hope you enjoy reading it and that you find it a valuable resource. Despite our best effort to avoid errors, we realize that things sometimes slip through the cracks, and we'd like to express, in advance, our regrets for any such slip-ups. We welcome your personal feedback, questions, and comments regarding this book's content and source code. You can contact us by sending us e-mail at prohtml5@gmail.com.

CHAPTER 1

Overview of HTML5

This book is about HTML5 Programming. Before you can understand HTML5 programming, however, you need to take a step back and understand what HTML5 is, a bit of the history behind it, and the differences between HTML 4 and HTML5.

In this chapter, we get right to the practical questions to which everyone wants answers. Why HTML5, and why all the excitement just now? What are the new design principles that make HTML5 truly revolutionary—but also highly accommodating? What are the implications of a plugin-free paradigm; what's in and what's out? What's new in HTML, and how does this kick off a whole new era for web developers? Let's get to it.

The Story So Far—The History of HTML5

HTML goes back a long way. It was first published as an Internet draft in 1993. The '90s saw an enormous amount of activity around HTML, with version 2.0, versions 3.2, and 4.0 (in the same year!), and finally, in 1999, version 4.01. In the course of its development, the World Wide Web Consortium (W3C) assumed control of the specification.

After the rapid delivery of these four versions though, HTML was widely considered a dead-end; the focus of web standards shifted to XML and XHTML, and HTML was put on the back burner. In the meantime, HTML refused to die, and the majority of content on the web continued to be served as HTML. To enable new web applications and address HTML's shortcomings, new features and specifications were needed for HTML.

Wanting to take the web platform to a new level, a small group of people started the Web Hypertext Application Working Group (WHATWG) in 2004. They created the HTML5 specification. They also began working on new features specifically geared to web applications—the area they felt was most lacking. It was around this time that the term Web 2.0 was coined. And it really *was* like a second new web, as static web sites gave way to more dynamic and social sites that required more features—a lot more features.

The W3C became involved with HTML again in 2006 and published the first working draft for HTML5 in 2008, and the XHTML 2 working group stopped in 2009. Another two years passed, and that is where we stand today. Because HTML5 solves very practical problems (as you will see later), browser vendors are feverishly implementing its new features, even though the specification has not been completely locked down. Experimentation by the browsers feeds back into and improves the specification. HTML5 is rapidly evolving to address real and practical improvements to the web platform.

MOMENTS IN HTML

Brian says: "Hi, I'm Brian, and I'm an HTML curmudgeon.

I authored my first home page back in 1995. At the time, a 'home page' was something you created to talk about yourself. It usually consisted of badly scanned pictures, `<blink>` tags, information about where you lived and what you were reading, and which computer-related project you were currently working on. Myself and most of my fellow 'World Wide Web developers' were attending or employed by universities.

At the time, HTML was primitive and tools were unavailable. Web applications hardly existed, other than a few primitive text-processing scripts. Pages were coded by hand using your favorite text editor. They were updated every few weeks or months, if ever.

We've come a long way in fifteen years.

Today, it isn't uncommon for users to update their online profiles many times a day. This type of interaction wouldn't have been possible if not for the steady, lurching advances in online tools that built on each previous generation.

Keep this in mind as you read this book. The examples we show here may seem simplistic at times, but the potential is limitless. Those of us who first used `<img>` tags in the mid-1990s probably had no idea that within ten years, many people would be storing and editing their photos online, but we should have predicted it.

We hope the examples we present in this book will inspire you beyond the basics and to create the new foundation of the Web for the next decade."

The Myth of 2022 and Why It Doesn't Matter

The HTML5 specification that we see today has been published as a working draft—it is not yet final. So when does it get cast in stone? Here are the key dates that you need to know. The first is 2012, which is the target date for the *candidate recommendation*. The second date is 2022, which is the *proposed recommendation*. Wait! Not so fast! Don't close this book to set it aside for ten years before you consider what these two dates actually mean.

The first and nearest date is arguably the most important one, because once we reach that stage, HTML5 will be complete. That's just around the corner. The significance of the proposed recommendation (which we can all agree is a bit distant) is that there will then be two interoperable implementations. In other words, two browsers equipped with completely interoperable implementations of the entire specifications—a lofty goal that actually makes the 2022 deadline seem ambitious. After all, we haven't even achieved that in HTML4 and only recently for CSS2!

What *is* important, right now, is that browser vendors are actively adding support for many very cool new features, and some of those are already in the Final Call for comments phase. Depending on your audience, you can start using many of these features today. Sure, any number of minor changes will need to be made down the road, but that's a small price to pay for enjoying the benefits of living on the cutting edge. Of course, if your audience uses Internet Explorer 6.0, many of the new features won't work and will require emulation—but that's still not a good reason to dismiss HTML5. After all, those users, too, will eventually be jumping to a later version. Many of them will probably move to Internet Explorer

9.0 right away, and that version of IE supports many more HTML5 features. In practice, the combination of new browsers and improving emulation techniques means you can use many HTML5 features today or in the very near future.

Who Is Developing HTML5?

We all know that a certain degree of structure is needed, and somebody clearly needs to be in charge of the specification of HTML5. That challenge is the job of three important organizations:

- *Web Hypertext Application Technology Working Group (WHATWG)*: Founded in 2004 by individuals working for browser vendors Apple, Mozilla, Google, and Opera, WHATWG develops HTML and APIs for web application development and provides open collaboration of browser vendors and other interested parties.

- *World Wide Web Consortium (W3C)*: The W3C contains the HTML working group that is currently charged with delivering their HTML5 specification.

- *Internet Engineering Task Force (IETF)*: This task force contains the groups responsible for Internet protocols such as HTTP. HTML5 defines a new WebSocket API that relies on a new WebSocket protocol, which is under development in an IETF working group.

A New Vision

HTML5 is based on various design principles, spelled out in the WHATWG specification, that truly embody a new vision of possibility and practicality.

- Compatibility
- Utility
- Interoperability
- Universal access

Compatibility and Paving the Cow Paths

Don't worry; HTML5 is not an upsetting kind of revolution. In fact, one of its core principles is to keep everything working smoothly. If HTML5 features are not supported, the behavior must degrade gracefully. In addition, since there is about 20 years of HTML content out there, supporting all that existing content is important.

A lot of effort has been put into researching common behavior. For example, Google analyzed millions of pages to discover the common ID and Class names for DIV tags and found a huge amount of repetition. For example, many people used DIV id="header" to mark up header content. HTML5 is all about solving real problems, right? So why not simply create a <header> element?

Although some features of the HTML5 standard are quite revolutionary, the name of the game is evolution not revolution. After all, why reinvent the wheel? (Or, if you must, then at least make a better one!)

3

Utility and the Priority of Constituencies

The HTML5 specification is written based upon a definite *Priority of Constituencies*. And as priorities go, "the user is king." This means, when in doubt, the specification values users over authors, over implementers (browsers), over specifiers (W3C/WHATWG), and over theoretical purity. As a result, HTML5 is overwhelmingly practical, though in some cases, less than perfect.

Consider this example. The following code snippets are all equally valid in HTML5:

```
id="prohtml5"
id=prohtml5
ID="prohtml5"
```

Sure, some will object to this relaxed syntax, but the bottom line is that the end user doesn't really care. We're not suggesting that you start writing sloppy code, but ultimately, it's the end user who suffers when any of the preceding examples generates errors and doesn't render the rest of the page.

HTML5 has also spawned the creation of XHTML5 to enable XML tool chains to generate valid HTML5 code. The serializations of the HTML or the XHTML version should produce the same DOM trees with minimal differences. Obviously, the XHTML syntax is a lot stricter, and the code in the last two examples would not be valid.

Secure by Design

A lot of emphasis has been given to making HTML5 secure right out of the starting gate. Each part of the specification has sections on security considerations, and security has been considered up front. HTML5 introduces a new origin-based security model that is not only easy to use but is also used consistently by different APIs. This security model allows us to do things in ways that used to be impossible. For example, it allows us to communicate securely across domains without having to revert to all kinds of clever, creative, but ultimately Non-secure hacks. In that respect, we definitely will not be looking back to the good old days.

Separation of Presentation and Content

HTML5 takes a giant step toward the clean separation of presentation and content. HTML5 strives to create this separation wherever possible, and it does so using CSS. In fact, most of the presentational features of earlier versions of HTML are no longer supported, but will still work, thanks to the compatibility design principle mentioned earlier. This idea is not entirely new, though; it was already in the works in HTML4 Transitional and XHTML1.1. Web designers have been using this as a best practice for a long time, but now, it is even more important to cleanly separate the two. The problems with presentational markup are:

- Poor accessibility

- Unnecessary complexity (it's harder to read your code with all the inline styling)

- Larger document size (due to repetition of style content), which translates into slower-loading pages

Interoperability Simplification

HTML5 is all about simplification and avoiding needless complexity. The HTML5 mantra? "Simple is better. Simplify wherever possible." Here are some examples of this:

- Native browser ability instead of complex JavaScript code

- A new, simplified DOCTYPE

- A new, simplified character set declaration

- Powerful yet simple HTML5 APIs

We'll say more about some of these later.

To achieve all this simplicity, the specification has become much bigger, because it needs to be much more precise—far more precise, in fact, than any previous version of the HTML specification. It specifies a legion of well-defined behaviors in an effort to achieve true browser interoperability by 2022. Vagueness simply will not make that happen.

The HTML5 specification is also more detailed than previous ones to prevent misinterpretation. It aims to define things thoroughly, especially web applications. Small wonder, then, that the specification is over 900 pages long!

HTML5 is also designed to handle errors well, with a variety of improved and ambitious error-handling plans. Quite practically, it prefers graceful error recovery to hard failure, again giving A-1 top priority to the interest of the end user. For example, errors in documents will not result in catastrophic failures in which pages do not display. Instead, error recovery is precisely defined so browsers can display "broken" markup in a standard way.

Universal Access

This principle is divided into three concepts:

- *Accessibility*: To support users with disabilities, HTML5 works closely with a related standard called Web Accessibility Initiative (WAI) Accessible Rich Internet Applications (ARIA). WAI-ARIA roles, which are supported by screen readers, can be already be added to your HTML elements.

- *Media Independence*: HTML5 functionality should work across all different devices and platforms if at all possible.

- *Support for all world languages*: For example, the new <ruby> element supports the Ruby annotations that are used in East Asian typography.

A Plugin–Free Paradigm

HTML5 provides native support for many features that used to be possible only with plugins or complex hacks (a native drawing API, native video, native sockets, and so on).

Plugins, of course, present many problems:

- Plugins cannot always be installed.

- Plugins can be disabled or blocked (for example, the Apple iPad does not ship with a Flash plugin).

- Plugins are a separate attack vector.

- Plugins are difficult to integrate with the rest of an HTML document (because of plugin boundaries, clipping, and transparency issues).

Although some plugins have high install rates (Adobe Flash, for example), they are often blocked in controlled corporate environments. In addition, some users choose to disable these plugins due to the unwelcome advertising displays that they empower. However, if users disable your plugin, they also disable the very program you're relying on to display your content.

Plugins also often have difficulty integrating their displays with the rest of the browser content, which causes clipping or transparency issues with certain site designs. Because plugins use a self-contained rendering model that is different from that of the base web page, developers face difficulties if pop-up menus or other visual elements need to cross the plugin boundaries on a page. This is where HTML5 comes on the scene, smiles, and waves its magic wand of *native* functionality. You can style elements with CSS and script with JavaScript. In fact, this is where HTML5 flexes its biggest muscle, showing us a power that just didn't exist in previous versions of HTML. It's not just that the new elements provide new functionality. It's also the added native interaction with scripting and styling that enables us to do much more than we could ever do before.

Take the new canvas element, for example. It enables us to do some pretty fundamental things that were not possible before (try drawing a diagonal line in a web page in HTML 4). However, what's most interesting is the power that we can unlock with the APIs and the styling we can apply with just a few lines of CSS code. Like well-behaved children, the HTML5 elements also play nicely together. For example, you can grab a frame from a video element and display it on a canvas, and the user can just click the canvas to play back the video from the frame you just showed. This is just one example of what a native code has to offer over a plugin. In fact, virtually *everything* becomes easier when you're not working with a black box. What this all adds up to is a truly powerful new medium, which is why we decided to write a book about HTML5 *programming*, and not just about the new elements!

What's In and What's Out?

So, what really *is* part of HTML5? If you read the specification carefully, you might not find all of the features we describe in this book. For example, you will not find Geolocation and Web Workers in there. So are we just making this stuff up? Is it all hype? No, not at all!

Many pieces of the HTML5 effort were originally part of the HTML5 specification and were then moved to separate standards documents to keep the specification focused. It was considered smarter to discuss and edit some of these features on a separate track before making them into official specifications. This way, one small contentious markup issue wouldn't hold up the show of the entire specification.

Experts in specific areas can come together on mailing lists to discuss a given feature without the crossfire of too much chatter. The industry still refers to the original set of features, including Geolocation, and so on as HTML5. Think of HTML5, then, as an umbrella term that covers the core markup, as well as many cool new APIs. At the time of this writing, these features are part of HTML5:

- Canvas (2D and 3D)

- Cross-document messaging

- Geolocation

- Audio and Video

- Forms

- MathML

- Microdata

- Server-Sent events

- Scalable Vector Graphics (SVG)

- WebSocket API and protocol

- Web origin concept

- Web storage

- Indexed database

- Application Cache (Offline Web Apps)

- Web Workers

- Drag and Drop

- XMLHttpRequest Level 2

As you can see, a lot of the APIs we cover in this book are on this list. How did we choose which APIs to cover? We chose to cover features that were at least somewhat baked. Translation? They're available in some form in more than one browser. Other (less-baked) features may only work in one special beta version of a browser, while others are still just ideas at this point.

As far as browser support goes, there are some excellent online resources that you can use to check current (and future) browser support. The site www.caniuse.com provides an exhaustive list of features and browser support broken down by browser version and the site www.html5test.com checks the support for HTML5 features in the browser you use to access it.

Furthermore, this book does not focus on providing you with the emulation workarounds to make your HTML5 applications run seamlessly on antique browsers. Instead, we will focus primarily on the specification of HTML5 and how to use it. That said, for each of the APIs we do provide some example code that you can use to detect its availability. Rather than using *user agent* detection, which is often unreliable, we use *feature* detection. For that, you can also use *Modernizr*—a JavaScript library that provides very advanced HTML5 and CSS3 feature detection. We highly recommend you use Modernizr in your applications, because it is hands-down the best tool for this.

MORE MOMENTS IN HTML

Frank says: "Hi, I'm Frank, and I sometimes paint.

One of the first HTML canvas demonstrations I saw was a basic painting application that mimicked the user interface of Microsoft Paint. Although it was decades behind the state of the art in digital painting and, at the time, ran in only a fraction of existing browsers, it got me thinking about the possibilities it represented.

When I paint digitally, I typically use locally installed desktop software. While some of these programs are excellent, they lack the characteristics that make web applications so great. In short, they are disconnected. Sharing digital paintings has, to date, involved exporting an image from a painting application and uploading it to the Web. Collaboration or critiques on a live canvas are out of the question. HTML5 applications can short-circuit the export cycle and make the creative process fit into the online world along with finished images.

The number of applications that cannot be implemented with HTML5 is dwindling. For text, the Web is already the ultimate two-way communication medium. Text-based applications are available in entirely web-based forms. Their graphical counterparts, like painting, video editing, and 3D modeling software, are just arriving now.

We can now build great software to create and enjoy images, music, movies, and more. Even better, the software we make will be on and off the Web: a platform that is ubiquitous, empowering, and online."

What's New in HTML5?

Before we start programming HTML5, let's take a quick look at what's new in HTML5.

New DOCTYPE and Character Set

First of all, the DOCTYPE for web pages has been greatly simplified. Compare, for example, the following HTML4 DOCTYPEs:

```
<!DOCTYPE HTML PUBLIC "-//W3C//DTD HTML 4.01 Transitional//EN"
 "http://www.w3.org/TR/html4/loose.dtd">
```

Who could ever remember any of these? We certainly couldn't. We would always just copy and paste some lengthy DOCTYPE into the page, always with a worry in the back of our minds, "Are you absolutely sure you pasted the right one?" HTML5 neatly solves this problem as follows:

```
<!DOCTYPE html>
```

Now *that's* a DOCTYPE you might just remember. Like the new DOCTYPE, the character set declaration has also been abbreviated. It used to be

```
<meta http-equiv="Content-Type" content="text/html; charset=utf-8">
```

Now, it is:

```
<meta charset="utf-8">
```

You can even leave off the quotation marks around "utf-8" if you want to. Using the new DOCTYPE triggers the browser to display pages in standards mode. For example, Figure 1-1 shows the information you will see if you open an HTML5 page in Firefox, and you click Tools ➤ Page Info. In this example, the page is rendered in standards mode.

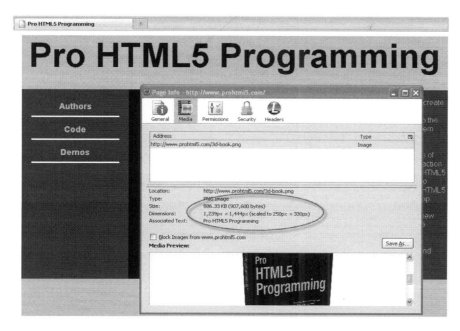

Figure 1-1. *A page rendered in standards-compliant mode*

When you use the new HTML5 DOCTYPE, it triggers browsers to render the page in standards-compliant mode. As you may know, Web pages can have different rendering modes, such as Quirks, Almost Standards, and Standards (or no-quirks) mode. The DOCTYPE indicates to the browser which mode to use and what rules are used to validate your pages. In Quirks mode, browsers try to avoid breaking pages and render them even if they are not entirely valid. HTML5 introduces new elements and has marked others as obsolete (more on this in the next section). If you use these obsolete elements, your page will not be valid. However, browsers will continue to render them as they used to.

New and Deprecated Elements

HTML5 introduces many new markup elements, which it groups into seven different content types. These are shown below in Table 1-1.

Table 1-1. *HTML5 Content Types*

Content Type	Description
Embedded	Content that imports other resources into the document, for example audio, video, canvas, and iframe
Flow	Elements used in the body of documents and applications, for example form, h1, and

	small
Heading	Section headers, for example h1, h2, and hgroup
Interactive	Content that users interact with, for example audio or video controls, button, and textarea
Metadata	Elements—commonly found in the head section— that set up the presentation or behavior of the rest of the document, for example script, style, and title
Phrasing	Text and text markup elements, for example mark, kbd, sub, and sup
Sectioning	Elements that define sections in the document, for example article, aside, and title

Most of these elements can be styled with CSS. In addition, some of them, such as canvas, audio, and video, can be used by themselves, though they are accompanied by APIs that allow for fine-grained native programmatic control. These APIs will be discussed in much more detail later in this book.

It is beyond the scope of this book to discuss all these new elements, but most of the sectioning elements (discussed in the next section) are new. The canvas, audio, and video elements are also new in HTML5.

Likewise, we're not going to provide an exhaustive list of all the deprecated tags (there are many good online resources online for this), but many of the elements that performed inline styling have been marked as obsolete in favor of using CSS, such as big, center, font, and basefont.

Semantic Markup

One content type that contains many new HTML5 elements is the *sectioning* content type. HTML5 defines a new *semantic* markup to describe an element's content. Using semantic markup doesn't provide any immediate benefits to the end user, but it does simplify the design of your HTML pages. What's more, it will make your pages more machine-readable and accessible. For example, search and syndication engines will definitely be taking advantage of these elements as they crawl and index pages.

As we said before, HTML5 is all about paving the cow paths. Google and Opera analyzed millions of pages to discover the common ID names for DIV tags and found a huge amount of repetition. For example, since many people used DIV id="footer" to mark up footer content, HTML5 provides a set of new sectioning elements that you can use in modern browsers right now. Table 1-2 shows the different semantic markup elements.

Table 1-2. New Sectioning HTML5 Elements

Sectioning Element	Description
header	Header content (for a page or a section of the page)
footer	Footer content (for a page or a section of the page)
section	A section in a web page

article	Independent article content
aside	Related content or pull quotes
nav	Navigational aids

All of these elements can be styled with CSS. In fact, as we described in the utility design principle earlier, HTML5 pushes the separation of content and presentation, so you have to style your page using CSS styles in HTML5. Listing 1-1 shows what an HTML5 page might look like. It uses the new DOCTYPE, character set, and semantic markup elements—in short, the new sectioning content. The code file (sample.html) is available in the code/intro folder.

Listing 1-1. An Example HTML5 Page

```
<!DOCTYPE html>
<html>

<head>
  <meta charset="utf-8" >
  <title>HTML5</title>
  <link rel="stylesheet" href="html5.css">
</head>

<body>
  <header>
    <h1>Header</h1>
    <h2>Subtitle</h2>
    <h4>HTML5 Rocks!</h4>
  </header>

  <div id="container">
      <nav>
        <h3>Nav</h3>
        <a href="http://www.example.com">Link 1</a>
        <a href="http://www.example.com">Link 2</a>
        <a href="http://www.example.com">Link 3</a>
      </nav>
        <section>
        <article>
          <header>
            <h1>Article Header</h1>
          </header>
          <p>Lorem ipsum dolor HTML5 nunc aut nunquam sit amet, consectetur adipiscing
elit. Vivamus at
                  est eros, vel fringilla urna.</p>
          <p>Per inceptos himenaeos. Quisque feugiat, justo at vehicula pellentesque,
turpis
                  lorem dictum nunc.</p>
          <footer>
            <h2>Article Footer</h2>
```

```
        </footer>
      </article>
      <article>
        <header>
          <h1>Article Header</h1>
        </header>
        <p>HTML5: "Lorem ipsum dolor nunc aut nunquam sit amet, consectetur
              adipiscing elit. Vivamus at est eros, vel fringilla urna. Pellentesque
odio</p>
        <footer>
          <h2>Article Footer</h2>
        </footer>
      </article>
    </section>
    <aside>
      <h3>Aside</h3>
        <p>HTML5: "Lorem ipsum dolor nunc aut nunquam sit amet, consectetur adipiscing
              elit. Vivamus at est eros, vel fringilla urna. Pellentesque odio
rhoncus</p>
    </aside>
    <footer>
      <h2>Footer</h2>
    </footer>
  </div>
</body>
</html>
```

Without styles, the page would be pretty dull to look at. Listing 1-2 shows some of the CSS code that can be used to style the content. The code file (html5.css) is available in the code/intro folder. This style sheet uses some of the new CSS3 features, such as rounded corners (border-radius) and rotate transformations (transform: rotate();). CSS3—just like HTML5 itself—is still under development, and it is modularized with subspecifications for easier browser uptake (for example, transformation, animation, and transition are all areas that are in separate subspecifications).

Experimental CSS3 features are prefixed with vendor strings to avoid namespace conflicts should the specifications change. To display rounded corners, gradients, shadows, and transformations, it is currently necessary to use prefixes such as -moz- (for Mozilla), o- (for Opera), -webkit- (for WebKit-based browsers such as Safari and Chrome), and -ms- (for Internet Explorer) in your declarations.

Listing 1-2. *CSS File for the HTML5 Page*

```
body {
        background-color:#CCCCCC;
        font-family:Geneva,Arial,Helvetica,sans-serif;
        margin: 0px auto;
        max-width:900px;
        border:solid;
        border-color:#FFFFFF;
}

header {
        background-color: #F47D31;
        display:block;
```

```css
        color:#FFFFFF;
        text-align:center;
}

header h2 {
        margin: 0px;
}

h1 {
        font-size: 72px;
        margin: 0px;
}

h2 {
        font-size: 24px;
        margin: 0px;
        text-align:center;
        color: #F47D31;
}

h3 {
        font-size: 18px;
        margin: 0px;
        text-align:center;
        color: #F47D31;
}

h4 {
        color: #F47D31;
        background-color: #fff;
        -webkit-box-shadow: 2px 2px 20px #888;
        -webkit-transform: rotate(-45deg);
        -moz-box-shadow: 2px 2px 20px #888;
        -moz-transform: rotate(-45deg);
        position: absolute;
        padding: 0px 150px;
        top: 50px;
        left: -120px;
        text-align:center;

}

nav {
        display:block;
        width:25%;
        float:left;
}

nav a:link, nav a:visited {
        display: block;
        border-bottom: 3px solid #fff;
        padding: 10px;
```

```
                text-decoration: none;
                font-weight: bold;
                margin: 5px;
        }

        nav a:hover {
                color: white;
                background-color: #F47D31;
        }

        nav h3 {
                margin: 15px;
                color: white;
        }

        #container {
                background-color: #888;
        }

        section {
                display:block;
                width:50%;
                float:left;
        }

        article {
                background-color: #eee;
                display:block;
                margin: 10px;
                padding: 10px;
                -webkit-border-radius: 10px;
                -moz-border-radius: 10px;
                border-radius: 10px;
                -webkit-box-shadow: 2px 2px 20px #888;
                -webkit-transform: rotate(-10deg);
                -moz-box-shadow: 2px 2px 20px #888;
                -moz-transform: rotate(-10deg);
        }

        article header {
                -webkit-border-radius: 10px;
                -moz-border-radius: 10px;
                border-radius: 10px;
                padding: 5px;

        }

        article footer {
                -webkit-border-radius: 10px;
                -moz-border-radius: 10px;
                border-radius: 10px;
                padding: 5px;
```

```
}

article h1 {
        font-size: 18px;
}


aside {
        display:block;
        width:25%;
        float:left;
}



aside h3 {
        margin: 15px;
        color: white;
}

aside p {
        margin: 15px;
        color: white;
        font-weight: bold;
        font-style: italic;
}


footer {
        clear: both;
        display: block;
        background-color: #F47D31;
        color:#FFFFFF;
        text-align:center;
        padding: 15px;
}

footer h2 {
        font-size: 14px;
        color: white;
}


/* links */
a {
        color: #F47D31;
}

a:hover {
        text-decoration: underline;
}
```

Figure 1-2 shows an example of the page in Listing 1-1, styled with CSS (and some CSS3) styles. Keep in mind, however, that there is no such thing as a typical HTML5 page. Anything goes, really, and this example uses many of the new tags mainly for purposes of demonstration.

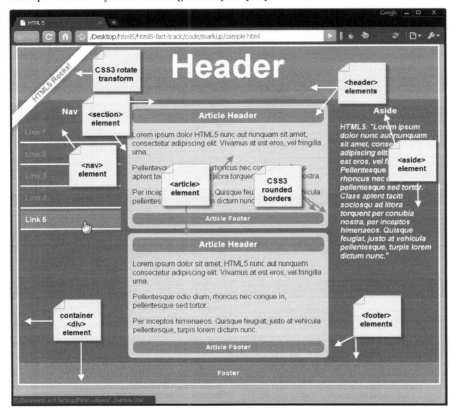

Figure 1-2. An HTML5 page with all the new semantic markup elements

One last thing to keep in mind is that browsers may seem to render things as if they actually understand these new elements. The truth is, however, that these elements could have been renamed foo and bar and then styled, and they would have been rendered the same way (but of course, they would not have any benefits in search engine optimization). The one exception to this is Internet Explorer, which requires that elements be part of the DOM. So, if you want to see these elements in IE, you must programmatically insert them into the DOM and display them as block elements. A handy script that does that for you is html5shiv (http://code.google.com/p/html5shiv/).

Simplifying Selection Using the Selectors API

Along with the new semantic elements, HTML5 also introduces new simple ways to find elements in your page DOM. Table 1-3 shows the previous versions of the document object allowed developers to make a few calls to find specific elements in the page.

Table 1-3. *Previous JavaScript Methods to Find Elements*

Function	Description	Example
getElementById()	Returns the element with the specified id attribute value	`<div id="foo">` `getElementById("foo");`
getElementsByName()	Returns all elements whose name attribute has the specified value	`<input type="text" name="foo">` `getElementsByName("foo");`
getElementsByTagName()	Return all elements whose tag name matches the specified value	`<input type="text">` `getElementsByTagName("input");`

With the new Selectors API, there are now more precise ways to specify which elements you would like to retrieve without resorting to looping and iterating through a document using standard DOM. The Selectors API exposes the same selector rules present in CSS as a means to find one or more elements in the page. For example, CSS already has handy rules for selecting elements based on their nesting, sibling, and child patterns. The most recent versions of CSS add support for more pseudo-classes—for example, whether an object is enabled, disabled, or checked—and just about any combination of properties and hierarchy you could imagine. To select elements in your DOM using CSS rules, simply utilize one of the functions shown in Table 1-4.

Table 1-4. *New QuerySelector Methods*

Function	Description	Example	Result
querySelector()	Return the first element in the page which matches the specified selector rules(s)	`document.querySelector("input.error");`	Return the first input field with a style class of "error"
querySelectorAll()	Returns all elements which match the specified rule or rules	`document.querySelectorAll("#results td");`	Return any table cells inside the element with id results

It is also possible to send more than one selector rule to the Selector API functions, for example:

```
// select the first element in the document with the
// style class highClass or the style class lowClass
var x = document.querySelector(".highClass", ".lowClass");
```

In the case of querySelector(), the first element that matches either rule is selected. In the case of querySelectorAll(), any element matching any of the listed rules is returned. Multiple rules are comma-separated.

The new Selector API makes it easy to select sections of the document that were painful to track before. Assume, for example, that you wanted the ability to find whichever cell of a table currently had the mouse hovering over it. Listing 1-3 shows how this is trivially easy with a selector. The example files for this (querySelector.html and querySelectorAll.html) are located in the code/intro directory.

Listing 1-3. Using the Selector API

```
<!DOCTYPE html>
<html>

<head>
  <meta charset="utf-8" />
  <title>Query Selector Demo</title>

  <style type="text/css">
    td {
      border-style: solid;
      border-width: 1px;
      font-size: 300%;
    }

    td:hover {
      background-color: cyan;
    }

    #hoverResult {
      color: green;
      font-size: 200%;
    }
  </style>
</head>

<body>
  <section>
    <!-- create a table with a 3 by 3 cell display -->
    <table>
      <tr>
        <td>A1</td> <td>A2</td> <td>A3</td>
      </tr>
      <tr>
        <td>B1</td> <td>B2</td> <td>B3</td>
      </tr>
      <tr>
        <td>C1</td> <td>C2</td> <td>C3</td>
      </tr>
    </table>

    <div>Focus the button, hover over the table cells, and hit Enter to identify them
```

```
using querySelector('td:hover').</div>
    <button type="button" id="findHover" autofocus>Find 'td:hover' target</button>
    <div id="hoverResult"></div>

    <script type="text/javascript">
      document.getElementById("findHover").onclick = function() {
        // find the table cell currently hovered in the page
        var hovered = document.querySelector("td:hover");
        if (hovered)
          document.getElementById("hoverResult").innerHTML = hovered.innerHTML;
      }
    </script>
  </section>

</body>
</html>
```

As you can see from this example, finding the element a user is hovering over is a one-line exercise using:

```
var hovered = document.querySelector("td:hover");
```

■ **Note** Not only are the Selector APIs handy, but they are often faster than traversing the DOM using the legacy child retrieval APIs. Browsers are highly optimized for selector matching in order to implement fast style sheets.

It should not be too surprising to find that the formal specification of selectors is separated from the specification for CSS at the W3C. As you've seen here, selectors are generally useful outside of styling. The full details of the new selectors are outside the scope of this book, but if you are a developer seeking the optimal ways to manipulate your DOM, you are encouraged to use the new Selectors API to rapidly navigate your application structure.

JavaScript Logging and Debugging

Though they're not technically a feature of HTML5, JavaScript logging and in-browser debugging tools have been improved greatly over the past few years. The first great tool for analyzing web pages and the code running in them was the Firefox add-on, Firebug.

Similar functionality can now be found in all the other browsers' built-in development tools: Safari's Web Inspector, Google's Chrome Developer Tools, Internet Explorer's Developer Tools, and Opera's Dragonfly. Figure 1-3 shows the Google Chrome Developer Tools (use the shortcut key CTRL + Shift + J on Windows or Command + Option + J on Mac to access this) that provide a wealth of information about your web pages; these include a debugging console, an elements View, a resource view, and a script view, to name just a few.

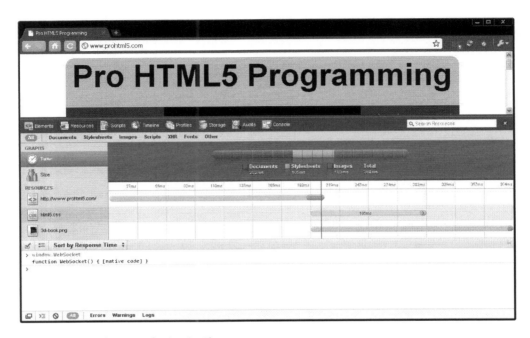

Figure 1-3. Developer Tools view in Chrome

Many of the debugging tools offer a way to set breakpoints to halt code execution and analyze the state of the program and the current state of the variables. The console.log API has become the de facto logging standard for JavaScript developers. Many browsers offer a split-pane view that allows you to see messages logged to the console. Using console.log is much better than making a call to alert(), since it does not halt program execution.

window.JSON

JSON is a relatively new and increasingly popular way to represent data. It is a subset of JavaScript syntax that represents data as object literals. Due to its simplicity and natural fit in JavaScript programming, JSON has become the de facto standard for data interchange in HTML5 applications. The canonical API for JSON has two functions, parse() and stringify() (meaning serialize or convert to string).

To use JSON in older browsers, you need a JavaScript library (several can be found at http://json.org). Parsing and serializing in JavaScript are not always as fast as you would like, so to speed up things, newer browsers now have a native implementation of JSON that can be called from JavaScript. The native JSON object is specified as part of the ECMAScript 5 standard covering the next generation of the JavaScript language. It is one of the first parts of ECMAScript 5 to be widely implemented. Every modern browser now has window.JSON, and you can expect to see quite a lot of JSON used in HTML5 applications.

DOM Level 3

One of the most maligned parts of web application development has been event handling. While most browsers support standard APIs for events and elements, Internet Explorer differs. Early on, Internet Explorer implemented an event model that differed from the eventual standard. Internet Explorer 9 (IE9) now supports DOM Level 2 and 3 features, so you can finally use the same code for DOM manipulation and event handling in all HTML5 browsers. This includes the ever-important addEventListener() and dispatchEvent() methods.

Monkeys, Squirrelfish, and Other Speedy Oddities

The latest round of browser innovations isn't just about new tags and new APIs. One of the most significant recent changes is the rapid evolution of JavaScript/ECMAScript engines in the leading browsers. Just as new APIs open up capabilities that were impossible in last-generation browsers, speedups in the execution of the overall scripting engine benefit both existing web applications and those using the latest HTML5 features. Think your browser can't handle complex image or data processing, or the editing of lengthy manuscripts? Think again.

For the last few years, browser vendors have been in a virtual arms race to see who could develop the fastest JavaScript engine. While the earliest iterations of JavaScript were purely interpreted, the newest engines compile script code directly to native machine code, offering speedups of orders of magnitude compared to the browsers of the mid-2000s.

The action pretty much began when Adobe donated its just-in-time (JIT) compilation engine and virtual machine for ECMAScript—code named Tamarin—to the Mozilla project in 2006. Although only pieces of the Tamarin technology remain in the latest versions of Mozilla, the donation of Tamarin helped spawn new scripting engines in each of the browsers, with names that are just as intriguing as the performance they claim.

Table 1-5. Web Browser JavaScript Engines

Browser	Engine Name	Notes
Apple Safari	Nitro (otherwise know as SquirrelFish Extreme)	Released in Safari 4 and refined in version 5, it introduces byte code optimizations and a context-threaded native compiler.
Google Chrome	V8	Since Chrome 2, it uses generational garbage collection for high memory scalability without interruptions.
Microsoft Internet Explorer	Chakra	Introduced in IE 9, Chakra focuses on background compilation and an efficient type system and demonstrates a tenfold improvement over IE8.
Mozilla Firefox	JägerMonkey	Refined from version 3.5, this combines fast interpretation with native compilation from trace trees.
Opera	Carakan	This one uses register-based byte code and selective native compilation and claims improvements of 75% on version 10.50.

All in all, this healthy competition among browser vendors is bringing the performance of JavaScript ever closer to that of native desktop application code.

STILL MORE MOMENTS IN HTML

Peter says: "Speaking of competition, and speedy oddities, my name is Peter and running is my thing—a lot of running.

Ultra running is a great sport where you meet great people. While running the last miles of a 100-mile race or a 165-mile trail run, you really get to know people in a very new way. At that point, you're really stripped down to your essence, the place where great friendships can happen. There's still the element of competition, to be sure, but most of all there's a deep sense of camaraderie. But I digress here.

To keep track of how my friends are doing in races that I can't attend (for example, when I am writing an HTML5 book), I usually follow along on the race websites. Not surprisingly, the 'live tracking' options are often quite unreliable.

A few years ago, I stumbled upon a site for a European race that had all the right ideas. They gave GPS trackers to the front runners and then displayed these racers on a map (we'll build some similar demonstrations in this book using Geolocation and WebSocket). Despite the fact that it was quite a primitive implementation (users had to actually click "refresh the page" to see updates!), I could instantly see the incredible potential.

Now, just a few years later, HTML5 provides us with tools to build these sorts of live race tracking websites with APIs such as Geolocation for location-aware applications and WebSockets for real-time updates. There's no doubt in my mind—HTML5 has crossed the finish line a winner!"

Summary

In this chapter, we have given you a general overview of the essentials of HTML5.

We charted the history of its development and some of the important dates coming up. We also outlined the four new design principles behind the HTML5 era that is now dawning: compatibility, utility, interoperability, and universal access. Each one of these principles opens the door to a world of possibilities and closes the door on a host of practices and conventions that are now rendered obsolete. We then introduced HTML5's startling new plugin-free paradigm, and we reviewed what's new in HTML5, such as a new DOCTYPE and character set, lots of new markup elements, and we discussed the race for JavaScript supremacy.

In the next chapter, we'll begin by exploring the programming side of HTML5, starting with the Canvas API.

CHAPTER 2

Using the Canvas API

In this chapter, we'll explore what you can do with the Canvas API—a cool API that enables you to dynamically generate and render graphics, charts, images, and animation. We'll walk you through using the basics of the rendering API to create a drawing that can scale and adjust to the browser environment. We'll show you how to create dynamic pictures based on user input in a heatmap display. Of course, we'll also alert you to the pitfalls of using Canvas and share tricks to overcome them.

This chapter presumes only a minimal amount of graphics expertise, so don't be afraid to jump in and try out one of the most powerful features of HTML5.

Overview of HTML5 Canvas

An entire book could be written about the use of the Canvas API (and it wouldn't be a small book). Because we have only a chapter, we're going to cover (what we think is) the most commonly used functionality in this very extensive API.

History

The canvas concept was originally introduced by Apple to be used in Mac OS X WebKit to create *dashboard widgets*. Before the arrival of canvas, you could only use drawing APIs in a browser through plug-ins such as Adobe plug-ins for Flash and Scalable Vector Graphics (SVG), Vector Markup Language (VML) only in Internet Explorer, or other clever JavaScript hacks.

Try, for example, to draw a simple diagonal line without a canvas element—it sounds easy, but it is a fairly complex task if you do not have a simple two-dimensional drawing API at your disposal. Canvas provides just that, and because it is an extremely useful thing to have in the browser, it was added to the HTML5 specification.

Early on, Apple hinted at possibly reserving the intellectual property rights in the WHATWG draft of the canvas specification, which caused concern at the time among some followers of web standardization. In the end, however, Apple disclosed the patents under the W3C's royalty-free patent licensing terms.

SVG versus Canvas

Peter says: "Canvas is essentially a *bitmap* canvas, and as such images that are drawn on a canvas are final and cannot be resized in the way that Scalable Vector Graphic (SVG) images can. Furthermore, objects drawn on a canvas are not part of the page's DOM or part of any namespace—something that is considered a weakness if you need hit detection or object-based updates. SVG images, on the other hand can be scaled seamlessly at different resolutions and allow for hit detection (knowing precisely where an image is clicked).

Why then, would the WHATWG HTML5 specification not use SVG exclusively? Despite its obvious shortcomings, the HTML5 Canvas API has two things going for it: it performs well because it does not have to store objects for every primitive it draws, and it is relatively easy to implement the Canvas API based on many of the popular two-dimensional drawing APIs found in other programming languages. Ultimately, it is better to have one bird in the hand than two in the bush."

What Is a Canvas?

When you use a canvas element in your web page, it creates a rectangular area on the page. By default, this rectangular area is 300 pixels wide and 150 pixels high, but you can specify the exact size and set other attributes for your canvas element. Listing 2-1 shows the most basic canvas element that can be added to an HTML page.

Listing 2-1. *A Basic Canvas Element*

```
<canvas></canvas>
```

Once you have added a canvas element to your page, you can use JavaScript to manipulate it any way you want. You can add graphics, lines, and text to it; you can draw on it; and you can even add advanced animations to it.

The Canvas API supports the same two-dimensional drawing operations that most modern operating systems and frameworks support. If you have ever programmed two-dimensional graphics in recent years, you will probably feel right at home with the Canvas API because it is designed to be similar to existing systems. If you haven't, you're about to discover how much more powerful a rendering system can be than the previous images and CSS tricks developers have used for years to create web graphics.

To programmatically use a canvas, you have to first get its *context*. You can then perform actions on the context and finally apply those actions to the context. You can think of making canvas modifications as similar to database transactions: you start a transaction, perform certain actions, and then commit the transaction.

Canvas Coordinates

As shown in Figure 2-1, coordinates in a canvas start at x=0,y=0 in the upper-left corner—which we will refer to as the *origin*—and increase (in pixels) horizontally over the x-axis and vertically over the y-axis.

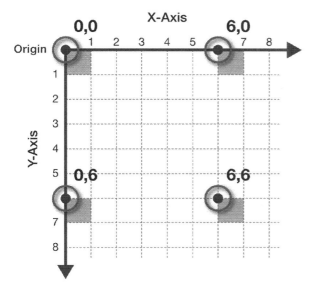

Figure 2-1. *x and y coordinates on a canvas*

When Not to Use Canvas

Although the canvas element is great and very useful, you should *not* use the canvas element when another element will suffice. For example, it would not be a good idea to dynamically draw all the different headings for an HTML document on a canvas instead of simply using heading styles (H1, H2, and so on) that are meant for that purpose.

Fallback Content

In case your web page is accessed by a browser that does not support the canvas element or a subset of the Canvas API features, it is a good idea to provide an alternate source. For example, you can provide an alternate image or just some text that explains what the user could be enjoying if they actually used a modern browser. Listing 2-2 shows how alternate text can be specified inside a canvas element. Browsers that do not support the canvas element will simply render this fallback content.

Listing 2-2. *Use of Fallback Text Inside a Canvas Element*

```
<canvas>
  Update your browser to enjoy canvas!
</canvas>
```

Instead of the previous text shown, you can also point to an image that can be displayed in case the browser does not support the canvas element.

What About Canvas Accessibility?

Peter says: "Providing alternate images or alternate text raises the subject of *accessibility*—an area in which the Canvas specification is, unfortunately, still lacking significantly. For example, there is no native method for inserting text alternatives for images that are being inserted into a canvas, and there is no native method to provide alternate text to match text generated with the canvas text API. At the time of this writing, there are no accessibility hooks that can be used with the dynamically generated content in a canvas, but a task force is working on designing them. Let's hope this improves with time."

One of the current proposals from the HTML5 designers for handling alternate, accessible canvas content is to use this fallback content section. However, in order for this to be useful for screen readers and other accessibility tools, the fallback content needs to be keyboard navigable even when a canvas is supported and displayed. While some browsers are supporting this capability now, you should not rely on it to support users with special needs. Using a separate section of the page to display canvas alternatives is recommended for now. As an added bonus, many users might enjoy using alternative controls or displays as a better way to quickly understand and navigate the page or application.

Future iterations of the Canvas API might also include focusable sub-areas of the canvas display and controls to interact with them. If your image display requires significant interaction, however, consider using SVG as an alternative to the Canvas API. SVG also allows drawing, but it integrates with the browser DOM as well.

CSS and Canvas

As with most HTML elements, CSS can be applied to the canvas element itself to add borders, padding, margins, etc. Additionally, some CSS values are inherited by the contents of the canvas; fonts are a good example, as fonts drawn into a canvas default to the settings of the canvas element itself.

Furthermore, properties set on the context used in canvas operations follow the syntax you may already be familiar with from CSS. Colors and fonts, for example, use the same notation on the context that they use throughout any HTML or CSS document.

Browser Support for HTML5 Canvas

With the arrival of Internet Explorer 9, all browser vendors now provide support for HTML5 Canvas, and it is already in the hands of a majority of users. This is a major milestone in web development, allowing 2D drawing to thrive on the modern Web.

In spite of the dwindling market share of previous versions of Internet Explorer, it is still a good idea to first test whether HTML5 Canvas is supported before you use the APIs. The section "Checking for Browser Support" later in this chapter will show you how you can programmatically check for browser support.

Using the HTML5 Canvas APIs

In this section, we'll explore the use of the Canvas APIs in more detail. For the sake of illustration—no pun intended—we will use the various Canvas APIs to build a logo-like display of a forest scene with trees and a beautiful trail-running path suitable for a long-distance race event. Although our example will not win any awards for graphical design, it should serve to illustrate the various capabilities of HTML5 Canvas in a reasonable order.

Checking for Browser Support

Before you use the canvas element, you will want to make sure there is support in the browser. This way, you can provide some alternate text in case there is no support in their antique browser. Listing 2-3 shows one way you can use to test for browser support.

Listing 2-3. Checking for Browser Support

```
try {
  document.createElement("canvas").getContext("2d");
  document.getElementById("support").innerHTML =
    "HTML5 Canvas is supported in your browser.";
} catch (e) {
  document.getElementById("support").innerHTML = "HTML5 Canvas is not supported ↵
                                      in your browser.";
}
```

In this example, you try to create a canvas object and access its context. If there is an error, you will catch it and know that Canvas is not supported. A previously defined support element on the page is updated with a suitable message to reflect whether there is browser support or not.

This test will indicate whether the canvas element itself is supported by the browser. It will not indicate which capabilities of the Canvas are supported. At the time of this writing, the API is stable and well-supported, so this should generally not be an issue to worry about.

Additionally, it is a good idea to supply fallback content to your canvas element, as shown in Listing 2-3.

Adding a Canvas to a Page

Adding a canvas element in an HTML page is pretty straight-forward. Listing 2-4 shows the canvas element that can be added to an HTML page.

Listing 2-4. The Canvas Element

```
<canvas height="200" width="200"></canvas>
```

The resulting canvas will show up as an "invisible" 200×200 pixel rectangle on your page. If you want to add a border around it, you could use the HTML code shown in Listing 2-5 to style the canvas with normal CSS borders.

Listing 2-5. Canvas Element with a Solid Border

```
<canvas id="diagonal" style="border: 1px solid;" width="200" height="200">
</canvas>
```

Note the addition of the ID diagonal to make it easy to locate this canvas element programmatically. An ID attribute is crucial to any canvas because all the useful operations on this element must be done through scripting. Without an ID, you will have difficulty locating the element to interoperate with it.

Figure 2-2 shows what the canvas in Listing 2-5 would look like in a browser.

Figure 2-2. A simple HTML5 canvas element on an HTML page

Not very exciting, but as any artist would tell you, it is full of potential. Now, let's do something with this pristine canvas. As mentioned before, it is not easy to draw a diagonal line on a web page without HTML5 Canvas. Let's see how easy it is now that we *can* use Canvas. Listing 2-6 shows how, with just a few lines of code, you can draw a diagonal line on the canvas we added to the page earlier.

Listing 2-6. Creating a Diagonal Line on a Canvas

```
<script>
  function drawDiagonal() {
    // Get the canvas element and its drawing context
    var canvas = document.getElementById('diagonal');
    var context = canvas.getContext('2d');

    // Create a path in absolute coordinates
    context.beginPath();
    context.moveTo(70, 140);
    context.lineTo(140, 70);

    // Stroke the line onto the canvas
    context.stroke();
  }

  window.addEventListener("load", drawDiagonal, true);
</script>
```

Let's examine the JavaScript code used to create the diagonal line. It is a simple example, but it captures the essential flow of working with the Canvas API:

You first gain access to the canvas object by referencing a particular canvas's ID value. In this example, the ID is diagonal. Next, you create a context variable and you call the canvas object's getContext method, passing in the type of canvas you are looking for. You pass in the string "2d" to get a two-dimensional context—the only available context type at this time.

▨ **Note** Much work has already been completed on a three-dimensional version of the Canvas context. Version 1.0 of the WebGL specification, a joint effort from browser vendors and the Khronos Group, was released in early 2011. WebGL is based on the same concepts and designs as the popular OpenGL library, bringing a similar API to JavaScript and HTML5. To create a three-dimensional drawing context in a supporting browser, you simply use the string "webgl" as the argument to getContext. The resulting context has an entirely new set of drawing APIs: capabilities that are thorough and complex enough for their own book. Although some browsers are shipping implementations of WebGL today, not all vendors are on board. However, the potential of three-dimensional rendering on the Web is compelling enough that we expect rapid uptake of support in the next few years. For more information, consult the WebGL site at the Khronos Group (http://www.khronos.org/webgl). We will touch on WebGL in a little more detail in the final chapter of this book.

You then use the context to perform drawing operations. In this case, you can create the diagonal line by calling three methods—beginPath, moveTo, and lineTo—passing in the line's start and end coordinates.

The drawing methods moveTo and lineTo do not actually create the line; you finalize a canvas operation and draw the line by calling the context.stroke(); method. Figure 2-3 shows the diagonal line created with the example code.

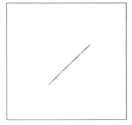

Figure 2-3. *Diagonal line on a canvas*

Triumph! Although this simple line may not appear to be the start of a revolution, keep in mind that drawing a diagonal line between two arbitrary points using classic HTML techniques was a very difficult maneuver involving stretched images, strange CSS and DOM objects, or other forms of black magic. Let us never speak of them again.

As you can see from this example's code, all operations on the canvas are performed via the context object. This will hold true for the rest of your interaction with the canvas because all the important functions with visual output are accessible only from the context, not the canvas object itself. This flexibility allows the canvas to support different types of drawing models in the future, based on the type of context that is retrieved from the canvas. Although we will frequently refer in this chapter to actions we will take on the canvas, keep in mind that this actually means that we will be working with the context object that the canvas supplies.

As demonstrated in the previous example, many operations on the context do not immediately update the drawing surface. Functions such as beginPath, moveTo, and lineTo do not modify the canvas appearance immediately. The same is true of many functions that set the styling and preferences of the canvas. Only when a path is *stroked* or *filled* does it appear on the display. Otherwise, the canvas will only be immediately updated when images are displayed, text is shown, or rectangles are drawn, filled, or cleared.

Applying Transformations to Drawings

Now let's look at another way to draw on the canvas using *transformation*. In the following example, the result is identical to the previous example, but the code used to draw the diagonal line is different. For this simple example, you could argue that the use of transformation adds unnecessary complexity. However, you can think of using transformation as a best practice for more complex canvas operations. You'll see that we'll use it a lot throughout the remaining examples, and it is critical to understanding the Canvas API's complex capabilities.

Perhaps the easiest way to think of the transformation system—at least, the easiest way that does not involve a great amount of mathematical formulae and hand-waving—is as a modification layer that sits between the commands you issue and the output on the canvas display. This modification layer is always present, even if you choose not to interact with it.

Modifications, or *transformations* in the parlance of drawing systems, can be applied sequentially, combined, and modified at will. Every drawing operation is passed through the modification layer to be modified before it appears on the canvas. Although this adds an extra layer of complexity, it also adds tremendous power to the drawing system. It grants access to the powerful modifications that modern image-editing tools support in real time, yet in an API that is only as complex as it absolutely needs to be.

Don't be fooled into thinking that you are optimizing performance if you don't use transformation calls in your code. The canvas implementation uses and applies transformations implicitly in its rendering engine, whether or not you call them directly. It is wiser to understand the system up front because it will be crucial to know if you step outside the most basic drawing operations.

A key recommendation for reusable code is that you usually want to *draw at the origin* (coordinate 0,0) and apply transformations—scale, translate, rotate, and so forth—to modify your drawing code into its final appearance, as shown in Figure 2-4.

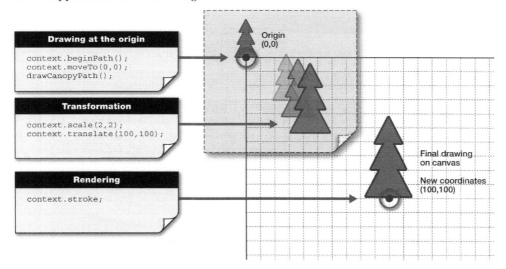

Figure 2-4. Overview of transformation and drawing at the origin

Listing 2-7 shows this best practice in action using the simplest transform: `translate`.

Listing 2-7. Using Translation to Create a Diagonal Line on a Canvas

```
<script>
  function drawDiagonal() {
    var canvas = document.getElementById('diagonal');
    var context = canvas.getContext('2d');

    // Save a copy of the current drawing state
    context.save();

    // Move the drawing context to the right, and down
    context.translate(70, 140);

    // Draw the same line as before, but using the origin as a start
    context.beginPath();
    context.moveTo(0, 0);
    context.lineTo(70, -70);
    context.stroke();

    // Restore the old drawing state
    context.restore();
  }

  window.addEventListener("load", drawDiagonal, true);
</script>
```

Let's examine the JavaScript code used to create this second, translated diagonal line.

1. First, you access the canvas object by referencing its ID value (in this case, diagonal).

2. You then retrieve a context variable by calling the canvas object's getContext function.

3. Next, you want to save the still unmodified context so you can get back to its original state at the end of the drawing and transformation operation. If you do not save the state, the modifications you're making during the operation (translate, scale, and so on) will continue to be applied to the context in future operations, and that might not be desirable. Saving the context state before transforming it will allow us to restore it later.

4. The next step is to apply the translate method to the context. With this operation, the translation coordinates you supply will be added to the eventual drawing coordinates (the diagonal line) at the time any drawing is rendered, thus moving the line to its final location, but only after the drawing operation is complete.

5. After the translation has been applied, you can perform the normal drawing operations to create the diagonal line. In this case, you can create the diagonal line by calling three methods—beginPath, moveTo, and lineTo—this time drawing at the origin (0,0) instead of coordinates 70,140.

31

6. After the line has been sketched, you can render it to the canvas (for example, draw the line) by calling the context.stroke method.

7. Finally, you restore the context to its clean original state, so that future canvas operations are performed without the translation that was applied in this operation. Figure 2-5 shows the diagonal line created with the example code.

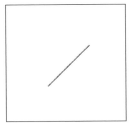

Figure 2-5. *Translated diagonal line on a canvas*

Even though your new line looks remarkably like the old one, you created it using the power of transformations, something that will become more apparent as we progress through the rest of this chapter.

Working with Paths

Although we could offer many more exciting examples for drawing lines, we are ready now to progress to something a bit more complex: *paths*. Paths in the HTML5 Canvas API represent any shape you care to render. Our original line example was a path, as you might have gathered from the conspicuous beginPath call used to start it off. But paths can be as complicated as you desire, with multiple line and curve segments and even subpaths. If you are looking to draw almost any shape on a canvas, the path API will be your focus point.

When embarking on any routine to draw a shape or path, the first call you make is beginPath. This simple function takes no arguments, but it signals to the canvas that you wish to start a new shape description. This function is mostly useful to the canvas so that it can calculate the interior and exterior of the shape you are creating for later fills and strokes.

A path always tracks the concept of a current location, which defaults to the origin. The canvas internally tracks the current location, but you will modify it with your drawing routines.

Once the shape is begun, you can use a variety of functions on the context to plot the layout of your shape. You've already seen the simplest context pathing functions in action:

- moveTo(x, y): moves the current location to a new destination of (x, y) without drawing.

- lineTo(x, y): moves the current location to a new destination of (x, y) drawing a straight line from the current position to the new one.

Essentially, the difference between these two calls is that the first is akin to lifting a drawing pen and moving to a new location, whereas the second tells the canvas to leave the pen on the paper and move it in a straight line to the new destination. However, it is worth pointing out again that *no actual drawing occurs until you stroke or fill the path*. At present, we are merely defining the positions in our path so that it can be drawn later.

The next special pathing function is a call to closePath. This command is very similar in behavior to the lineTo function, with the difference being that the destination is automatically assumed to be the origination of the path. However, the closePath also informs the canvas that the current shape has closed or formed a completely contained area. This will be useful for future fills and strokes.

At this point, you are free to continue with more segments in your path to create additional subpaths. Or you can beginPath at any time to start over and clear the path list entirely.

As with most complex systems, it is often better to see them in action. Let's depart from our line examples and use the Canvas API to start to create a new scene that illustrates a forest with a trail-running path. This scene will serve as a logo of sorts for our race event. And as with any picture, we will start with a basic element, which in this case is the canopy of a simple pine tree. Listing 2-8 shows how to draw the pine tree's canopy.

Listing 2-8. Function That Creates a Path for a Tree Canopy

```
function createCanopyPath(context) {
  // Draw the tree canopy
  context.beginPath();

  context.moveTo(-25, -50);
  context.lineTo(-10, -80);
  context.lineTo(-20, -80);
  context.lineTo(-5, -110);
  context.lineTo(-15, -110);

  // Top of the tree
  context.lineTo(0, -140);

  context.lineTo(15, -110);
  context.lineTo(5, -110);
  context.lineTo(20, -80);
  context.lineTo(10, -80);
  context.lineTo(25, -50);

  // Close the path back to its start point
  context.closePath();
}
```

As you can see from the code, we used the same move and line commands from before, but more of them. These lines form the branches of a simple tree shape, and we close the path back at the end. Our tree will leave a notable gap at the bottom, and we will use this in future sections to draw the trunk. Listing 2-9 shows how to use that canopy drawing function to actually render our simple tree shape onto a canvas.

Listing 2-9. Function That Draws a Tree on the Canvas

```
function drawTrails() {
  var canvas = document.getElementById('trails');
  var context = canvas.getContext('2d');

  context.save();
  context.translate(130, 250);
```

```
// Create the shape for our canopy path
createCanopyPath(context);

// Stroke the current path
context.stroke();
context.restore();
}
```

All the calls in this routine should be familiar to you already. We fetch the canvas context, save it for future reference, translate our position to a new location, draw the canopy, stroke it onto the canvas, and then restore our state. Figure 2-6 shows the results of our handiwork, a simply line representation of a tree canopy. We'll expand on this as we go forward, but it's a good first step.

Figure 2-6. *A simple path of a tree canopy*

Working with Stroke Styles

The Canvas API wouldn't be powerful or popular if developers were stuck using simple stick drawings and black lines. Let's use the stroke styling capabilities to make our canopy a little more tree-like. Listing 2-10 shows some basic commands that can modify the properties of the context in order to make the stroked shape look more appealing.

Listing 2-10. *Using a Stroke Style*

```
// Increase the line width
context.lineWidth = 4;

// Round the corners at path joints
context.lineJoin = 'round';

// Change the color to brown
context.strokeStyle = '#663300';

// Finally, stroke the canopy
context.stroke();
```

By adding the above properties before stroking, we change the appearance of any future stroked shapes—at least until we restore the context back to a previous state.

First, we increase the width of the stroked lines to four pixels.

Next, we set the lineJoin property to round, which causes the joints of our shape's segments to take on a more rounded corner shape. We could also set the lineJoin to bevel or miter (and the corresponding context.miterLimit value to tweak it) to choose other corner options.

Finally, we change the color of the stroke by using the strokeStyle property. In our example, we are setting the color to a CSS value, but as you will see in later sections, it is also possible to set the strokeStyle to be an image pattern or a gradient for fancier displays.

Although we are not using it here, we could also set the lineCap property to be either butt, square, or round to specify how lines should display at the endpoints. Alas, our example has no dangling line ends. Figure 2-7 shows our spruced-up tree canopy, nowstroked with a wider, smoother, brown line instead of the flat black line from before.

Figure 2-7. Stylish stroked tree canopy

Working with Fill Styles

As you might expect, stroking is not the only way to affect the appearance of canvas shapes. The next common way to modify a shape is to specify how its paths and subpaths are filled. Listing 2-11 shows how simple it is to fill our canopy with a pleasant, green color.

Listing 2-11. Using a Fill Style

```
// Set the fill color to green and fill the canopy
context.fillStyle = '#339900';
context.fill();
```

First, we set the fillStyle to the appropriate color. As we will see later, it is also possible to set the fill to be a gradient or an image pattern. Then, we simply call the context's fill function to let the canvas fill all the pixels inside all the closed paths of our current shape, as shown in Figure 2-8.

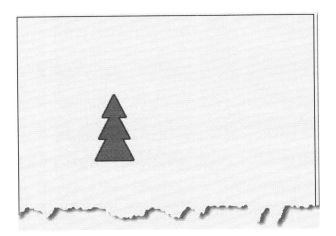

Figure 2-8. *Filled tree canopy*

Because we stroked our canopy before filling it, the fill covers part of the stroked path. This is due to the fact that the wide stroke—in our case, four pixels wide—is centered along the line of the path shape. The fill applies to all pixels on the interior of the shape, and as such it will cover half of the stroked line pixels. Should you prefer the full stroke to appear, you can simply fill *before* stroking the path.

Filling Rectangular Content

Every tree deserves a strong foundation. Thankfully, we left space for our tree trunk in the original shape path. Listing 2-12 shows how we can add the simplest rendering of a tree trunk by using the `fillRect` convenience function.

Listing 2-12. *Using the fillRect Convenience Function*

```
// Change fill color to brown
context.fillStyle = '#663300';

// Fill a rectangle for the tree trunk
context.fillRect(-5, -50, 10, 50);
```

Here, we once again set a brown fill style. But instead of explicitly drawing the corners of our trunk rectangle using the `lineTo` ability, we will draw the entire trunk in one step by using `fillRect`. The `fillRect` call takes the x and y location, as well as the width and height, and then immediately fills it with the current fill style.

Although we are not using them here, corresponding functions exist to `strokeRect` and `clearRect`. The former will draw the outline of the rectangle based on a given position and dimension, while the latter will remove any content from the rectangular area and reset it to its original, transparent color.

Canvas Animations

Brian says: "The ability to clear rectangles in the canvas is core to creating animations and games using the Canvas API. By repeatedly drawing and clearing sections of the canvas, it is possible to present the illusion of animation, and many examples of this already exist on the Web. However, to create animations that perform smoothly, you will need to utilize *clipping* features and perhaps even a secondary buffered canvas to minimize the flickering caused by frequent canvas clears. Although animations are not the focus of this book, check out the 'Practical Extra' sections of this chapter for some tips on using HTML5 to animate your pages."

Figure 2-9 shows our simple, flatly filled tree trunk attached to our previous canopy path.

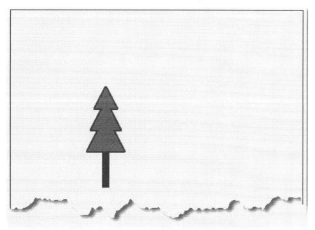

Figure 2-9. *Tree with filled rectangular trunk*

Drawing Curves

The world, particularly the natural world, is not filled with straight lines and rectangles. Fortunately, the canvas provides a variety of functions for creating curves in our paths. We will demonstrate the simplest option—a *quadratic* curve—to form a path through our virtual forest. Listing 2-13 demonstrates the addition of two quadratic curves.

Listing 2-13. *Drawing a Curve*

```
// Save the canvas state and draw the path
context.save();

context.translate(-10, 350);
context.beginPath();

// The first curve bends up and right
```

```
context.moveTo(0, 0);
context.quadraticCurveTo(170, -50, 260, -190);

// The second curve continues down and right
context.quadraticCurveTo(310, -250, 410,-250);

// Draw the path in a wide brown stroke
context.strokeStyle = '#663300';
context.lineWidth = 20;
context.stroke();

// Restore the previous canvas state
context.restore();
```

As before, one of the first things we will do is save our canvas context state, because we will be modifying the translation and stroke options here. For our forest path, we will start by moving back to the origin and drawing a first quadratic curve up and to the right.

As shown in Figure 2-10, the quadraticCurveTo function begins at the current drawing location and takes two x, y point locations as its parameters. The second one is the final stop in our curve. The first one represents a *control point*. The control point sits to the side of the curve (not on it) and acts almost as a gravitational pull for the points along the curve path. By adjusting the location of the control point, you can adjust the curvature of the path you are drawing. We draw a second quadratic curve up and to the right to complete our path; then stroke it just as we did for our tree canopy before (only wider).

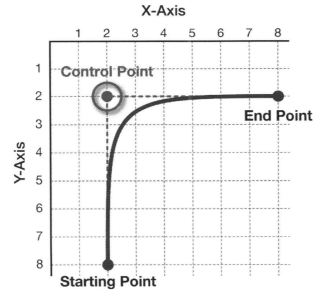

Figure 2-10. Quadratic curve start, end, and control points

Other options for curves in the HTML5 Canvas API include the bezierCurveTo, arcTo, and arc functions. These curves take additional control points, a radius, or angles to determine the characteristics of the curve. Figure 2-11 shows the two quadratic curves stroked on our canvas to create a path through the trees.

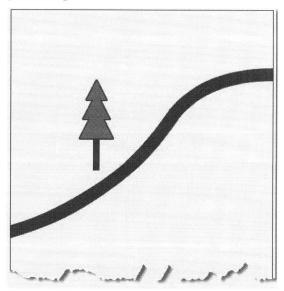

Figure 2-11. *Quadratic curves for a path*

Inserting Images into a Canvas

Images can be extremely handy to display inside a canvas. They can be stamped, stretched, modified with transformations, and often be the focus of the entire canvas. Thankfully, the Canvas API includes a few simple commands for adding image content to the canvas.

But images also add a complication to the canvas operations: you must wait for them to load. Browsers will usually be loading images asynchronously as your page script is rendering. However, if you attempt to render an image onto a canvas before it has completely loaded, the canvas will fail to render any image at all. As such, you should be careful to make sure the image is loaded completely before you attempt to render it.

To solve this problem in our simple forest trail example, we will load an image of a bark texture to use directly in the canvas. In order to make sure that the image has completed loading before we render, we will switch the loading code to only execute as a callback from image loading completion, as shown in Listing 2-14.

Listing 2-14. *Loading the Image*

```
// Load the bark image
var bark = new Image();
bark.src = "bark.jpg";

// Once the image is loaded, draw on the canvas
```

```
bark.onload = function () {
  drawTrails();
}
```

As you can see, we've added an onload handler to the bark.jpg image to call the main drawTrails function only when the image loading has completed. This guarantees that the image will be available to the next calls we add to the canvas rendering, as shown in Listing 2-15.

Listing 2-15. *Drawing an Image on a Canvas*

```
// Draw the bark pattern image where
//  the filled rectangle was before
context.drawImage(bark, -5, -50, 10, 50);
```

Here, we have replaced the previous call to fillRect with a simple routine to display our bark image as the new trunk for our tree. Although the image is a subtle replacement, it provides more texture to our display. Note that in this call, we are specifying an x, y, width, and height argument in addition to the image itself. This option will scale the image to fit into the 10×50 pixel space that we have allocated for our trunk. We could also have passed in source dimensions to have more control over the clipping area of the incoming image to be displayed.

As you can see in Figure 2-12, the change to the appearance of our trunk is only slightly different from the filled rectangle we used before.

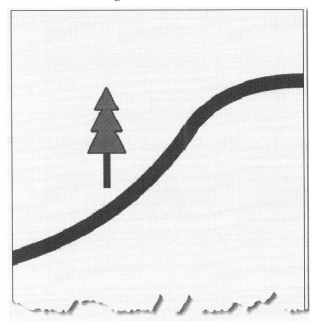

Figure 2-12. *Tree with an image used for trunk*

Using Gradients

Not satisfied with the tree trunk? Well, neither are we. Let's take another approach to drawing our tree trunk that uses a little more finesse: gradients. Gradients allow you to apply a gradual algorithmic sampling of colors as either a stroke or fill style, just like the patterns were applied in the last section. Creating gradients requires a three-step process:

1. Create the gradient object itself.

2. Apply color stops to the gradient object, signaling changes in color along the transition.

3. Set the gradient as either a fillStyle or a strokeStyle on the context.

It is perhaps easiest to think of gradients as a smooth change of color that moves along a line. For example, if you supply points A and B as the arguments to the creation of a gradient, the color will be transitioned for any stroke or fill that moves in the direction of point A to point B.

To determine what colors are displayed, simply use the addColorStop function on the gradient object itself. This function allows you to specify an offset and a color. The color argument is the color you want to be applied in the stroke or fill at the offset position. The offset position is a value between 0.0 and 1.0, representing how far along the gradient line the color should be reached.

If you create a gradient from point (0,0) to point (0,100) and specify a white color stop at offset 0.0 and a black offset at offset 1.0, then when the stroke or fill occurs, you will see the color gradually shift from white (the beginning color stop) to black (the end color stop) as the rendering moves from point (0,0) to point (0,100).

As with other color values, it is possible to supply an alpha (for example, transparency) value as part of the color and make that alpha value transition as well. To do so, you will need to use another textual representation of the color value, such as the CSS rgba function that includes an alpha component.

Let's see this in more detail with a code sample that applies two gradients to a fillRect representing our final tree trunk, as shown in Listing 2-16.

Listing 2-16. *Using a Gradient*

```
// Create a 3 stop gradient horizontally across the trunk
var trunkGradient = context.createLinearGradient(-5, -50, 5, -50);

// The beginning of the trunk is medium brown
trunkGradient.addColorStop(0, '#663300');

// The middle-left of the trunk is lighter in color
trunkGradient.addColorStop(0.4, '#996600');

// The right edge of the trunk is darkest
trunkGradient.addColorStop(1, '#552200');

// Apply the gradient as the fill style, and draw the trunk
context.fillStyle = trunkGradient;
context.fillRect(-5, -50, 10, 50);

// A second, vertical gradient creates a shadow from the
//   canopy on the trunk
var canopyShadow = context.createLinearGradient(0, -50, 0, 0);
```

```
// The beginning of the shadow gradient is black, but with
//   a 50% alpha value
canopyShadow.addColorStop(0, 'rgba(0, 0, 0, 0.5)');

// Slightly further down, the gradient completely fades to
//   fully transparent. The rest of the trunk gets no shadow.
canopyShadow.addColorStop(0.2, 'rgba(0, 0, 0, 0.0)');

// Draw the shadow gradient on top of the trunk gradient
context.fillStyle = canopyShadow;
context.fillRect(-5, -50, 10, 50);
```

Applying these two gradients creates a nice, smooth light source on our rendered tree as shown in Figure 2-13, making it appear curved and covered by a slight shadow from the canopy above. Let's keep it.

Figure 2-13. *Tree with gradient trunk*

Besides the linear gradient used in our example, the Canvas API also supports a radial gradient option that allows you to specify two circular representations in which the color stops are applied to the cone between the two circles. The radial gradient uses the same color stops as the linear gradient, but takes its arguments in the form shown in Listing 2-17.

Listing 2-17. *Example of Applying a Radial Gradient*

```
createRadialGradient(x0, y0, r0, x1, y1, r1)
```

In this example, the first three arguments represent a circle centered at (x0, y0) with radius r0, and the last three arguments represent a second circle centered at (x1, y1) with radius r1. The gradient is drawn across the area between the two circles.

Using Background Patterns

Direct rendering of images has many uses, but in some cases it is beneficial to use an image as a background tile, similar to the capability available in CSS. We've already seen how it is possible to set a stroke or fill style to be a solid color. The HTML5 Canvas API also includes an option to set an image as a repeatable pattern for either a path stroke or fill.

To make our forest trail appear a bit more rugged, we will demonstrate the capability by replacing the previous stroked trail curve with one that uses a background image fill. In doing so, we'll swap out our now-unused bark image for a gravel image that we will put to use here. Listing 2-18 shows we replace the call to drawImage with a call to createPattern.

Listing 2-18. Using a Background Pattern

```
// Replace the bark image with
// a trail gravel image
var gravel = new Image();
gravel.src = "gravel.jpg";
gravel.onload = function () {
    drawTrails();
}

// Replace the solid stroke with a repeated
// background pattern
context.strokeStyle = context.createPattern(gravel, 'repeat');
context.lineWidth = 20;
context.stroke();
```

As you can see, we are still calling stroke() for our path. However, this time we have set a strokeStyle property on the context first, passing in the result of a call to context.createPattern. Oh, and once again the image needs to be previously loaded in order for the canvas to perform the operation. The second argument is a repetition pattern that can be one of the choices shown in Table 2-1.

Table 2-1. Repetition Patterns

Repeat	Value
repeat	(Default) The image is repeated in both directions
repeat-x	The image is repeated only in the X dimension
repeat-y	The image is repeated only in the Y dimension
no-repeat	The image is displayed once and not repeated

Figure 2-14 shows the result of the use of a background image rather than an explicitly drawn image to represent our trail.

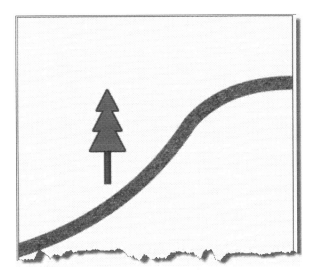

Figure 2-14. A trail with a repeating background pattern

Scaling Canvas Objects

What kind of forest has only one tree? Let's fix that right away. To make this a little easier, we will adjust our code sample to isolate the tree drawing operations to a single routine, called drawTree, as shown in Listing 2-19.

Listing 2-19. Function to Draw the Tree Object

```
// Move tree drawing into its own function for reuse
function drawTree(context) {
  var trunkGradient = context.createLinearGradient(-5, -50, 5, -50);
  trunkGradient.addColorStop(0, '#663300');
  trunkGradient.addColorStop(0.4, '#996600');
  trunkGradient.addColorStop(1, '#552200');
  context.fillStyle = trunkGradient;
  context.fillRect(-5, -50, 10, 50);

  var canopyShadow = context.createLinearGradient(0, -50, 0, 0);
  canopyShadow.addColorStop(0, 'rgba(0, 0, 0, 0.5)');
  canopyShadow.addColorStop(0.2, 'rgba(0, 0, 0, 0.0)');
  context.fillStyle = canopyShadow;
  context.fillRect(-5, -50, 10, 50);

  createCanopyPath(context);

  context.lineWidth = 4;
  context.lineJoin = 'round';
  context.strokeStyle = '#663300';
```

```
    context.stroke();

    context.fillStyle = '#339900';
    context.fill();
}
```

As you can see, the drawTree function contains all the code we previously created to draw the canopy, trunk, and trunk gradient. Now we will use one of the transformation routines—context.scale—to draw a second tree at a new location and with a larger size, as shown in Listing 2-20.

Listing 2-20. *Drawing the Tree Objects*

```
// Draw the first tree at X=130, Y=250
context.save();
context.translate(130, 250);
drawTree(context);
context.restore();

// Draw the second tree at X=260, Y=500
context.save();
context.translate(260, 500);

// Scale this tree twice normal in both dimensions
context.scale(2, 2);
drawTree(context);
context.restore();
```

The scale function takes two factors for the x and y dimensions as its arguments. Each factor tells the canvas implementation how much larger (or smaller) to make the size in that dimension; an X factor of 2 would make all subsequent draw routines twice as wide, while a Y factor of 0.5 would make all subsequent operations half as tall as before. Using these routines, we now have an easy way to create a second tree in our trails canvas, as shown in Figure 2-15.

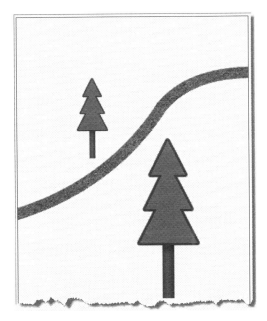

Figure 2-15. *Tree with a larger scale*

Always Perform Shape and Path Routines at the Origin

Brian says (and really means it, this time): "This example illustrates one of the reasons why it is a good idea to perform shape and path routines at the origin; then translate them when complete, as we do here in our code. The reason is that transforms such as `scale` and `rotate` operate from the origin.

If you perform a `rotate` transform to a shape drawn off origin, a `rotate` transform will rotate the shape around the origin rather than rotating in place. Similarly, if you performed a scale operation to shapes before translating them to their proper position, all locations for path coordinates would also be multiplied by the scaling factor. Depending on the scale factor applied, this new location could even be off the canvas altogether, leaving you wondering why your scale operation just 'deleted' the image."

Using Canvas Transforms

Transform operations are not limited to scales and translates. It is also possible to rotate the drawing context using the context.rotate(angle) function or even to modify the underlying transform directly for more advanced operations such as shearing of the rendered paths. If you wanted to rotate the display of an image, you would merely need to call the series of operations shown in Listing 2-21.

Listing 2-21. A Rotated Image

```
context.save();

// rotation angle is specified in radians
context.rotate(1.57);
context.drawImage(myImage, 0, 0, 100, 100);

context.restore();
```

In Listing 2-22, however, we will show how you can apply an arbitrary transform to the path coordinates to radically alter the display of our existing tree path in order to create a shadow effect.

Listing 2-22. Using a Transform

```
// Create a 3 stop gradient horizontally across the trunk
// Save the current canvas state for later
context.save();

// Create a slanted tree as the shadow by applying
//  a shear transform, changing X values to increase
//  as Y values increase
// With this transform applied, all coordinates are
//  multiplied by the matrix.
context.transform(1, 0,-0.5, 1, 0, 0);

// Shrink the shadow down to 60% height in the Y dimension
context.scale(1, 0.6);

// Set the tree fill to be black, but at only 20% alpha
context.fillStyle = 'rgba(0, 0, 0, 0.2)';
context.fillRect(-5, -50, 10, 50);

// Redraw the tree with the shadow effects applied
createCanopyPath(context);
context.fill();

// Restore the canvas state
context.restore();
```

Modifying the context transform directly as we've done here is something you should attempt only if you are familiar with the matrix mathematics underpinning two-dimensional drawing systems. If you check the math behind this transform, you will see that we are shifting the X values of our drawing by a factor of the corresponding Y values in order to shear the gray tree being used as a shadow. Then, by applying a scale factor of 60%, the sheared tree is decreased in size.

Note that the sheared "shadow" tree is rendered first, so that the actual tree appears above it in *Z-order* (the order in which the canvas objects overlap). Also, the shadow tree is drawn using the CSS notation for RGBA, which allows us to set the alpha value to only 20% of normal. This creates the light, semitransparent look for the shadow tree. Once applied to our scaled trees, the output renders as shown in Figure 2-16.

Figure 2-16. Trees with transformed shadows

Using Canvas Text

As we approach the end of our trail creation, let's demonstrate the power of the Canvas API text functions by adding a fancy title to the top of our display. It is important to note that text rendering on a canvas is treated the same way as any other path object: text can be stroked or filled, and all rendering transformations and styles can apply to text just as they do to any other shape.

As you might expect, the text drawing routines consist of two functions on the context object:

- `fillText (text, x, y, maxwidth)`

- `strokeText (text, x, y, maxwidth)`

Both functions take the text as well as the location at which it should be drawn. Optionally, a `maxwidth` argument can be provided to constrain the size of the text by automatically shrinking the font to fit the given size. In addition, a `measureText` function is available to return a metrics object containing the width of the given text should it be rendered using the current context settings.

As is the case with all browser text display, the actual appearance of the text is highly configurable using context properties that are similar to their CSS counterparts, as shown in Table 2-2.

Table 2-2. Possible Settings for Background Pattern Repetition

Property	Values	Note
font	CSS font string	Example: italic Arial, sans-serif
textAlign	start, end, left, right, center	Defaults to start
textBaseline	top, hanging, middle, alphabetic, ideographic, bottom	Defaults to alphabetic

All these context properties can be set to alter the context or accessed to query the current values. In Listing 2-23, we will create a large text message with the font face Impact and fill it with the background pattern of our existing bark image. In order to center the text across the top of our canvas, we will declare a maximum width and a center alignment.

Listing 2-23. Using Canvas Text

```
// Draw title text on our canvas
context.save();

// The font will be 60 pixel, Impact face
context.font = "60px impact";

// Use a brown fill for our text
context.fillStyle = '#996600';
// Text can be aligned when displayed
context.textAlign = 'center';

// Draw the text in the middle of the canvas with a max
//  width set to center properly
context.fillText('Happy Trails!', 200, 60, 400);
context.restore();
```

As you can see from the result in Figure 2-17, the trail drawing just got a whole lot—you guessed it—happier.

Figure 2-17. Background pattern-filled text

Applying Shadows

Finally, we will use the built-in canvas shadow API to add a blurred shadow effect to our new text display. Like many graphical effects, shadows are best applied in moderation, even though the Canvas API allows you to apply shadows to any operation we have already covered.

Once again, shadows are controlled by a few global context properties, as shown in Table 2-3.

Table 2-3. Shadow Properties

Property	Values	Note
shadowColor	Any CSS color	Can include an alpha component
shadowOffsetX	Pixel count	Positive values move shadow to the right, negative left
shadowOffsetY	Pixel count	Positive values move shadow down, negative up
shadowBlur	Gaussian blur	Higher values cause blurrier shadow edges

The shadow effect is triggered on any path, text, or image render if the shadowColor and at least one of the other properties is set to a nondefault value. Listing 2-24 shows how we can apply a shadow to our new trails title text.

Listing 2-24. *Applying a Shadow*

```
// Set some shadow on our text, black with 20% alpha
context.shadowColor = 'rgba(0, 0, 0, 0.2)';

// Move the shadow to the right 15 pixels, up 10
context.shadowOffsetX = 15;
context.shadowOffsetY = -10;

// Blur the shadow slightly
context.shadowBlur = 2;
```

With these simple additions, the canvas renderer will automatically apply shadows until the canvas state is restored or the shadow properties are reset. Figure 2-18 shows the newly applied shadows.

Figure 2-18. *Title with shadowed text*

As you can see, the shadow generated by CSS is positional only and not in sync with the transformational shadow we created for our tree. For the sake of consistency, you should probably only use one approach to drawing shadows in a given canvas scene.

Working with Pixel Data

One of the most useful—albeit nonobvious—aspects of the Canvas API is the ability for developers to easily get access to the underlying pixels in the canvas. This access works in both directions: it is trivial to get access to the pixel values as a numerical array, and it is equally easy to modify those values and apply them back to the canvas. In fact, it is entirely possible to manipulate the canvas entirely through the pixel value calls and forgo the rendering calls we've discussed in this chapter. This is made possible by the existence of three functions on the context API.

First up is context.getImageData(sx, sy, sw, sh). This function returns a representation of the current state of the canvas display as a collection of integers. Specifically, it returns an object containing three properties:

- width: The number of pixels in each row of the pixel data

- height: The number of pixels in each column of the pixel data

- data: A one-dimensional array containing the actual RGBA values for each pixel retrieved from the canvas. This array contains four values for each pixel—a red, green, blue, and alpha component—each with a value from 0 to 255. Therefore, each pixel retrieved from the canvas becomes four integer values in the data array. The data array is populated by pixels from left to right and top to bottom (for example, across the first row, then across the second row, and so on), as shown in Figure 2-19.

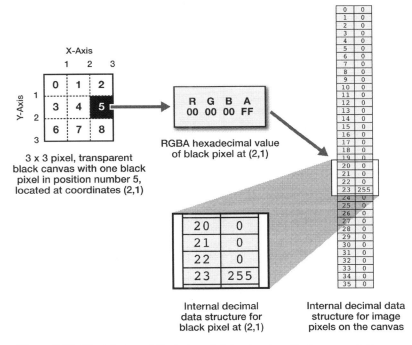

Figure 2-19. Pixel data and the internal data structure that represents it

The data returned by the call to getImageData is limited to the region defined by the four parameters. Only canvas pixels contained in the rectangular region surrounded by the source x, y, width, and height parameters will be retrieved. Therefore, to access all pixel values as data, you should pass in getImageData(0, 0, canvas.width, canvas.height).

Because there are four image data values representing each pixel, it can be a little tricky to calculate exactly which index represents the values for a given pixel. The formula is as follows.

For any pixel at coordinate (x,y) in a canvas with a given width and height, you can locate the component values:

- **Red component**: ((width * y) + x) * 4

- **Green component**: ((width * y) + x) * 4 + 1

- **Blue component**: ((width * y) + x) * 4 + 2

- **Alpha component**: ((width * y) + x) * 4 + 3

Once you have access to the object with image data, it is quite easy to modify the pixel values in the data array mathematically, because they are each simply integers from 0 to 255. Changing the red, green, blue, or alpha values for one or more pixels makes it easy to update the canvas display by using the second function: context.putImageData(imagedata, dx, dy).

putImageData allows you to pass in a set of image data in the same format as it was originally retrieved; that's quite handy because you can modify the values the canvas originally gave you and put them back. Once this function is called, the canvas will immediately update to reflect the new values of the pixels you passed in as the image data. The dx and dy parameters allow you to specify an offset for where to start applying your data array into the existing canvas, should you choose to use one.

Finally, if you want to start from scratch with a set of blank canvas data, you can call context.createImageData(sw, sh) to create a new set of image data tied to the canvas object. This set of data can be programmatically changed as before, even though it does not represent the current state of the canvas when retrieved.

There is yet another way to get data out of a canvas: the canvas.toDataURL API. This function gives you a programmatic way to retrieve the current rendering data of a canvas in a text format, but in this case the format is a standard representation of the data that browsers can interpret as images.

A data URL is a string containing the data of an image—such as a PNG—that a browser can display just like a normal image file. The format of a data URL is best illustrated with an example:

```
data:image/png;base64, WCAYAAABkY9jZxn…
```

This example shows that the format is the string data: followed by a MIME type (such as image/png), followed by a flag indicating whether or not the data is encoded in base64 format, and then the text representing the data itself.

Don't worry about the format, as you won't be generating it yourself. The important point is that with a simple call, you can get the content of a canvas delivered to you in one of these special URLs. When you call canvas.toDataURL(type), you can pass in a type of image you would like the canvas data generated in, such as image/png (the default) or image/jpeg. The data URL returned to you can be used as the source of image elements in a page or CSS styles, as shown in Listing 2-25.

Listing 2-25. Creating an Image from a Canvas

```
var myCanvas = document.getElementById("myCanvas");

// draw operations into the canvas...
```

```
// get the canvas data as a data URL
var canvasData = myCanvas.toDataURL();

// set the data as the source of a new image
var img = new Image();
img.src = canvasData;
```

You don't have to use a data URL right away. You could even store the URL in your browser's local storage for later retrieval and manipulation. Browser storage will be covered later in this book.

Implementing Canvas Security

There is an important caveat to using pixel manipulation, as described in the previous section. Although most developers would use pixel manipulation for legitimate means, it is quite possible that the ability to fetch and update data from a canvas could be used for nefarious purposes. For this reason, the concept of an *origin-clean* canvas was specified, so that canvases that are *tainted* with images from origins other than the source of the containing page cannot have their data retrieved.

As shown in Figure 2-20, if a page served up from http://www.example.com contains a canvas element, it is entirely possible that the code in the page could try to render an image from http://www.remote.com inside the canvas. After all, it is perfectly acceptable to render images from remote sites inside any given web page.

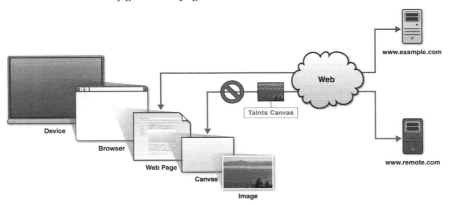

Figure 2-20. *Local and remote image sources*

However, before the arrival of the Canvas API, it was not possible to programmatically retrieve the pixel values of a downloaded image. Private images from other sites could be displayed in a page but not read or copied. Allowing scripts to read image data from other origins would effectively share users' photographs and other sensitive online image file with the entire web.

In order to prevent this, any canvas that contains images rendered from remote origins will throw a security exception if the getImageData or toDataURL functions are called. It is perfectly acceptable to render remote images into a canvas from another origin as long as you (or any other scriptwriter) do not attempt to fetch the data from that canvas after it has been tainted. Be aware of this limitation and practice safe rendering.

Building an Application with HTML5 Canvas

There are many different application possibilities for using the Canvas API: graphs, charts, image editing, and so on. However, one of the most intriguing uses for the canvas is to modify or overlay existing content. One popular type of overlay is known as a heatmap. Although the name implies a temperature measurement, the heat in this case can refer to any level of measurable activity. Areas on the map with high levels of activity are colored as hot (for example, red, yellow, or white). Areas with less activity show no color change at all, or minimal blacks and grays.

For example, a heatmap can be used to indicate traffic on a city map, or storm activity on a global map. And situations such as these are easy to implement in HTML5 by combining a canvas display with an underlying map source. Essentially, the canvas can be used to overlay the map and draw the heat levels based on the appropriate activity data.

Let's build a simple heatmap using the capabilities we learned about in the Canvas API. In this case, our heat data source will be not external data, but the movement of our mouse across the map. Moving the mouse over a portion of the map will cause the heat to increase, and holding the mouse at a given position will rapidly increase the temperature to maximum levels. We can overlay such a heatmap display(shown in Figure 2-21) on a nondescript terrain map, just to provide a sample case.

Heatmap

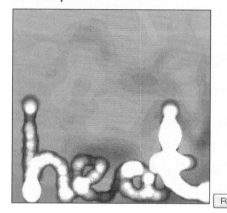

Figure 2-21. The heatmap application

Now that you've seen the end result of our heatmap application, let's step through the code sample. As usual, the working examples are available online for your download and perusal.

Let's start with the HTML elements declared in this example. For this display, the HTML consists of only a title, a canvas, and a button we can use to reset the heatmap. The background display for the canvas consists of a simple mapbg.jpg applied to the canvas via CSS as shown in Listing 2-26.

Listing 2-26. The Heatmap Canvas Element

```
<style type="text/css">
  #heatmap {
      background-image: url("mapbg.jpg");
  }
```

```
</style>

<h2>Heatmap </h2>
<canvas id="heatmap" class="clear" style="border: 1px solid ; " height="300"↵
 width="300"> </canvas>
<button id="resetButton">Reset</button>
```

We also declare some initial variables to be used later in the example.

```
var points = {};
var SCALE = 3;
var x = -1;
var y = -1;
```

Next, we will set the canvas to have a high transparency value for its global drawing operations, and set the composite mode to cause new draws to lighten the underlying pixels rather than replace them.

Then, as shown in Listing 2-27, we will set a handler to change the display—addToPoint—every time the mouse moves or one-tenth of a second passes.

Listing 2-27. The loadDemo Function

```
function loadDemo() {
  document.getElementById("resetButton").onclick = reset;

  canvas = document.getElementById("heatmap");
  context = canvas.getContext('2d');
  context.globalAlpha = 0.2;
  context.globalCompositeOperation = "lighter"

function sample() {
  if (x != -1) {
    addToPoint(x,y)
  }
  setTimeout(sample, 100);
}

canvas.onmousemove = function(e) {
  x = e.clientX - e.target.offsetLeft;
  y = e.clientY - e.target.offsetTop;
  addToPoint(x,y)
}

  sample();
}
```

If the user clicks **Reset**, the entire canvas area is cleared and reset to its original state by using the canvas' clearRect function, as shown in Listing 2-28.

Listing 2-28. The reset Function

```
function reset() {
  points = {};
  context.clearRect(0,0,300,300);
```

```
  x = -1;
  y = -1;
}
```

Next we create a lookup table of colors to use when drawing heat on the canvas. Listing 2-29 shows how the colors range in brightness from least to greatest, and they will be used to represent varying levels of heat on the display. The greater the value of the intensity, the brighter the returned color.

Listing 2-29. The getColor Function

```
function getColor(intensity) {
  var colors = ["#072933", "#2E4045", "#8C593B", "#B2814E", "#FAC268", "#FAD237"];
  return colors[Math.floor(intensity/2)];
}
```

Whenever the mouse moves or hovers over an area of the canvas, a point is drawn. The point grows in size (and brightness) the longer the mouse stays in the immediate area. As shown in Listing 2-30, we use the context.arc function to draw a circle of a given radius, and we draw a brighter, hotter color for larger radius values by passing the radius to our getColor function.

Listing 2-30. The drawPoint Function

```
function drawPoint(x, y, radius) {
  context.fillStyle = getColor(radius);
  radius = Math.sqrt(radius)*6;

  context.beginPath();
  context.arc(x, y, radius, 0, Math.PI*2, true)

  context.closePath();
  context.fill();
}
```

In the addToPoint function—which you will recall is accessed every time the mouse moves or hovers over a point—a heat value is increased and stored for that particular point on the canvas. Listing 2-31 shows that the maximum point value is 10. Once the current value of heat for a given pixel is found, the appropriate pixel is passed to drawPoint with its corresponding heat/radius value.

Listing 2-31. The addToPoint Function

```
function addToPoint(x, y) {
  x = Math.floor(x/SCALE);
  y = Math.floor(y/SCALE);

  if (!points[[x,y]]) {
    points[[x,y]] = 1;
  } else if (points[[x,y]]==10) {
    return
  } else {
    points[[x,y]]++;
  }
  drawPoint(x*SCALE,y*SCALE, points[[x,y]]);
}
```

Finally, the initial `loadDemo` function is registered to be called whenever the window completes loading.

```
window.addEventListener("load", loadDemo, true);
```

Together, these one hundred or so lines of code illustrate how much you can do with the Canvas API in a short amount of time, without using any plug-ins or external rendering technology. With an infinite number of data sources available it is easy to see how they can be visualized simply and effectively.

Practical Extra: Full Page Glass Pane

In the example application, you saw how you can apply a canvas on top of a graphic. You can also apply a canvas on top of the entire browser window or portions of the same—a technique commonly referred to as glass pane. Once you have positioned the glass pane canvas on top of a web page, you can do all kinds of cool and handy things with it.

For example, you can use a routine to retrieve the absolute position of all the DOM elements on a page and create a step-by-step help function that can guide users of a web application through the steps they must perform to start and use the application.

Or, you can use the glass pane canvas to scribble feedback on someone's web page using the mouse events for drawing input. Some things to keep in mind if you try to use a canvas in this capacity:

- You will need to set the canvas positioning to absolute and give it a specific position, width, and height. Without an explicit width and height setting, the canvas will remain at a zero pixel size.

- Don't forget to set a high Z-index on the canvas so that it floats above all the visible content. A canvas rendered under all the existing content doesn't get much chance to shine.

- Your glass pane canvas can block access to events in the content below, so be sparing in how you use it and remove it when it is unnecessary.

Practical Extra: Timing Your Canvas Animation

Earlier in the chapter, we mentioned that it is a common practice to animate elements on a canvas. This could be used for gaming, transitional effects, or simply to replace animated GIFs in an existing web page. But one area where JavaScript has been lacking is a reliable way to schedule your animation updates.

Today, most developers use the classic `setTimeout` or `setInterval` calls to schedule changes to a web page or application. Both of these calls allow you to schedule a callback after a certain number of milliseconds, which then allows you to make changes to the page during the callback. However, there are some significant problems with using that approach:

- As a developer, you need to guess at the appropriate number of milliseconds in the future to schedule the next update. With the modern Web running on a wider variety of devices than ever, it is tricky to know the suggested frame rate for a high-powered desktop device versus a mobile phone. And even if you guess how many frames to schedule per second, you may end up competing with other pages or machine load.

- It is more common than ever for users to browse with multiple windows or tabs, even on mobile devices. If you use setTimeout and setInterval to schedule your page updates, these will continue to happen even when the page is in the background. Running your scripts when they aren't even visible is a great way to convince users that your web application is draining their phone battery!

As an alternative, many browsers now offer a requestAnimationFrame function on the window object. This function takes a callback as its argument, and the callback will be invoked whenever the browser deems it appropriate for the animation to be updated.

Let's add another example (Listing 2-32) of our trail scene, this one with a crudely animated rain storm to signify the cancellation of our upcoming race. This code builds on the previous examples, and redundant code is not listed here.

Listing 2-32. *Basic Animation Frame Request*

```
// create an image for our rain texture
var rain = new Image();
rain.src = "rain.png";
rain.onload = function () {
  // Start off the animation with a single frame request
  // once the rain is loaded
  window.requestAnimFrame(loopAnimation, canvas);
}

// Previous code omitted...

// this function allows us to cover all browsers
// by aliasing the different browser-specific
// versions of the function to a single function
window.requestAnimFrame = (function(){
  return  window.requestAnimationFrame       ||
          window.webkitRequestAnimationFrame ||
          window.mozRequestAnimationFrame    ||
          window.oRequestAnimationFrame      ||
          window.msRequestAnimationFrame     ||
          // fall back to the old setTimeout technique if nothing
          // else is available
          function(/* function */ callback, /* DOMElement */ element){
            window.setTimeout(callback, 1000 / 60);
          };
})();

// This function is where we update the content of our canvas
function drawAFrame() {
  var context = canvas.getContext('2d');

  // do some drawing on the canvas, using the elapsedTime
  // as a guide for changes.
  context.save();

  // draw the existing trails picture first
  drawTrails();
```

```
  // Darken the canvas for an eerie sky.
  // By only darkening most of the time, we create lightning flashes
  if (Math.random() > .01) {
    context.globalAlpha = 0.65;
    context.fillStyle = '#000000';
    context.fillRect(0, 0, 400, 600);
    context.globalAlpha = 1.0;
  }

  // then draw a rain image, adjusted by the current time
  var now = Date.now();
  context.fillStyle = context.createPattern(rain, 'repeat');

  // We'll draw two translated rain images at different rates to
  // show thick rain and snow
  // Our rectangle will be bigger than the display size, and
  // repositioned based on the time
  context.save();
  context.translate(-256 + (0.1 * now) % 256, -256 + (0.5 * now) % 256);
  context.fillRect(0, 0, 400 + 256, 600 + 256);
  context.restore();

  // The second rectangle translates at a different rate for
  // thicker rain appearance
  context.save();
  context.translate(-256 + (0.08 * now) % 256, -256 + (0.2 * now) % 256);
  context.fillRect(0, 0, 400 + 256, 600 + 256);
  context.restore();

  // draw some explanatory text
  context.font = '32px san-serif';
  context.textAlign = 'center';
  context.fillStyle = '#990000';
  context.fillText('Event canceled due to weather!', 200, 550, 400);
  context.restore();
}

// This function will be called whenever the browser is ready
// for our application to render another frame.
function loopAnimation(currentTime) {
  // Draw a single frame of animation on our canvas
  drawAFrame();

  // After this frame is drawn, let the browser schedule
  // the next one
  window.requestAnimFrame(loopAnimation, canvas);
}
```

Once we update our drawing, we can see the animating rain on top of our trail (see Figure 2-22).

Figure 2-22. Still shot of canvas with rain animation

It is up to the browser to decide how often to call the animation frame callback. Pages in the background will be called less frequently, and the browser may clip the rendering to the element provided to the `requestAnimationFrame` call ("canvas" in our example) to optimize drawing resources. You aren't guaranteed a frame rate, but you are spared the work of scheduling for different environments!

This technique is not limited to the Canvas API. You can use `requestAnimationFrame` to make changes anywhere on the page content or CSS. There are other ways to produce movement on a web page—CSS animations come to mind—but if you are working with script-based changes, the `requestAnimationFrame` function is the way to go.

Summary

As you can see, the Canvas API provides a very powerful way to modify the appearance of your web application without resorting to odd document hacks. Images, gradients, and complex paths can be combined to create nearly any type of display you may be looking to present. Keep in mind that you generally need to draw at the origin, load any images you want to display before attempting to draw them, and be mindful of tainting your canvas with foreign image sources. However, if you learn to harness the power of the canvas, you can create applications that were never possible in a web page before.

CHAPTER 3

Working with Scalable Vector Graphics

In this chapter, we'll explore what you can do with another graphics feature in HTML5: *Scalable Vector Graphics*. Scalable Vector Graphics, or SVG, is an expressive language for two dimensional graphics.

Overview of SVG

In this section we'll look at the standard vector graphics support in HTML5 browsers, but first, let's review a couple of graphics concepts: raster and vector graphics.

In raster graphics, an image is represented by a two dimensional grid of pixels. The HTML5 Canvas 2d API is an example of a raster graphics API. Drawing with the Canvas API updates the canvas's pixels. PNG and JPEG are examples of raster image formats. The data in PNG and JPEG images also represents pixels.

Vector graphics are quite different. Vector graphics represent images with mathematical descriptions of geometry. A vector image contains all of the information needed to draw an image from high-level geometric objects such as lines and shapes. As you can tell by the name, SVG is an example of vector graphics. Like HTML, SVG is a file format that also has an API. SVG combined with the DOM APIs form a vector graphics API. It is possible to embed raster graphics such as PNG images inside of SVG, but SVG is primarily a vector format.

History

SVG has been around for a few years. SVG 1.0 was published as a W3C recommendation in 2001. SVG was originally available in browsers with the use of a plugin. Shortly afterward, browsers added native support for SVG images.

Inline SVG in HTML has a shorter history. A defining characteristic of SVG is that it is based on XML. HTML, of course, has a different syntax, and you cannot simply embed XML syntax inside of HTML documents. Instead, it has special rules for SVG. Prior to HTML5, it was possible to embed SVG as <img> elements inside an HTML page or link to self-contained .svg documents. HTML5 introduced inline SVG, in which SVG elements themselves can appear in HTML markup. Of course, in HTML, the syntax rules are more relaxed than in XML. You can have unquoted attributes, mixed capitalization, and so on. You will still need to use self-closing tags when appropriate. For example, you can embed a circle into your HTML document with just a little markup:

```
<svg height=100 width=100><circle cx=50 cy=50 r=50 /></svg>
```

Understanding SVG

Figure 3-1 shows an HTML5 document with the *Happy Trails!* image we drew with the canvas API in Chapter 2. If you read the title of this chapter, you can probably guess that this version was drawn with SVG. SVG lets you do many of the same drawing operations as the canvas API. Much of the time, the results can be visually identical. There are some important invisible differences, however. For one thing, the text is selectable. You don't get that with canvas! When you draw text onto a canvas element, the characters are frozen as pixels. They become part of the image and cannot change unless you redraw a region of the canvas. Because of that, text drawn onto a canvas is invisible to search engines. SVG, on the other hand, is searchable. Google, for instance, indexes the text in SVG content on the web.

***Figure 3-1.** SVG version of Happy Trails!*

SVG is closely related to HTML. If you choose, you can define the content of an SVG document with markup. HTML is a declarative language for structuring pages. SVG is a complimentary language for creating visual structures. You can interact with both SVG and HTML using DOM APIs. SVG documents are live trees of elements that you can script and style, just like HTML. You can attach event handlers to SVG elements. For example, you can use click event handlers to make SVG buttons or shaped clickable regions. That is essential for building interactive applications that use mouse input.

Additionally, you can view and edit the structure of the SVG in your browser's development tool. As you can see in Figure 3-2, inline SVG embeds directly into the HTML DOM. It has a structure you can observe and change at runtime. You can dig into SVG and see its source, unlike an image that is just a grid of pixels.

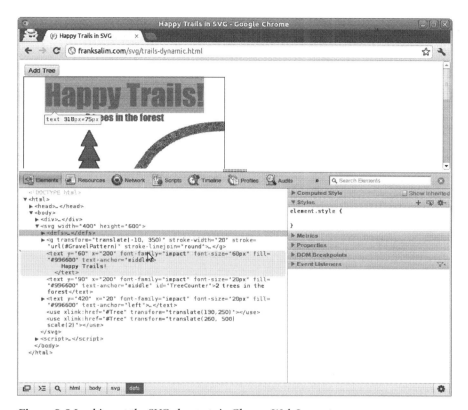

Figure 3-2.*Looking at the SVG elements in ChromeWeb Inspector*

In Figure 3-2, the highlighted text element contains the following code:

```
< text y="60" x="200" font-family="impact" font-size="60px"
  fill="#996600" text-anchor="middle">
    Happy Trails
</text>
```

In the development environment you can add, remove, and edit SVG elements. The changes take effect instantly in the active page. This is extremely convenient for debugging and experimenting.

RETAINED-MODE GRAPHICS

Frank says: "There are two schools of thought in graphics API design. Immediate-mode graphics like canvas provide a drawing interface. API calls cause a drawing action to occur *immediately*, hence the name. The counter style to immediate mode-graphics is called retained-mode. In retained-mode graphics, there is a model of the visual objects in the scene that is retained over time. There is an API to manipulate the scene graph, and the graphics engine redraws the scene when it changes. SVG is retained-mode graphics in which its scene graph is the document. The API to manipulate SVG is the W3C DOM API.

There are JavaScript libraries that build-retained mode APIs on top of canvas. Some also provide sprites, input handling, and layers. You may choose to use such a library, but remember that these features and more are native in SVG!"

Scalable Graphics

When you magnify, rotate, or otherwise transform SVG content, all of the lines making up the image are crisply redrawn. SVG scales without losing quality. The vector information that makes up an SVG document is preserved when it is rendered. Contrast that with pixel graphics. If you magnify a pixel graphic like a canvas or an image, it becomes blurry. That is because the image is composed of pixels that can only be resampled at a higher resolution. The underlying information—the paths and shapes that went into making the image—is lost after drawing (see Figure 3-3).

Figure 3-3. *Closeups of SVG and canvas at 500% magnification*

Creating 2D Graphics with SVG

Let's look again at the *Happy Trails!* image from Figure 3-1.Every visible part of this SVG drawing has some corresponding markup. The complete SVG language is quite extensive, and all of its details and nuances will not fit in this chapter. However, to get a glimpse of the breadth of the SVG vocabulary, here are some of the features used to draw Happy Trails:

- Shapes
- Paths
- Transformations
- Patterns and Gradients
- Reusable Content
- Text

Let's look at each of these in turn before we combine them into a complete scene. Before we can do that, though, we'll need to see how to add SVG to a page.

Adding SVG to a Page

Adding inline SVG to an HTML page is as simple as adding any other element.

There are several ways to use SVG on the Web, including as <img> elements. We will use inline SVG in HTML, because it will integrate into the HTML document. That will let us later write an interactive application that seamlessly combines HTML, JavaScript, and SVG (see Listing 3-1).

Listing 3-1. *SVG Containing a Red Rectangle*

```
<!doctype html>
<svg width="200" height="200">
</svg>
```

That's it! No XML namespace necessary. Now, between the start and end svg tags, we can add shapes and other visual objects. If you want to split the SVG content out into a separate .svg file, you will need to change it like so:

```
<svg width="400" height="600" xmlns="http://www.w3.org/2000/svg"
    xmlns:xlink="http://www.w3.org/1999/xlink">
</svg>
```

Now it is a valid XML document with the proper namespace attributes. You will be able to open that document with a wide variety of image viewers and editors. You can also refer to an SVG file from HTML as a static image with code such as `<img src="example.svg">`. One downside to that approach is that the SVG document is not integrated into the DOM the way inline SVG content is. You won't be able to script interaction with the SVG elements.

Simple Shapes

The SVG language includes basic shape elements such as rectangles, circles, and ellipses. The size and position of shape elements are defined with attributes. For rectangles, these are width and height. For circles, there is an r attribute for radius. All of these use the CSS syntax for distances, so they can be pixels, points, ems, and so on. Listing 3-2 is a very short HTML document containing inline SVG. It is just a gray rectangle with a red outline that is 100 pixels by 80 pixels in size, and it is displayed in Figure 3-4.

Listing 3-2. *SVG Containing a Red Rectangle*

```
<!doctype html>
<svg width="200" height="200">
  <rect x="10" y="20" width="100" height="80" stroke="red" fill="#ccc" />
</svg>
```

Figure 3-4. *An SVG rectangle in an HTML document*

SVG draws objects in the order they appear in the document. If we add a circle after the rectangle, it appears on top of the first shape. We will give that circle an 8 pixel wide blue stroke and no fill style (see Listing 3-3), so it stands out, as shown in Figure 3-5.

Listing 3-3. *A Rectangle and a Circle*

```
<!doctype html>
<svg width="200" height="200">
  <rect x="10" y="20" width="100" height="80" stroke="red" fill="#ccc" />
  <circle cx="120" cy="80" r="40" stroke="#00f" fill="none" stroke-width="8" />
</svg>
```

Figure 3-5. *A rectangle and a circle*

Note that the x and y attributes define the position of the top-left corner of the rectangle. The circle, on the other hand, has cx and cy attributes, which are the x and y values for the center of the circle. SVG uses the same coordinate system as the canvas API. The top-left corner of the svg element is position 0,0. See Chapter 2 for the details of the canvas coordinate system.

Transforming SVG Elements

There are organizational elements in SVG intended to combine multiple elements so that they can be transformed or linked to as units. The <g> element stands for "group." Groups can be used to combine multiple related elements. As a group, they can be referred to by a common ID. A group can also be transformed as a unit. If you add a transform attribute to a group, all of that group's contents are transformed. The transform attribute can include commands to rotate (see Listing 3-4 and Figure 3-6), translate, scale, and skew. You can also specify a transformation matrix, just as you can with the canvas API.

Listing 3-4. *A Rectangle and a Circle Within a Rotated Group*

```
<svg width="200" height="200">
  <g transform="translate(60,0) rotate(30) scale(0.75)" id="ShapeGroup">
    <rect x="10" y="20" width="100" height="80" stroke="red" fill="#ccc" />
    <circle cx="120" cy="80" r="40" stroke="#00f" fill="none" stroke-width="8" />
  </g>
</svg>
```

Figure 3-6. *A rotated group*

Reusing Content

SVG has a <defs> element for defining content for future use. It also has an element named <use> that you can link to your definitions. This lets you reuse the same content multiple times and eliminate redundancy. Figure 3-7 shows a group used three times at different transformed positions and scales. The group has the id ShapeGroup, and it contains a rectangle and a circle. The actual rectangle and circle shapes are just defined the one time inside of the <defs> element. The defined group is not, by itself, visible. Instead, there are three <use> elements linked to the shape group, so three rectangles and three circles appear rendered on the page (see Listing 3-5).

Listing 3-5. *Using a Group Three Times*

```
<svg width="200" height="200">
  <defs>
    <g id="ShapeGroup">
      <rect x="10" y="20" width="100" height="80" stroke="red" fill="#ccc" />
      <circle cx="120" cy="80" r="40" stroke="#00f" fill="none" stroke-width="8" />
    </g>
  </defs>

  <use xlink:href="#ShapeGroup" transform="translate(60,0) scale(0.5)"/>
  <use xlink:href="#ShapeGroup" transform="translate(120,80) scale(0.4)"/>
  <use xlink:href="#ShapeGroup" transform="translate(20,60) scale(0.25)"/>
</svg>
```

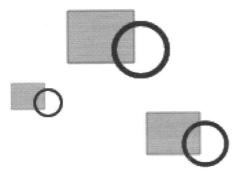

Figure 3-7. Three use elements referencing the same group

Patterns and Gradients

The circle and rectangle in Figure 3-7 have simple fill and stroke styles. Objects can be painted with more complex styles, including gradients and patterns (see Listing 3-6). Gradients can be linear or radial. Patterns can be made up of pixel graphics or even other SVG elements. Figure 3-8 shows a rectangle with a linear color gradient as well as a circle with a gravel texture. The texture comes from a JPEG image that is linked to from an SVG image element.

Listing 3-6. Texturing the Rectangle and Circle

```
<!doctype html>
<svg width="200" height="200">
  <defs>
    <pattern id="GravelPattern" patternUnits="userSpaceOnUse"
        x="0" y="0" width="100" height="67" viewBox="0 0 100 67">
      <image x="0" y="0" width="100" height="67" xlink:href="gravel.jpg"></image>
    </pattern>

    <linearGradient id="RedBlackGradient">
        <stop offset="0%" stop-color="#000"></stop>
        <stop offset="100%" stop-color="#f00"></stop>
    </linearGradient>
  </defs>

  <rect x="10" y="20" width="100" height="80"
      stroke="red"
      fill="url(#RedBlackGradient)" />
  <circle cx="120" cy="80" r="40" stroke="#00f"
      stroke-width="8"
      fill="url(#GravelPattern)" />
</svg>
```

Figure 3-8. A rectangle with a gradient fill and a circle with a pattern fill

SVG Paths

SVG has freeform paths as well as simple shapes. Path elements have d attributes. The "d" stands for data. Inside the value of the d attribute, you can specify a series of path drawing commands. Each command might take coordinate arguments. Some of the commands are M for moveto, L for lineto, Q for quadratic curve, and Z for closing the path. If these remind you of the canvas drawing API, that is no coincidence. Listing 3-7 uses a path element to draw a closed tree canopy shape using a series of lineto commands.

Listing 3-7. SVG Path Defining a Tree Canopy

```
<path d="M-25, -50
        L-10, -80
        L-20, -80
        L-5, -110
        L-15, -110
        L0, -140
        L15, -110
        L5, -110
        L20, -80
        L10, -80
        L25, -50
        Z" id="Canopy"></path>
```

You can fill a path by closing it with the Z command and giving it a fill attribute, just like the rectangle we drew earlier. Figure 3-9 shows how to draw a tree by combining a stroked closed path and a filled closed path.

Figure 3-9. A stroked path, a filled path, and both paths

Similarly, we can create an open path with two quadratic curves to form a trail. We can even give it texture. Note the stroke-linejoin attribute in Listing 3-8. This makes a round connection between the two quadratic curves. Figure 3-10 shows a mountain trail drawn as an open path.

Listing 3-8. SVG Path Defining a Twisting Trail

```
<g transform="translate(-10, 350)" stroke-width="20" stroke="url(#GravelPattern)" stroke-
linejoin="round">
        <path d="M0,0 Q170,-50 260, -190 Q310, -250 410,-250" fill="none"></path>
    </g>
```

Figure 3-10. An open path containing two quadratic curves

Using SVG Text

SVG also supports text. Text in SVG is selectable within the browser (see Figure 3-11). Should they choose to, browsers and search engines could also allow users to search for text inside of SVG text elements. This has major usability and accessibility benefits.

SVG Text has attributes that are similar to CSS style rules for HTML. Listing 3-9 shows a text element that has font-weight and font-family attributes. As in CSS, font-family can be a single font-family name like "sans-serif" or a list of fallbacks like "Droid Sans, sans-serif" in the order you prefer.

Listing 3-9. SVG Text

```
<svg width="600" height="200">
  <text
    x="10" y="80"
    font-family="Droid Sans"
    stroke="#00f"
    fill="#0ff"
    font-size="40px"
    font-weight="bold">
    Select this text!
  </text>
</svg>
```

Figure 3-11. Selecting SVG text

Putting the Scene Together

We can combine all of the preceding elements to make an image of happy trails. The text is, naturally, a text element. The tree trunks are composed of two rectangles. The tree canopies are two paths. The trees cast shadows, which use the same geometry given a gray fill color and a transformation that skews them down and to the right. The winding path that cuts across the image is another path with an image pattern for texture. There is also a little bit of CSS to give the scene an outline.

Listing 3-10 provides the complete code for trails-static.html.

***Listing 3-10.** Complete Code for trails-static.html*

```
<title>Happy Trails in SVG</title>

<style>
  svg {
      border: 1px solid black;
  }
</style>

<svg width="400" height="600">

  <defs>
      <pattern id="GravelPattern" patternUnits="userSpaceOnUse" x="0" y="0" width="100"
height="67" viewBox="0 0 100 67">
      <image x=0 y=0 width=100 height=67 xlink:href="gravel.jpg" />
      </pattern>
      <linearGradient id="TrunkGradient">
      <stop offset="0%" stop-color="#663300" />
      <stop offset="40%" stop-color="#996600" />
      <stop offset="100%" stop-color="#552200" />
      </linearGradient>

      <rect x="-5" y="-50" width=10 height=50 id="Trunk" />
      <path d="M-25, -50
              L-10, -80
              L-20, -80
              L-5, -110
              L-15, -110
              L0, -140
              L15, -110
              L5, -110
              L20, -80
              L10, -80
              L25, -50
              Z"
      id="Canopy"
      />
      <linearGradient id="CanopyShadow" x=0 y=0 x2=0 y2=100%>
      <stop offset="0%" stop-color="#000" stop-opacity=".5" />
      <stop offset="20%" stop-color="#000" stop-opacity="0" />
      </linearGradient>
```

```
      <g id="Tree">
      <use xlink:href="#Trunk" fill="url(#TrunkGradient)" />
      <use xlink:href="#Trunk" fill="url(#CanopyShadow)" />
      <use xlink:href="#Canopy" fill="none" stroke="#663300"
      stroke-linejoin="round" stroke-width="4px" />
      <use xlink:href="#Canopy" fill="#339900" stroke="none" />
      </g>

      <g id="TreeShadow">
      <use xlink:href="#Trunk" fill="#000" />
      <use xlink:href="#Canopy" fill="000" stroke="none" />
      </g>
</defs>


<g transform="translate(-10, 350)"
      stroke-width="20"
      stroke="url(#GravelPattern)"
      stroke-linejoin="round">
      <path d="M0,0 Q170,-50 260, -190 Q310, -250 410,-250"
      fill="none" />
</g>

<text y=60 x=200
      font-family="impact"
      font-size="60px"
      fill="#996600"
      text-anchor="middle" >
      Happy Trails!
</text>

<use xlink:href="#TreeShadow"
      transform="translate(130, 250) scale(1, .6) skewX(-18)"
      opacity="0.4" />
<use xlink:href="#Tree" transform="translate(130,250)" />

<use xlink:href="#TreeShadow"
      transform="translate(260, 500) scale(2, 1.2) skewX(-18)"
      opacity="0.4" />

<use xlink:href="#Tree" transform="translate(260, 500) scale(2)" />
</svg>
```

Building an Interactive Application with SVG

In this section, we'll expand on the static example. We will add HTML and JavaScript to make the document interactive. We will take advantage of the capabilities of SVG in an application that would require considerably more code to implement with the canvas API.

Adding Trees

We need just a single button element in this interactive application. The click handler for the button adds a new tree at a random location within the 600x400 pixel SVG region. The new tree is also randomly scaled by an amount between 50% and 150%. Each new tree is actually a <use> element referencing the "Tree" group containing multiple paths. The code uses the namespaced document.createElementNS() call to create a <use> element. It links it with the xlink:href attribute to the previously defined Tree group. It then appends the new element to the SVG element tree (see Listing 3-11).

Listing 3-11. Add Tree Function

```
document.getElementById("AddTreeButton").onclick = function() {
  var x = Math.floor(Math.random() * 400);
  var y = Math.floor(Math.random() * 600);
  var scale = Math.random() + .5;
  var translate = "translate(" +x+ "," +y+ ") ";

  var tree = document.createElementNS("http://www.w3.org/2000/svg", "use");
  tree.setAttributeNS("http://www.w3.org/1999/xlink", "xlink:href", "#Tree");
  tree.setAttribute("transform", translate + "scale(" + scale + ")");
  document.querySelector("svg").appendChild(tree);
  updateTrees();
}
```

Elements are rendered in the order they appear in the DOM. This function always adds trees as new child nodes at the end of the SVG element's list of child nodes. That means that newer trees will appear on top of older trees.

This function ends with a call to updateTrees(), which we will see next.

Adding the updateTrees Function

The updateTrees function runs when the document initially loads as well as any time trees are added or removed. It is responsible for updating the text that displays the number of trees in the forest. It also attaches a click handler function to each tree (see Listing 3-12).

Listing 3-12 updateTrees Function

```
function updateTrees() {
  var list = document.querySelectorAll("use");
  var treeCount = 0;
  for (var i=0; i<list.length; i++) {
    if(list[i].getAttribute("xlink:href")=="#Tree") {
      treeCount++;
      list[i].onclick = removeTree;
    }
  }
  var counter = document.getElementById("TreeCounter");
  counter.textContent = treeCount + " trees in the forest";
}
```

An important thing to note about this code is that it keeps no state in JavaScript regarding the tree count. Every time an update occurs, this code selects and filters all of the trees from the live document to get the latest count.

Adding the removeTree Function

Now, let's add the function that removes trees when they are clicked (see Listing 3-13).

Listing 3-13. removeTree Function

```
function removeTree(e) {
  var elt = e.target;
  if (elt.correspondingUseElement) {
    elt = elt.correspondingUseElement;
  }
  elt.parentNode.removeChild(elt);
  updateTrees();

}
```

The first thing we do here is check the target of the click event. Due to differences in DOM implementations, the event target could be either the tree group or a use element linked to that group. Either way, this function simply removes that element from the DOM and calls the updateTrees() function.

If you remove a tree that is on top of another tree, you don't have to do anything to redraw the lower content. This is one of the benefits of developing against a retained-mode API. You simply manipulate the tree (no pun intended) of elements, and the browser takes care of drawing the necessary pixels. Similarly, when the text updates to display the latest tree count, it stays below the trees. If you want the text to appear above the trees, you will have to append the trees to the document before the text element.

Adding the CSS Styles

To make the interaction more discoverable, we will add some CSS that changes the appearance of the tree beneath the mouse cursor:

```
g[id=Tree]:hover  {
      opacity: 0.9;
      cursor: crosshair;
  }
```

Whenever you hover over an element with an id attribute equal to "Tree," that element will become partially transparent, and the mouse cursor will change to a crosshair.

The one pixel black border around the entire SVG element is also defined in CSS.

```
svg {
  border: 1px solid black;
}
```

And that's it! Now you have an interactive application using inline SVG in HTML5 (see Figure 3-12).

Figure 3-12. *The final document with a few trees added*

The Final Code

For completeness, Listing 3-14 provides the entire `trails-dynamic.html` file. It contains all of the SVG from the static version as well as the script that makes it interactive.

Listing 3-14. *The Entire `trails-dynamic.html` Code*

```
<!doctype html>
<title>Happy Trails in SVG</title>

<style>
  svg {
    border: 1px solid black;
  }
  g[id=Tree]:hover  {
    opacity: 0.9;
    cursor: crosshair;
  }
</style>

<div>
  <button id="AddTreeButton">Add Tree</button>
```

```
    </div>

    <svg width="400" height="600">

      <defs>
        <pattern id="GravelPattern" patternUnits="userSpaceOnUse" x="0" y="0" width="100"
    height="67" viewBox="0 0 100 67">
          <image x=0 y=0 width=100 height=67 xlink:href="gravel.jpg" />
        </pattern>
        <linearGradient id="TrunkGradient">
          <stop offset="0%" stop-color="#663300" />
          <stop offset="40%" stop-color="#996600" />
          <stop offset="100%" stop-color="#552200" />
        </linearGradient>

        <rect x="-5" y="-50" width=10 height=50 id="Trunk" />
        <path d="M-25, -50
                L-10, -80
                L-20, -80
                L-5, -110
                L-15, -110
                L0, -140
                L15, -110
                L5, -110
                L20, -80
                L10, -80
                L25, -50
                Z"
          id="Canopy"
        />
        <linearGradient id="CanopyShadow" x=0 y=0 x2=0 y2=100%>
          <stop offset="0%" stop-color="#000" stop-opacity=".5" />
          <stop offset="20%" stop-color="#000" stop-opacity="0" />
        </linearGradient>
        <g id="Tree">
          <use xlink:href="#Trunk" fill="url(#TrunkGradient)" />
          <use xlink:href="#Trunk" fill="url(#CanopyShadow)" />
          <use xlink:href="#Canopy" fill="none" stroke="#663300"
            stroke-linejoin="round" stroke-width="4px" />
          <use xlink:href="#Canopy" fill="#339900" stroke="none" />
        </g>
      </defs>


      <g transform="translate(-10, 350)"
          stroke-width="20"
          stroke="url(#GravelPattern)"
          stroke-linejoin="round">
          <path d="M0,0 Q170,-50 260, -190 Q310, -250 410,-250"
            fill="none" />
      </g>
```

```
  <text y=60 x=200
    font-family="impact"
    font-size="60px"
    fill="#996600"
    text-anchor="middle" >
    Happy Trails!
  </text>
  <text y=90 x=200
    font-family="impact"
    font-size="20px"
    fill="#996600"
    text-anchor="middle" id="TreeCounter">
  </text>

  <text y=420 x=20
    font-family="impact"
    font-size="20px"
    fill="#996600"
    text-anchor="left">
    <tspan>You can remove a</tspan>
    <tspan y=440 x=20>tree by clicking on it.</tspan>
  </text>

  <use xlink:href="#Tree" transform="translate(130,250)" />
  <use xlink:href="#Tree" transform="translate(260, 500) scale(2)" />
</svg>

<script>
  function removeTree(e) {
    var elt = e.target;
    if (elt.correspondingUseElement) {
      elt = elt.correspondingUseElement;
    }
    elt.parentNode.removeChild(elt);
    updateTrees();
  }

  document.getElementById("AddTreeButton").onclick = function() {
    var x = Math.floor(Math.random() * 400);
    var y = Math.floor(Math.random() * 600);
    var scale = Math.random() + .5;
    var translate = "translate(" +x+ "," +y+ ") ";

    var tree = document.createElementNS("http://www.w3.org/2000/svg", "use");
    tree.setAttributeNS("http://www.w3.org/1999/xlink", "xlink:href", "#Tree");
    tree.setAttribute("transform", translate + "scale(" + scale + ")");
    document.querySelector("svg").appendChild(tree);
    updateTrees();
  }

  function updateTrees() {
    var list = document.querySelectorAll("use");
```

```
  var treeCount = 0;
  for (var i=0; i<list.length; i++) {
    if(list[i].getAttribute("xlink:href")=="#Tree") {
      treeCount++;
      list[i].onclick = removeTree;
    }
  }
  var counter = document.getElementById("TreeCounter");
  counter.textContent = treeCount + " trees in the forest";
}

updateTrees();
</script>
```

SVG TOOLS

Frank says: "Because of SVG's long history as a standard format for vector graphics, there are many useful tools for working with SVG images. There is even an open-source editor called SVG-edit that runs in the browser. You can embed it in your own applications! On the desktop, Adobe Illustrator and Inkscape are two powerful vector graphics applications that can both import and export SVG. I've found Inkscape to be very useful for creating new graphics (see Figure 3-13).

SVG tools tend to work with standalone .svg files, not SVG embedded in HTML, so you may need to convert between the two formats."

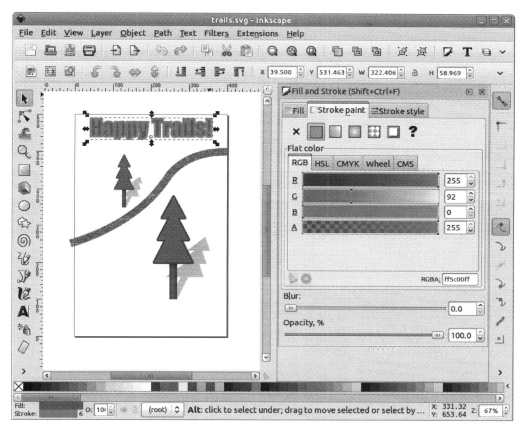

***Figure 3-13.** Modifying the stroke of a text element in Inkscape*

Summary

In this chapter, you have seen how SVG in HTML5 provides a powerful way to create applications with interactive two dimensional graphics.

First we looked at a scene drawn using SVG embedded in an HTML5 document. We examined the elements and attributes that made up the drawing. We saw how you can define and reuse content definitions, group and transform elements, and draw with shapes, paths, and text.

Finally, we added JavaScript to an SVG document to make an interactive application. We used CSS, DOM manipulation, and events to take advantage of SVG's nature as a live document.

Now that we've seen how SVG brings vector graphics to HTML5, we'll turn our attention to audio-visual elements that bring more complex media to your application.

CHAPTER 4

Working with Audio and Video

In this chapter, we'll explore what you can do with two important HTML5 elements—*audio* and *video*—and we'll show you how they can be used to create compelling applications. The audio and video elements add new media options to HTML5 applications that allow you to use audio and video without plugins while providing a common, integrated, and scriptable API.

First, we'll discuss audio and video container files and codecs, and why we ended up with the codecs supported today. We'll go on to describe lack of common codec support—the most important drawback for using the media elements—and we'll discuss how we hope that this won't be such a big issue in the future. We'll also show you a mechanism for switching to the most appropriate type of content for the browser to display.

Next, we'll show you how you can use control audio and video programmatically using the APIs and finally we'll explore the use of the audio and video in your applications.

Overview of Audio and Video

In the following sections, we'll discuss some of the key concepts related to Audio and video: containers and codecs.

Video Containers

An audio or video file is really just a *container* file, similar to a ZIP archive file that contains a number of files. Figure 4-1 shows how a video file (a video container) contains audio tracks, video tracks, and additional metadata. The audio and video tracks are combined at runtime to play the video. The metadata contains information about the video such as cover art, title and subtitle, captioning information, and so on.

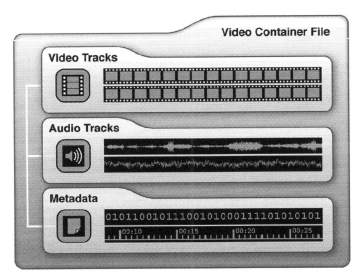

Figure 4-1. Overview of the video container

Some of the popular video container formats include the following:

- Audio Video Interleave (.avi)
- Flash Video (.flv)
- MPEG 4 (.mp4)
- Matroska (.mkv)
- Ogg (.ogv)

Audio and Video Codecs

Audio and video *coders/decoders* (*codecs*) are algorithms used to encode and decode a particular audio or video stream so that they can be played back. Raw media files are enormous, so without encoding, a video or audio clip would consist of tremendous amounts of data that could be too large to transmit across the Internet in a reasonable amount of time. Without a decoder, the recipient would not be able to reconstitute the original media source from the encoded form. A codec is able to understand a specific container format and decodes the audio and video tracks that it contains.

Some example audio codecs are the following:

- AAC
- MPEG-3
- Ogg Vorbis

Example video codecs are the following:

- H.264
- VP8
- Ogg Theora

The Codec Wars and the Tentative Truce

Some of the codecs are patent-encumbered, while others are freely available. For example, the Vorbis audio codec and the Theora video codec are freely available, while the use of the MPEG-4 and H.264 codecs are subject to license fees.

Originally, the HTML5 specification was going to require that certain codecs were supported. However, some vendors did not wish to include Ogg Theora as it was not part of their existing hardware and software stacks. Apple's iPhone, for example, includes hardware accelerated decoding for h264 video but not Theora. Free systems, on the other hand, cannot include proprietary for-pay codecs without hurting downstream distribution. On top of that, the performance that certain proprietary codecs provide is a factor in the browser uptake of free codecs. This situation has led to a stalemate; there does not appear to be a single codec that all browser vendors are willing to implement.

For now, the codec requirement has been dropped from the specification. However, this decision may be revisited in the future. For now, understand the current browser support and understand that you may need to re-encode your media for different environments. (You should probably be doing this already.)

We do expect that support for different codecs will increase and converge over time, making the choice of common media types easy and ubiquitous. It is also possible that one codec will grow to be the de facto standard codec for the Web. Additionally, the media tags have a built in mechanism for switching to the most appropriate type of content for the browser to display to make supporting different environments easy.

Here Comes WebM

Frank says: "Google introduced the WebM video format in May 2010. WebM is a new format for audio and video intended to clear up the murky media format situation on the Web. WebM files have the `.webm` extension and consist of VP8 video and Ogg Vorbis audio in a container based on Matroska. Google released the WebM specification and software under permissive licenses covering source code and patent rights. As a high quality format that is free for both implementers and publishers, WebM represents a significant development in the codec landscape."

Audio and Video Restrictions

There are a few things that are not supported in the Audio and video specification:

- *Streaming* audio and video. That is, there is currently no standard for bitrate switching in HTML5 video; only full media files are supported by current implementations. However, there are aspects of the spec that are designed to support streaming media in the future once the formats are supported.

- Media is restricted by HTTP cross-origin resource sharing. See Chapter 6 for more information about cross-origin resource sharing (CORS).

- Full-screen video is not scriptable because it could be considered a security violation to let a scriptable element take over the full screen. However, browsers have the option of letting users choose to view videos in full screen through additional controls.

Browser Support for Audio and Video

Due to the fractured codec support, simply knowing which browsers support the new audio and video elements is not enough; you also need to know which codecs are supported. Table4-1 shows which browsers support which codecs at the time of this writing.

Table 4-1. Audio and Video Codec and Container Support

Browser	Codec and Container Support
Chrome	Ogg (Theora and Vorbis) WebM (VP8 and Vorbis) MPEG 4 (H.264 and AAC)
Firefox	Ogg (Theora and Vorbis) WebM (VP8 and Vorbis)
Internet Explorer	MPEG 4 (H.264 and AAC)
Opera	Ogg (Theora and Vorbis) WebM (VP8 and Vorbis)
Safari	MPEG 4 (H.264 and AAC)

Note also that Google announced it will drop support for the MP4 format, but that has not happened yet. Also, there is a plugin that can be used to play WebM in Internet Explorer 9. It is always good idea to first test whether audio and video are supported. The section "Checking for Browser Support" later in this chapter will show you how you can programmatically check for browser support.

Using the Audio and Video API

In this section, we'll explore the use of the audio and video in your applications. There are two main benefits to using the new media tags over previous video-embedding techniques—usually videos are embedded using the Flash, QuickTime, or Windows Media plugins—that aim to make life easier for users and developers:

- *The new audio and video tags remove deployment hurdles by being part of the native browser environment.* Although some plugins have high install rates, they are often blocked in controlled corporate environments. Some users choose to disable these plugins due to the... ostentatious... advertising displays those plugins are also capable of, which also removes their capability to be used for media playback. Plugins are also separate vectors of attack for security issues. And plugins often have difficulty integrating their displays with the rest of browser content, causing clipping or transparency issues with certain site designs. Because plugins use a self-contained rendering model that is different from that of the base web page, developers face difficulties if elements such as popup menus or other visual elements need to cross plugin boundaries in a page.

- *The media elements expose a common, integrated, and scriptable API to the document.* As a developer, your use of the new media elements allows very simple ways to script the control and playback of content. We will see multiple examples of this later in the chapter.

Of course, there is one primary drawback to using the media tags: lack of common codec support, as discussed in the earlier sections of this chapter. However, we expect that support for codecs will increase and converge over time, making the choice of common media types easy and ubiquitous. Plus, the media tags have a built-in mechanism for switching to the most appropriate type of content for the browser to display, as you will soon see.

Checking for Browser Support

The easiest way to check for support of the video and audio tags is to dynamically create one or both with scripting and check for the existence of a function:

```
var hasVideo = !!(document.createElement('video').canPlayType);
```

This simple code line will dynamically create a video element and check for the existence of the canPlayType() function. By using the !! operator, the result is converted to a Boolean value, which indicates whether or not a video object could be created.

However, if video or audio support is not present, you may choose to use an enabling script that introduces media script tags into older browsers, allowing the same scriptability but using technologies such as Flash for playback.

Alternatively, you can choose to include alternate content between your audio or video tags, and the alternate content will display in place of the unsupported tag. This alternate content can be used for a Flash plugin to display the same video if the browser doesn't support the HTML5 tags. If you merely wish to display a text message for nonsupporting browsers, it is quite easy to add content inside the video or audio elements as shown in Listing 4-1.

Listing 4-1. *Simple Video Element*

```
<video src="video.webm" controls>
  Your browser does not support HTML5 video.
</video>
```

However, if you choose to use an alternative method to render video for browsers without HTML5 media support, you can use the same element content section to provide a reference to an external plugin displaying the same media as shown in Listing 4-2.

Listing 4-2. Video Element with Flash Fallback

```
<video src="video.webm" controls>
  <object data="videoplayer.swf" type="application/x-shockwave-flash">
    <param name="movie" value="video.swf"/>
  </object>
  Your browser does not support HTML5 video.
</video>
```

By embedding an object element that displays a Flash video inside the video element, the HTML5 video will be preferred if it is available, and the Flash video will be used as a fallback. Unfortunately, this requires multiple versions of the video to be served up until HTML5 support is ubiquitous.

Accessibility

Making your web applications accessible to everyone isn't just the right thing to do; it's good business, and, in some cases, it's the law! Users with limited vision or hearing should be presented with alternative content that meets their needs. Keep in mind that the alternative content located between the video and audio elements is only displayed if the browser does *not* support those elements at all and, therefore, is not suitable for accessible displays where the browser may support HTML5 media but the user may not.

The emerging standard for video accessibility is Web Video Text Tracks (WebVTT), formerly known as Web SubRip Text (WebSRT) format. At the time of this writing, it is only just starting to appear in some early builds of browsers. WebVTT uses a simple text file (*.vtt) that starts with the word WEBVTT on the first line. The vtt file must be served up with the mime type text/vtt. Listing 4-3 shows the contents of an example vtt file.

Listing 4-3. WebVTT File

```
WEBVTT

1
00:00:01,000 --> 00:00:03,000
What do you think about HTML5 Video and WebVTT?...

2
00:00:04,000 --> 00:00:08,000
I think it's great. I can't wait for all the browsers to support it!
```

To use the vtt file in your video element, add the track element pointing to the vtt file as shown in the following example:

```
<video src="video.webm" controls>
  <track label="English" kind="subtitles" srclang="en" src="subtitles_en.vtt" default>
  Your browser does not support HTML5 video.
</video>
```

You can add multiple track elements. Listing 4-4 shows how you can support English and Dutch subtitles using track elements pointing to a vtt file.

Listing 4-4. Using WebVTT Tracks in a Video Element

```
<video src="video.ogg" controls>
  <track label="English" kind="subtitles" srclang="en" src="subtitles_en.vtt">
  <track label="Dutch" kind="subtitles" srclang="nl" src="subtitles_nl.vtt">
  Your browser does not support HTML5 video.
</video>
```

The WebVTT standard supports more than just subtitles. It also allows for captions and cue settings (instructions for how text is rendered). The full WebVTT syntax is beyond the scope of this book. See the WHATWG specification at `www.whatwg.org/specs/web-apps/current-work/webvtt.html` for more details.

Understanding Media Elements

Due to a wise design decision, there is much commonality between the `audio` and `video` elements in HTML5. Both audio and video support many of the same operations—play, pause, mute/unmute, load, and so on—and therefore, the common behavior was separated out into the *media* element section of the specification. Let's start examining the media elements by observing what they have in common.

The Basics: Declaring Your Media Element

For the sake of example, we will use an `audio` tag to try out the common behaviors of HTML5 media. The examples in this section will be very media-heavy (surprise!), and they are included in the `code/av` folder of the support files that come with this book.

For the very simplest example (the example file `audio.html`), let's create a page that shows an audio player for a soothing, satisfying, and very public domain audio clip: Johann Sebastian Bach's "Air" (shown in Listing 4-5).

Listing 4-5. HTML Page with an Audio Element

```
<!DOCTYPE html>
<html>
  <title>HTML5 Audio </title>
  <audio controls src="johann_sebastian_bach_air.ogg">
          An audio clip from Johann Sebastian Bach.
  </audio>
</html>
```

This clip assumes that the HTML document and the audio file—in this case, johann_sebastian_bach_air.ogg—are served from the same directory. As shown in Figure 4-2, viewing this in a browser supporting the audio tag will show a simple control and play bar representing the audio to play. When the user clicks the play button, the audio track starts as expected.

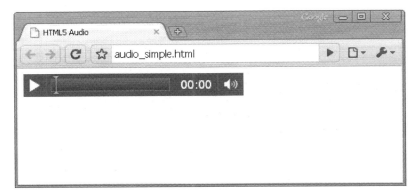

Figure 4-2. Simple audio controls

The controls attribute tells the browser to display common user controls for starting, stopping, and seeking in the media clip, as well as volume control. Leaving out the controls attribute hides them, and leaves the clip with no way for the user to start playing.

The content between the audio tags is a text representation of what the browser will display if it does not support the media tag. This is what you and your users will see if they are running an older browser. It also gives the opportunity to include an alternate renderer for the media, such as a Flash player plugin or a direct link to the media file.

Using the Source

Finally, we come to the most important attribute: src. In the simplest setup, a single src attribute points to the file containing the media clip. But what if the browser in question does not support that container or codec (in this case, Ogg and Vorbis)? Then, an alternate declaration is shown in Listing 4-6; it includes multiple sources from which the browser can choose (see the example file audio_multisource.html).

Listing 4-6. An Audio Element with Multiple Source Elements

```
<audio controls>
    <source src="johann_sebastian_bach_air.ogg">
    <source src="johann_sebastian_bach_air.mp3">
    An audio clip from Johann Sebastian Bach.
</audio>
```

In this case, we include two new source elements instead of the src attribute on the audio tag. This allows the browser to choose which source best suits the playback capabilities it has and use the best fit as the actual media clip. Sources are processed in order, so a browser that can play multiple listed source types will use the first one it encounters.

■ **Note** Place the media source files with the best user experience or lowest server load highest in any source list.

Running this clip in a supported browser may not change what you see. But if a browser supports the MP3 format and not the Ogg Vorbis format, the media playback will now be supported. The beauty of this declaration model is that as you write code to interact with the media file, it doesn't matter to you which container or codec was actually used. The browser provides a unified interface for you to manipulate the media, no matter which source was matched for playback.

However, there is another way to give the browser hints about which media source to use. Recall that a container for media can support many different codec types, and you will understand that a browser may be misled into which types it does or does not support based on the extension of the declared source file. If you specify a type attribute that does not match your source, the browser may refuse to play the media. It may be wise to include the type only if you know it with certainty. Otherwise, it is better to omit this attribute and let the browser detect the encoding as shown in Listing 4-7 (in the example file audio_type.html). Also note that the WebM format allows only one audio codec and one video codec. That means the .webm extension or the video/webm content-type tells you everything you need to know about the file. If a browser can play .webm, it should be able to play any valid .webm file.

Listing 4-7. Including Type and Codec Information in an Audio Element

```
<audio controls>
    <source src="johann_sebastian_bach_air.ogg" type="audio/ogg; codecs=vorbis">
    <source src="johann_sebastian_bach_air.mp3" type="audio/mpeg">
    An audio clip from Johann Sebastian Bach.
</audio>
```

As you can see, the type attribute can declare both the container and codec type. The values here represent Ogg Vorbis and MP3, respectively. The full list is governed by RFC 4281, a document maintained by the Internet Engineering Task Force (IETF), but some common combinations are listed in Table 4-2.

Table 4-2. Media Types and Attribute Values

Type	Attribute Value
Theora video and Vorbis audio in an Ogg container	type='video/ogg; codecs="theora, vorbis"'
Vorbis audio in an Ogg container	type='audio/ogg; codecs=vorbis'
WebM video in a Matroska container	type='video/webm; codecs="vp8, vorbis"'
Simple baseline H.264 video and low complexity AAC audio in an MP4 container	type='video/mp4; codecs="avc1.42E01E, mp4a.40.2"'
MPEG-4 visual simple profile and low complexity AAC audio in an MP4 container	type='video/mp4; codecs="mp4v.20.8, mp4a.40.2"'

Taking Control

You've already seen that the default playback controls can be displayed by using the controls attribute in the video or audio tag. As you might expect, leaving out this attribute will not display controls when the media is displayed, but it will also not show anything at all in the case of *audio* files, as the only visual representation of an audio element is its controls. (A video without controls still displays the video content.) Leaving out the controls attribute should not display any content that affects the normal rendering of the page. One way to cause the media to play is to set another attribute in the tag: autoplay (see Listing 4-8 and the example file audio_no_control.html).

Listing 4-8. Using the Autoplay Attribute

```
<audio autoplay>
    <source src="johann_sebastian_bach_air.ogg" type="audio/ogg; codecs=vorbis">
    <source src="johann_sebastian_bach_air.mp3" type="audio/mpeg">
    An audio clip from Johann Sebastian Bach.
</audio>
```

By including the autoplay attribute, the media file will play as soon as it is loaded, without any user interaction. (Note that autoplay is not supported everywhere. For example, it is disabled on iOS.) However, most users will find this highly annoying, so use autoplay with caution. Playing audio without prompting may be intended to create an atmospheric effect or, worse, to force an advertisement on the user. But it also interferes with other audio playing on the user's machine, and can be quite detrimental to users who rely on audible screen readers to navigate web content. Note also that some devices, like the iPad, prevent autoplay and even automatically playing a media file (triggered by a page load event, for example).

If the built-in controls do not suit the layout of your user interface, or if you need to control the media element using calculations or behaviors that are not exposed in the default controls, there are many built-in JavaScript functions and attributes to help you, too. Table 4-3 lists some of the most common functions.

Table 4-3. Common Control Functions

Function	Behavior
load()	Loads the media file and prepares it for playback. Normally does not need to be called unless the element itself is dynamically created. Useful for loading in advance of actual playback.
play()	Loads (if necessary) and plays the media file. Plays from the beginning unless the media is already paused at another position.
pause()	Pauses playback if currently active.
canPlayType(type)	Tests to see whether the video element can play a hypothetical file of the given MIME type.

The canPlayType(type) method has a non-obvious use case: by passing in a MIME type of an arbitrary video clip to a dynamically created video element, you can use a simple script to determine whether the current browser supports that type. For example, the following code provides a quick way to determine whether the current browser can support playing videos with MIME type of fooType without displaying any visible content in the browser window:

```
var supportsFooVideo = !!(document.createElement('video').canPlayType('fooType'));
```

Note that this function returns the very non-binary "null," "maybe," or "probably," with probably being the best possible scenario.

Table 4-4 shows a few of the read-only attributes on media elements.

Table 4-4. Read-only Media Attributes

Read-only Attribute	Value
duration	The duration of the full media clip, in seconds. If the full duration is not known, NaN is returned.
paused	Returns true if the media clip is currently paused. Defaults to true if the clip has not started playing.
ended	Returns true if the media clip has finished playing.
startTime	Returns the earliest possible value for playback start time. This will usually be 0.0 unless the media clip is streamed and earlier content has left the buffer.
error	An error code, if an error has occurred.
currentSrc	Returns the string representing the file that is currently being displayed or loaded. This will match the source element selected by the browser.

Table 4-5 shows some of the attributes on the media elements that allow scripts to modify them and affect the playback directly. As such, they behave similar to functions.

Table 4-5. Scriptable Attribute Values

Attribute	Value
autoplay	Sets the media clip to play upon creation or query whether it is set to autoplay.
loop	Returns true if the clip will restart upon ending or sets the clip to loop (or not loop).
currentTime	Returns the current time in seconds that has elapsed since the beginning of the playback. Sets currentTime to seek to a specific position in the clip playback.
controls	Shows or hides the user controls, or queries whether they are currently visible.
volume	Sets the audio volume to a relative value between 0.0 and 1.0, or queries the value of the same.
muted	Mutes or unmutes the audio, or determines the current mute state.
autobuffer	Tells the player whether or not to attempt to load the media file before playback is initiated. If the media is set for auto-playback, this attribute is ignored.

Between the various functions and attributes, it is possible for a developer to create any media playback user interface and use it to control any audio or video clip that is supported by the browser.

Working with Audio

If you understand the shared attributes for both audio and video media elements, you've basically seen all that the audio tag has to offer. So let's look at a simple example that shows control scripting in action.

Audio Activation

If your user interface needs to play an audio clip for users, but you don't want to affect the display with a playback timeline or controls, you can create an invisible audio element—one with the controls attribute unset or set to false—and present your own controls for audio playback. Consider the simple code in Listing 4-9, also available in the sample code file audioCue.html.

Listing 4-9. Adding Your Own Play Button to Control Audio

```
<!DOCTYPE html>
<html>
  <link rel="stylesheet" href="styles.css">
  <title>Audio cue</title>

  <audio id="clickSound">
    <source src="johann_sebastian_bach_air.ogg">
    <source src="johann_sebastian_bach_air.mp3">
  </audio>

  <button id="toggle" onclick="toggleSound()">Play</button>

  <script type="text/javascript">
    function toggleSound() {
        var music = document.getElementById("clickSound");
        var toggle = document.getElementById("toggle");

        if (music.paused) {
          music.play();
          toggle.innerHTML = "Pause";
        }
        else {
          music.pause();
          toggle.innerHTML ="Play";
        }
    }
  </script>
</html>
```

Once again, we are using an audio element to play our favorite Bach tune. However, in this example we hide user controls and don't set the clip to autoplay on load. Instead, we have created a toggle button to control the audio playback with script:

```
<button id="toggle" onclick="toggleSound()">Play</button>
```

Our simple button is initialized to inform the user that clicking it will start playback. And each time the button is pressed, the toggleSound() function is triggered. Inside the toggleSound() function, we first gain access to the audio and button elements in the DOM:

```
if (music.paused) {
    music.play();
    toggle.innerHTML = "Pause";
}
```

By accessing the paused attribute on the audio element, we can check to see whether the user has already paused playback. The attribute defaults to true if no playback is initiated, so this condition will be met on the first click. In that case, we call the play() function on the clip and change the text of the button to indicate that the next click will pause the clip:

```
else {
    music.pause();
    toggle.innerHTML ="Play";
}
```

Conversely, if the music clip is not paused (if it is playing), we will actively pause() it and change the button text to indicate that the next click will restart play. Seems simple, doesn't it? That's the point of the media elements in HTML5: to create simple display and control across media types where once a myriad of plugins existed. Simplicity is its own reward.

Working with Video

Enough with simplicity. Let's try something more complicated. The HTML5 video element is very similar to the audio element, but with a few extra attributes thrown in. Table 4-6 shows some of these attributes.

Table 4-6. Additional Video Attributes

Attribute	Value
poster	The URL of an image file used to represent the video content before it has loaded. Think "movie poster." This attribute can be read or altered to change the poster.
width, height	Read or set the visual display size. This may cause centering, letterboxing, or pillaring if the set width does not match the size of the video itself.
videoWidth, videoHeight	Return the intrinsic or natural width and height of the video. They cannot be set.

The video element has one other key feature that is not applicable to the audio element: it can be provided to many functions of the HTML5 Canvas (see Chapter 2).

Creating a Video Timeline Browser

In this more complex example, we'll show how a video element can have its frames grabbed and displayed in a dynamic canvas. To demonstrate this capability, we'll build a simple video timeline viewer. While the video plays, periodic image frames from its display will be drawn onto a nearby canvas. When the user clicks any frame displayed in the canvas, we'll jump the playback of the video to that precise moment in time. With only a few lines of code, we can create a timeline browser that users can use to jump around inside a lengthy video.

Our sample video clip is the tempting concession advert from the mid-20th century movie theaters, so let's all go to the lobby to get ourselves a treat (see Figure 4-3).

Figure 4-3. The video timeline application

Adding the Video and the Canvas Element

We start with a simple declaration to display our video clip:

```
<video id="movies" autoplay oncanplay="startVideo()" onended="stopTimeline()"
autobuffer="true" width="400px" height="300px">
    <source src="Intermission-Walk-in.ogv">
    <source src="Intermission-Walk-in_512kb.mp4">
</video>
```

As most of this markup will look familiar to you from the audio example, let's focus on the differences. Obviously, the <audio> element has been replaced with <video>, and the <source> elements point to the Ogg and MPEG movies that will be selected by the browser.

The video has, in this case, been declared to have autoplay so that it starts as soon as the page loads. Two additional event handler functions have been registered. When the video is loaded and ready to begin play, the oncanplay function will trigger and start our routine. Similarly, when the video ends, the onended callback will allow us to stop creating video frames.

Next, we'll add a canvas called timeline into which we will draw frames of our video at regular intervals.

```
<canvas id="timeline" width="400px" height="300px">
```

Adding Variables

In the next section of our demo, we begin our script by declaring some values that will let us easily tweak the demo and make the code more readable:

```
// # of milliseconds between timeline frame updates
var updateInterval = 5000;
// size of the timeline frames
var frameWidth = 100;
var frameHeight = 75;

// number of timeline frames
var frameRows = 4;
var frameColumns = 4;
var frameGrid = frameRows * frameColumns;
```

updateInterval controls how often we will capture frames of the video—in this case, every five seconds. The frameWidth and frameHeight set how large the small timeline video frames will be when displayed in the canvas. Similarly, the frameRows, frameColumns, and frameGrid determine how many frames we will display in our timeline:

```
// current frame
var frameCount = 0;

// to cancel the timer at end of play
var intervalId;

var videoStarted = false;
```

To keep track of which frame of video we are viewing, a frameCount is made accessible to all demo functions. (For the sake of our demo, a frame is one of our video samples taken every five seconds.) The intervalId is used to stop the timer we will use to grab frames. And finally, we add a videoStarted flag to make sure that we only create one timer per demo.

Adding the updateFrame Function

The core function of our demo—where the video meets the canvas—is where we grab a video frame and draw it onto our canvas:

```
// paint a representation of the video frame into our canvas
function updateFrame() {
    var video = document.getElementById("movies");
    var timeline = document.getElementById("timeline");

    var ctx = timeline.getContext("2d");

    // calculate out the current position based on frame
    // count, then draw the image there using the video
    // as a source
    var framePosition = frameCount % frameGrid;
    var frameX = (framePosition % frameColumns) * frameWidth;
    var frameY = (Math.floor(framePosition / frameRows)) * frameHeight;
```

```
        ctx.drawImage(video, 0, 0, 400, 300, frameX, frameY, frameWidth, frameHeight);

        frameCount++;
}
```

As you've seen in Chapter 2, the first thing to do with any canvas is to grab a two-dimensional drawing context from it:

```
var ctx = timeline.getContext("2d");
```

Because we want to populate our canvas grid with frames from left to right, top to bottom, we need to figure out exactly which of the grid slots will be used for our frame based on the number of the frame we are capturing. Based on the width and height of each frame, we can then determine exact X and Y coordinates at which to begin our drawing:

```
var framePosition = frameCount % frameGrid;
var frameX = (framePosition % frameColumns) * frameWidth;
var frameY = (Math.floor(framePosition / frameRows)) * frameHeight;
```

Finally, we reach the key call to draw an image onto the canvas. We've seen the position and scaling arguments before in our canvas demos, but instead of passing an image to the drawImage routine, we here pass the video object itself:

```
ctx.drawImage(video, 0, 0, 400, 300, frameX, frameY, frameWidth, frameHeight);
```

Canvas drawing routines can take video sources as images or patterns, which gives you a handy way to modify the video and redisplay it in another location.

■ **Note** When a canvas uses a video as an input source, it draws only the currently displayed video frame. Canvas displays will not dynamically update as the video plays. Instead, if you want the canvas content to update, you must redraw your images as the video is playing.

Adding the startVideo Function

Finally, we update frameCount to reflect that we've taken a new snapshot for our timeline. Now, all we need is a routine to regularly update our timeline frames:

```
function startVideo() {

    // only set up the timer the first time the
    // video is started
    if (videoStarted)
        return;

    videoStarted = true;

    // calculate an initial frame, then create
    // additional frames on a regular timer
    updateFrame();
```

```
    intervalId = setInterval(updateFrame, updateInterval);
```

Recall that the startVideo() function is triggered as soon as the video has loaded enough to begin playing. First, we make sure that we are going to handle the video start only once per page load, just in case the video is restarted:

```
// only set up the timer the first time the
// video is started
if (videoStarted)
    return;

videoStarted = true;
```

When the video starts, we will capture our first frame. Then, we will start an interval timer—a timer that repeats continuously at the specified update interval—which will regularly call our updateFrame() function. The end result is that a new frame will be captured every five seconds:

```
    // calculate an initial frame, then create
    // additional frames on a regular timer
    updateFrame();
    intervalId = setInterval(updateFrame, updateInterval);
```

Handling User Input

Now all we need to do is handle user clicks for the individual timeline frames:

```
// set up a handler to seek the video when a frame
// is clicked
var timeline = document.getElementById("timeline");
timeline.onclick = function(evt) {
    var offX = evt.layerX - timeline.offsetLeft;
    var offY = evt.layerY - timeline.offsetTop;

    // calculate which frame in the grid was clicked
    // from a zero-based index
    var clickedFrame = Math.floor(offY / frameHeight) * frameRows;
    clickedFrame += Math.floor(offX / frameWidth);

    // find the actual frame since the video started
    var seekedFrame = (((Math.floor(frameCount / frameGrid)) *
                            frameGrid) + clickedFrame);

    // if the user clicked ahead of the current frame
    // then assume it was the last round of frames
    if (clickedFrame > (frameCount % 16))
        seekedFrame -= frameGrid;

        // can't seek before the video
        if (seekedFrame < 0)
            return;
```

Things get a little more complicated here. We retrieve the timeline canvas and set a click-handling function on it. The handler will use the event to determine which X and Y coordinates were clicked by the user:

```
var timeline = document.getElementById("timeline");
timeline.onclick = function(evt) {
    var offX = evt.layerX - timeline.offsetLeft;
    var offY = evt.layerY - timeline.offsetTop;
```

We then use the frame dimensions to figure out which of the 16 frames was clicked by the user:

```
        // calculate which frame in the grid was clicked
        // from a zero-based index
        var clickedFrame = Math.floor(offY / frameHeight) * frameRows;
        clickedFrame += Math.floor(offX / frameWidth);
```

The clicked frame should be only one of the most recent video frames, so determine the most recent frame that corresponds to that grid index:

```
    // find the actual frame since the video started
    var seekedFrame = (((Math.floor(frameCount / frameGrid)) *
                                        frameGrid) + clickedFrame);
```

If the user clicks ahead of the current frame, jump back one complete cycle of grid frames to find the actual time:

```
    // if the user clicked ahead of the current frame
    // then assume it was the last round of frames
    if (clickedFrame > (frameCount % 16))
        seekedFrame -= frameGrid;
```

And finally, we have to safeguard against any case in which the user clicks a frame that would be before the start of the video clip:

```
    // can't seek before the video
    if (seekedFrame < 0)
        return;
```

Now that we know what point in time the user wants to seek out, we can use that knowledge to change the current playback time. Although this is the key demo function, the routine itself is quite simple:

```
    // seek the video to that frame (in seconds)
    var video = document.getElementById("movies");
    video.currentTime = seekedFrame * updateInterval / 1000;

    // then set the frame count to our destination
    frameCount = seekedFrame;
```

By setting the currentTime attribute on our video element, we cause the video to seek to the specified time and reset our current frame count to the newly chosen frame.

▓ **Note** Unlike many JavaScript timers that deal with milliseconds, the `currentTime` of a video is specified in seconds.

Adding the stopTimeline Function

All that remains for our video timeline demo is to stop capturing frames when the video finishes playing. Although not required, if we don't take this step, the demo will continue capturing frames of the finished demo, blanking out the entire timeline after a while:

```
// stop gathering the timeline frames
function stopTimeline() {
    clearInterval(intervalId);
}
```

The stopTimeline handler will be called when another of our video handlers—onended—is triggered by the completion of video playback.

Our video timeline is probably not full-featured enough to satisfy power users, but it took only a short amount of code to accomplish. Now, on with the show.

The Final Code

Listing 4-10 shows the complete code for the video timeline page.

Listing 4-10. The Complete Video Timeline Code

```
<!DOCTYPE html>
<html>
  <link rel="stylesheet" href="styles.css">
  <title>Video Timeline</title>

  <video id="movies" autoplay oncanplay="startVideo()" onended="stopTimeline()"
autobuffer="true"
    width="400px" height="300px">
    <source src="Intermission-Walk-in.ogv">
    <source src="Intermission-Walk-in_512kb.mp4">
  </video>

  <canvas id="timeline" width="400px" height="300px">

  <script type="text/javascript">

    // # of milliseconds between timeline frame updates
    var updateInterval = 5000;

    // size of the timeline frames
    var frameWidth = 100;
    var frameHeight = 75;
```

101

```javascript
// number of timeline frames
var frameRows = 4;
var frameColumns = 4;
var frameGrid = frameRows * frameColumns;

// current frame
var frameCount = 0;

// to cancel the timer at end of play
var intervalId;

var videoStarted = false;

function startVideo() {

    // only set up the timer the first time the
    // video is started
    if (videoStarted)
      return;

    videoStarted = true;

    // calculate an initial frame, then create
    // additional frames on a regular timer
    updateFrame();
    intervalId = setInterval(updateFrame, updateInterval);

    // set up a handler to seek the video when a frame
    // is clicked
    var timeline = document.getElementById("timeline");
    timeline.onclick = function(evt) {
        var offX = evt.layerX - timeline.offsetLeft;
        var offY = evt.layerY - timeline.offsetTop;

        // calculate which frame in the grid was clicked
        // from a zero-based index
        var clickedFrame = Math.floor(offY / frameHeight) * frameRows;
        clickedFrame += Math.floor(offX / frameWidth);

        // find the actual frame since the video started
        var seekedFrame = (((Math.floor(frameCount / frameGrid)) *
                            frameGrid) + clickedFrame);

        // if the user clicked ahead of the current frame
        // then assume it was the last round of frames
        if (clickedFrame > (frameCount % 16))
            seekedFrame -= frameGrid;

        // can't seek before the video
        if (seekedFrame < 0)
          return;
```

```
                // seek the video to that frame (in seconds)
                var video = document.getElementById("movies");
                video.currentTime = seekedFrame * updateInterval / 1000;

                // then set the frame count to our destination
                frameCount = seekedFrame;
            }
        }

        // paint a representation of the video frame into our canvas
        function updateFrame() {
            var video = document.getElementById("movies");
            var timeline = document.getElementById("timeline");

            var ctx = timeline.getContext("2d");

            // calculate out the current position based on frame
            // count, then draw the image there using the video
            // as a source
            var framePosition = frameCount % frameGrid;
            var frameX = (framePosition % frameColumns) * frameWidth;
            var frameY = (Math.floor(framePosition / frameRows)) * frameHeight;
            ctx.drawImage(video, 0, 0, 400, 300, frameX, frameY, frameWidth, frameHeight);

            frameCount++;
        }

        // stop gathering the timeline frames
        function stopTimeline() {
            clearInterval(intervalId);
        }

    </script>

</html>
```

Practical Extras

Sometimes there are techniques that don't fit into our regular examples, but which nonetheless apply to many types of HTML5 applications. We present to you some short, but common, practical extras here.

Background Noise in a Page

Many a web site has attempted to entertain its viewers by playing audio by default for any visitors. While we don't condone this practice, Audio support makes it quite easy to achieve this, as shown in Listing 4-11.

Listing 4-11. Using the Loop and Autoplay Attributes

```
<!DOCTYPE html>
<html>
  <link rel="stylesheet" href="styles.css">
  <title>Background Music</title>

  <audio autoplay loop>
      <source src="johann_sebastian_bach_air.ogg">
      <source src="johann_sebastian_bach_air.mp3">
  </audio>

  <h1>You're hooked on Bach!</h1>

</html>
```

As you can see, playing a looping background sound is as easy as declaring a single audio tag with the autoplay and loop attributes set (see Figure 4-4).

Figure 4-4. Using autoplay to play music when a page loads

Losing Viewers in the <Blink> of an eye

Brian says: "With great power comes great responsibility, and just because you *can*, doesn't mean you *should*. If you want an example, just remember the <blink> tag!"

Don't let the power of easy audio and video playback seduce you into using it where it isn't appropriate. If you have a compelling reason to enable media with autoplay—perhaps a media browser in which the user is expecting content to start on load—make sure to provide a clear means for disabling that feature. Nothing will turn users from your site faster than annoying content that they can't easily turn off."

Mouseover Video Playback

Another way to use simple scripting effectively with video clips is to trigger the play and pause routines, based on mouse movement over the video. This could be useful in a site that needs to display many video clips and let the user choose which ones to play. The video gallery can display short preview clips on when a user moves the mouse over them and a full video display when the user clicks. It is quite easy to achieve this affect using a code sample similar to Listing 4-12 (see the example file mouseoverVideo.html).

Listing 4-12. *Mouse Detection on a Video Element*

```
<!DOCTYPE html>
<html>
  <link rel="stylesheet" href="styles.css">
  <title>Mouseover Video</title>

  <video id="movies" onmouseover="this.play()" onmouseout="this.pause()"
        autobuffer="true"
    width="400px" height="300px">
    <source src="Intermission-Walk-in.ogv" type='video/ogg; codecs="theora, vorbis"'>
    <source src="Intermission-Walk-in_512kb.mp4" type='video/mp4; codecs="avc1.42E01E,
                mp4a.40.2"'>
  </video>
</html>
```

By simply setting a few extra attributes, the preview playback can trigger when a user points at the video, as shown in Figure 4-5.

Point at the video to play it!

Figure 4-5. Mouseover video playback

Summary

In this chapter, we have explored what you can do with the two important HTML5 elements audio and video. We have shown you how they can be used to create compelling web applications. The audio and video elements add new media options to HTML5 applications that allow you to use audio and video without plugins, while at the same time providing a common, integrated, and scriptable API.

First, we discussed the audio and video container files and codecs and why we ended up with the codecs supported today. We then showed you a mechanism for switching to the most appropriate type of content for the browser to display, and we showed you how to make video accessible using WebVTT.

Next, we showed you how you can use control audio and video programmatically using the APIs and finally we looked at how you can use of the HTML5 audio and video in your applications.

In the next chapter, we'll show how you can use Geolocation to tailor your application's output to the whereabouts of your users with a minimal amount of code.

CHAPTER 5

Using the Geolocation API

Let's say you want to create a web application that offers discounts and special deals on running shoes in stores that your application's users are within walking (or running) distance away from. Using the Geolocation API, you can request users to share their location and, if they agree, you can provide them with instructions on how to get to a nearby store to pick up a new pair of shoes at a discounted rate.

Another example of the use of Geolocation could be an application that tracks how far you have run (or walked). You can picture using an application in a browser on a mobile phone that you turn on when you start a run. While you're on the move, the application tracks how far you have run. The coordinates for the run can even be overlaid on a map, perhaps even with an elevation profile. If you're running a race against other competitors, the application might even show your opponents' locations.

Other Geolocation application ideas could be turn-by-turn GPS-style navigation, social networking applications that allow you to see exactly where your friends are, so you can pick the coffee shop you want to visit, and many more unusual applications.

In this chapter, we'll explore what you can do with Geolocation—an exciting API that allows users to share their location with web applications so that they can enjoy location-aware services. First, we'll take a look at the source of Geolocation location information—the latitude, longitude and other attributes—and where they can come from (GPS, Wi-Fi, cellular triangulation, and so on). Then, we'll discuss the privacy concerns around using Geolocation data and how browsers work with this data.

After that, we'll dive into a practical discussion about the two different position request functions (methods) within the Geolocation API: the one-shot position request and repeated position updates, and we'll show you how and when to use them. Next, we'll show you how to build a practical Geolocation application using the same API, and we'll finish up with a discussion about a few additional use cases and tips.

About Location Information

Using the Geolocation API is fairly straightforward. You request a position and, if the user agrees, the browser returns location information. The position is provided to the browser by the underlying device (for example, a laptop or a mobile phone) on which the Geolocation–enabled browser is running. The location information is provided as a set of latitude and longitude coordinates along with additional metadata. Armed with this location information, you can then build a compelling, location-aware application.

Latitude and Longitude Coordinates

The location information consists primarily of a pair of latitude and longitude coordinates like the ones shown in the following example, which shows the coordinates for beautiful Tahoe City, located on the shore of Lake Tahoe, America's most beautiful mountain lake:

```
Latitude: 39.17222, Longitude: -120.13778
```

In the preceding example, the latitude (the numerical value indicating distance north or south of the equator is 39.17222) and the longitude (the numerical value indicating distance east or west of Greenwich, England) is -120.13778.

Latitude and longitude coordinates can be expressed in different ways:

- Decimal format (for example, 39.17222)

- Degree Minute Second (DMS) format (for example, 39° 10' 20')

▪ **Note** When you use the Geolocation API, coordinates are always returned in the decimal format.

In addition to latitude and longitude coordinates, Geolocation always provides the *accuracy* of the location coordinates. Additional metadata may also be provided, depending on the device that your browser is running on. These include *altitude, altitudeAccuracy, heading,* and *speed.* If this additional metadata is not available it will be returned as a null value.

Where Does Location Information Come From?

The Geolocation API does not specify which underlying technology a device has to use to locate the application's user. Instead, it simply exposes an API for retrieving location information. What is exposed, however, is the level of accuracy with which the location was pinpointed. There is no guarantee that the device's actual location returns an accurate location.

Location, Location

Peter says: "Here is a funny example of that. At home, I use a wireless network. I opened the Geolocation example application shown in this chapter in Firefox and it figured out that I was in Sacramento (about 75 miles from my actual physical location). Wrong, but not too surprising, because my Internet Service Provider is located in downtown Sacramento.

Then, I asked my sons, Sean and Rocky, to browse to the same page on their iPhones (using the same Wi-Fi network). In Safari, it looked like they were located in Marysville, California—a town that is located 30 miles from Sacramento. Go figure!"

A device can use any of the following sources:

- IP address
- Coordinate triangulation
  - Global Positioning System (GPS)
  - Wi-Fi with MAC addresses from RFID, Wi-Fi, and Bluetooth
  - GSM or CDMA cell phone IDs
- User defined

Many devices use a combination of one or more sources to ensure an even higher accuracy. Each of these methods has its own pros and cons, as explained in the next sections.

IP Address Geolocation Data

In the past, IP address–based geolocation was the only way to get a possible location, but the returned locations often proved unreliable. IP address–based geolocation works by automatically looking up a user's IP address and then retrieving the registrant's physical address. Therefore, if you have an ISP that provides you with an IP address, your location is often resolved to the physical address of your service provider that could be miles away. Table 5-1 shows the pros and cons of IP address–based geolocation data.

Table 5-1. *Pros and Cons of IP Address–based Geolocation Data*

Pros	Cons
Available everywhere	Not very accurate (wrong many times, but also accurate only to the city level)
Processed on the server side	Can be a costly operation

Many websites advertise based on IP address locations. You can see this in action when you travel to another country and suddenly see advertisements for local services (based on the IP address of the country or region you are visiting).

GPS Geolocation Data

As long as you can see the sky, GPS can provide very accurate location results. A GPS fix is acquired by acquiring the signal from multiple GPS satellites that fly around the earth. However, it can take awhile to get a fix, which does not lend itself particularly well for applications that must start up rapidly.

Because it can take a long time to get a GPS location fix, you might want to query for the user's location asynchronously. To show your application's users that a fix is being acquired, you can add a status bar. Table 5-2 shows the pros and cons of GPS–based geolocation data.

Table 5-2. Pros and Cons of GPS–based Geolocation Data

Pros	Cons
Very accurate	It can take a long time getting a location fix, which can drain a user's device's batteries
	Does not work well indoors
	May require additional hardware

Wi-Fi Geolocation Data

Wi-Fi–based geolocation information is acquired by triangulating the location based on the user's distance from a number of known Wi-Fi access points, mostly in urban areas. Unlike GPS, Wi-Fi is very accurate indoors as well as in urban areas. Table 5-3 shows the pros and cons of Wi-Fi–based geolocation data.

Table 5-3. Pros and Cons of Wi-Fi–based Geolocation Data

Pros	Cons
Accurate	Not good in rural areas with few wireless access points
Works indoors	
Can get fix quickly and cheaply	

Cell Phone Geolocation Data

Cell phone–based geolocation information is acquired by triangulating the location based on the user's distance from a number of cell phone towers. This method provides a general location result that is fairly accurate. This method is often used in combination with Wi-Fi– and GPS–based geolocation information. Table 5-4 shows the pros and cons of cell phone–based geolocation data.

Table 5-4. Pros and Cons of Cell Phone–based Geolocation Data

Pros	Cons
Fairly accurate	Requires a device with access to a cell phone or cell modem
Works indoors	Not good in rural areas with fewer cell phone towers
Can get fix quickly and cheaply	

User–Defined Geolocation Data

Instead of programmatically figuring out where the user is, you can also allow users to define their location themselves. An application may allow users to enter their address, ZIP code, or some other details; your application can then use that information to provide location-aware services. Table 5-5 shows the pros and cons of user–defined geolocation data.

Table 5-5. Pros and Cons of User–defined Geolocation Data

Pros	Cons
Users may have more accurate location data than programmatic services	Can also be very inaccurate, especially if the location changes
Allows geolocation services for alternate locations	
User entry might be faster than detection	

Browser Support for Geolocation

Geolocation was one of the first HTML5 features to be fully embraced and implemented, and it is available in all the major browsers now. For a complete overview of the current browser support, including mobile support, refer to http://caniuse.com and search for Geolocation.

If you have to support older browsers, it's always a good idea to first see whether Geolocation is supported before you use the API. The section "Checking for Browser Support" later in this chapter will show you how you can programmatically check for browser support.

111

Privacy

The Geolocationspecification mandates that a mechanism is provided to protect the user's privacy. Furthermore, location information should not be made available unless the application's users grant their express permission.

This makes sense and addresses the "big brother" concerns users often raise about Geolocation applications. However, as you can see from some of the possible use cases for HTML 5 Geolocation applications, there is usually an incentive for the user to share this information. For example, users might be OK with sharing their location if this could let them know about a rare 50% discount on a pair of running shoes that are ready to be picked up in a store located just a few blocks away from where they happen to be drinking coffee. Let's take a closer look at the browser and device privacy architecture shown in Figure 5-1.

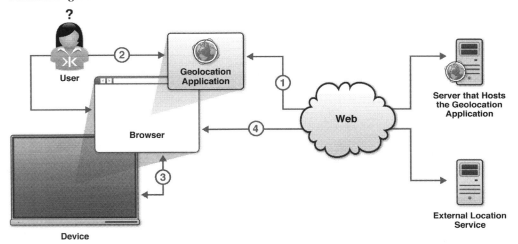

Figure 5-1. *Geolocation browser and device privacy architecture*

The following steps are shown in the diagram:

1. A user navigates to a location-aware application in the browser.

2. The application web page loads and requests coordinates from the browser by making a Geolocation function call. The browser intercepts this and requests user permission. Let's assume, in this case, that the permission is granted.

3. The browser retrieves coordinate information from the device it is running on. For example, a combination of IP address, Wi-Fi, and possibly GPS coordinates. This is an internal function of the browser.

4. The browser sends these coordinates to a trusted external location service, which returns location coordinates that can now be sent back to the host of the Geolocation application.

■ **Important** The application does *not* have direct access to the device; it can only query the browser to access the device on its behalf.

Triggering the Privacy Protection Mechanism

When you access a web page that uses the Geolocation API, the privacy protection mechanism should kick in. Figure 5-2 shows what this looks like in Firefox.

Figure 5-2. *The notification bar is triggered in Firefox when the Geolocation API is used.*

The mechanism is triggered when the Geolocation code is executed. Simply adding Geolocation code that is not called anywhere (for example, in an onload method) does not do anything. If, however, the Geolocation code is executed, for example, in a call to navigator.geolocation.getCurrentPosition (explained in more detail later on), the user is prompted to share their location with the application. Figure 5-3 shows what happens on Safari, running on an iPhone.

Figure 5-3. *The notification dialog box is triggered in Safari when the Geolocation API is used.*

Apart from providing the necessary mechanism to request permission to share your location, some implementations (Firefox, for example) also allow you to remember the permission granted to the site for the next time you enter. This is similar to how you can remember passwords for certain sites in your browser.

■ **Note** if you've given permission to always give your location to a site in Firefox and later change your mind, you can easily revoke that permission by going back to the site and selecting **Page Info** from the **Tools** menu. Then change the setting for **Share Location** on the **Permissions** tab.

Dealing with Location Information

Location data is sensitive information, so when you receive it, you must be careful about handling, storing, and retransmitting the data. Unless users give permission to store data, you should always dispose of the data after the task for which it was required is complete.

Therefore, if you retransmit the location data, it is recommended that you first encrypt the data. Regarding the collection of geolocation data, your application should prominently show the following:

- That you are collecting location data

- Why you are collecting location data

- How long the location data is kept

- How you are securing the data

- How and with whom the location data is shared (if it is)

- How users can check and update their location data

Using the Geolocation API

In this section, we'll explore the use of the Geolocation API in more detail. For the sake of illustration, we've created a simple browser page—geolocation.html. Remember that you can download all the code from the book's page on apress.com or on the companion website http://prohtml5.com.

Checking for Browser Support

Before you call the Geolocation API functions, you will want to make sure that there is support in the browser for what you're about to do. This way, you can provide some alternate text, prompting the users of your application to dump their dinosaur-like browsers or install a plugin such as Gears, which augments the existing browser functionality. Listing 5-1 shows one way you can use to test for browser support.

Listing 5-1. Checking for Browser Support

```
function loadDemo() {
  if(navigator.geolocation) {
    document.getElementById("support").innerHTML = "Geolocation supported.";

} else {
    document.getElementById("support").innerHTML = "Geolocation is not supported in
                                 your browser.";
  }
}
```

In this example, you test for browser support in the loadDemo function, which might be called when the application's page is loaded. A call to navigator.geolocation (you can also use Modernizr) will return the Geolocation object if it exists, or trigger the failure case if it does not. In this case, the page is updated to reflect whether there is browser support or not by updating a previously defined support element on the page with a suitable message.

Position Requests

There are two types of position requests:

- One-shot position request
- Repeated position updates

One-Shot Position Requests

In many applications, it will be acceptable to retrieve the user's location only once, or only by request. For example, if someone is looking for the nearest movie theater showing today's popular movie in the next hour, the simplest form of the Geolocation API shown in Listing 5-2 can be used.

Listing 5-2. One-Shot Position Request

```
void getCurrentPosition(in PositionCallback successCallback,
                in optional PositionErrorCallback errorCallback,
                in optional PositionOptions options);
```

Let's take a look at this core function call in more detail.

First, this is a function that is available on the `navigator.geolocation` object, so you will need to have already retrieved this object in your script. As noted previously, make sure that you have a good fallback handler if your browser does not support Geolocation.

The function takes one required parameter, and two optional ones.

- The `successCallback` function parameter tells the browser which function you want called when the location data is made available. This is important because operations such as fetching location data may take a long time to complete. No user wants the browser to be locked up while the location is retrieved, and no developer wants his program to pause indefinitely—especially because fetching the location data will often be waiting on a user to grant permission. The `successCallback` is where you will receive the actual location information and act on it.

- However, as in most programming scenarios, it is good to plan for failure cases. It is quite possible that the request for location information may not complete for reasons beyond your control, and for those cases you will want to provide an `errorCallback` function that can present the user with an explanation, or perhaps make an attempt to try again. While optional, it is recommended that you provide one.

- Finally, an `options` object can be provided to the Geolocation service to fine-tune the way it gathers data. This is an optional parameter that we will examine later.

Let's say that you've created a JavaScript function on our page named `updateLocation()` in which you update the contents of the page with the new location data. Similarly, you've created a `handleLocationError()` function to handle the error cases. We'll examine the details of those functions next, but that means that your core request to access the user's position would look something like this:

```
navigator.geolocation.getCurrentPosition(updateLocation, handleLocationError);
```

The updateLocation() Function

So, what happens in our updateLocation() call? It's actually quite simple. As soon as the browser has access to the location information, it will call updateLocation() with a single parameter: a position object. The position will contain coordinates—as the attribute coords—and a timestamp for when the location data was gathered. While you may or may not need the timestamp, the coords attribute contains the crucial values for the location.

The coordinates always have multiple attributes on them, but it is up to the browser and the hardware of the user's device whether they will have meaningful values. The following are the first three attributes:

- latitude
- longitude
- accuracy

These attributes are guaranteed to have values and are fairly self-explanatory. latitude and longitude will contain the Geolocation service's best determined value of the user's location specified in decimal degrees. accuracy will contain a value in meters that specifies how close the latitude and longitude values are to the actual location, with a 95% confidence level. It can therefore be used to display a proximity radius around the location to give people a visual clue about the accuracy. Due to the nature of Geolocation implementations, approximation will be common and coarse. Make sure to check the accuracy of the returned values before you present them with any certainty. Recommending a user to visit a "nearby" shoe store that is actually hours away could have unintended consequences.

The other attributes of the coordinates are not guaranteed to be supported, but they will return a null value if they are not available (for example, if you're on a desktop computer, you're unlikely to have access to this information):

- altitude—the height of the user's location, in meters
- altitudeAccuracy—once again in meters, or null if no altitude is provided
- heading—direction of travel, in degrees relative to true north
- speed—ground speed in meters per second

Unless you are sure that your users have devices with access to such information, it is recommended that you not rely on them as critical to your application. While global positioning devices are likely to provide this level of detail, simple network triangulation will not.

Now let's take a look at a code implementation of our updateLocation() function that performs some trivial updates with the coordinates (see Listing 5-3).

Listing 5-3. Example of Using the updateLocation() Function

```
function updateLocation(position) {
  var latitude = position.coords.latitude;
  var longitude = position.coords.longitude;
  var accuracy = position.coords.accuracy;
  var timestamp = position.timestamp;

  document.getElementById("latitude").innerHTML = latitude;
  document.getElementById("longitude").innerHTML = longitude;
```

```
    document.getElementById("accuracy").innerHTML = accuracy
    document.getElementById("timestamp").innerHTML = timestamp;•
}
```

In this example, the updateLocation() callback is used to update the text in different elements of our page; we put the value of the longitude attribute in the longitude element, the latitude attribute in the latitude element, and accuracy and timestamp in their corresponding fields.

The handleLocationError() Function

Handling errors is very important for a Geolocation application because there are many moving parts and therefore many possibilities for the location calculation services to go awry. Fortunately, the API defines error codes for all the cases you will need to handle, and it sets them on the error object passed to your error handler as the code attribute. Let's look at them in turn:

- PERMISSION_DENIED (error code 1)—The user chose not to let the browser have access to the location information.

- POSITION_UNAVAILABLE (error code 2)—The technique used to determine the user's location was attempted, but failed.

- TIMEOUT (error code 3)—A timeout value was set as an option, and the attempt to determine the location exceeded that limit.

In these cases, you will probably want to let the user know that something went wrong. You may want to retry getting the values in the case of an unavailable or timed-out request.

Listing 5-4 shows an example of an error handler in action.

Listing 5-4. Using an Error Handler

```
function handleLocationError(error) {
    switch(error.code){
    case 0:
      updateStatus("There was an error while retrieving your location: " +
                                error.message);
    break;
    case 1:
    updateStatus("The user prevented this page from retrieving a location.");
    break;
    case 2:
    updateStatus("The browser was unable to determine your location: " +
                                error.message);
    break;
    case 3:
    updateStatus("The browser timed out before retrieving the location.");
    break;
    }
}
```

The error codes are accessed from the code attribute of the provided error object, while the message attribute will give access to a more detailed description of what went wrong. In all cases, we call our own routine to update the status of the page with the necessary info.

Optional Geolocation Request Attributes

With both the normal and error cases handled, you should turn your attention to the three optional attributes that you can pass to the Geolocation service in order to fine-tune how it gathers its data. Note that these three attributes can be passed using shorthand object notation, making it trivial to add them to your Geolocation request calls.

- enableHighAccuracy—This is a hint to the browser that, if available, you would like the Geolocation service to use a higher accuracy-detection mode. This defaults to false, but when turned on, it may not cause any difference, or it may cause the machine to take more time or power to determine location. Use with caution.

> ■ **Note** Curiously, the high accuracy setting is only a toggle switch: true or false. The API was not created to allow the accuracy to be set to various values or a numeric range. Perhaps this will be addressed in future versions of the specification.

- timeout—This optional value, provided in milliseconds, tells the browser the maximum amount of time it is allowed to calculate the current location. If the calculation does not complete in this amount of time, the error handler is called instead. This value defaults to Infinity, or no limit.
- maximumAge—This value indicates how old a location value can be before the browser must attempt to recalculate. Again, it is a value in milliseconds. This value defaults to zero, meaning that the browser must attempt to recalculate a value immediately.

> ■ **Note** You might be wondering what the difference is between the timeout and maximumAge options. Although similarly named, they do have distinct uses. The timeout value deals with the *duration* needed to calculate the location value, while maximumAge refers to the *frequency* of the location calculation. If any single calculation takes longer than the timeout value, an error is triggered. However, if the browser does not have an up-to-date location value that is younger than maximumAge, it must refetch another value. Special values apply here: setting the maximumAge to "0" requires the value to always be re-fetched, while setting it to Infinity means it should never be refetched.

The Geolocation API does not allow you to tell the browser how often to recalculate the position. This is left entirely up to the browser implementation. All we can do is tell the browser what the maximumAge is of the value it returns. The actual frequency is a detail we cannot control.

Let's update our location request to include an optional parameter using shorthand notation, as shown in the following example:

```
navigator.geolocation.getCurrentPosition(updateLocation,handleLocationError,
                          {timeout:10000});
```

This new call ensures that any request for location that takes longer than 10 seconds (10,000 milliseconds) should trigger an error, in which case the handleLocationError function will be called with the TIMEOUT error code. We can combine the Geolocation calls that we discussed so far and display the relevant data on a page as shown in Figure 5-4.

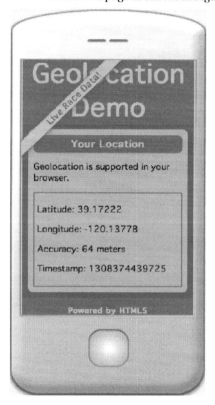

Figure 5-4. Geolocation data displayed on a mobile device

Repeated Position Updates

Sometimes you have to make repeated position requests. Thankfully, the designers of the Geolocation API made it trivial to switch from an application that requests a user location one time to one that requests the location at regular intervals. In fact, it's largely as trivial as switching the request call, as shown in the following examples:

- One-shot update:
  ```
  navigator.geolocation.getCurrentPosition(updateLocation,
  handleLocationError);
  ```

- Repeated updates:
  `navigator.geolocation.`**`watchPosition`**`(updateLocation, handleLocationError);`

This simple change will cause the Geolocation service to call your `updateLocation` handler repeatedly as the user's location changes, rather than one time. It acts as though your program is *watching* the location and will let you know whenever the location changes.

Why would you want to do this?

Consider a web page that gives turn-by-turn directions as the viewer moves around town. Or a page that constantly updates to show you the nearest gas station as you drive down the highway. Or even a page that records and sends your location so that you can retrace your steps. All these services become easy to build once the location updates flow into your application right as they are changing.

Turning off the updates is also simple. Should your application no longer need to receive regular updates about the user's location, you need merely make a call to the `clearWatch()` function, as shown in the following example:

```
navigator.geolocation.clearWatch(watchId);
```

This function will inform the Geolocation service that you no longer want to receive updates on a user's location. But what is the `watchID` and where did it come from? It is actually the return value from the `watchPosition()` call. It identifies the unique monitor request in order to allow us to cancel it later. So, if your application ever needs to stop receiving location updates, you would write some code, as shown in Listing 5-5.

Listing 5-5. *Using watchPostion*

```
var watchId = navigator.geolocation.watchPosition(updateLocation,
                                            handleLocationError);
// do something fun with the location updates!

// OK, now we are ready to stop receiving location updates
navigator.geolocation.clearWatch(watchId);
```

Building an Application with Geolocation

So far, we've mainly focused on single-shot location requests. Let's see how powerful the Geolocation API can really be by using its multirequest feature to build a small but useful application: a web page with a distance tracker.

If you've ever wanted a quick way to determine how far you've traveled in a certain amount of time, you would normally use a dedicated device such as a GPS navigation system or a pedometer. Using the power of the Geolocation service, you can create a web page that tracks how far you have traveled from where the page was originally loaded. Although less useful on a desktop computer, this page is ideal for the millions of web-enabled phones that ship with Geolocation support today. Simply point your smartphone browser to this example page, grant the page permission to access your location, and every few seconds it will update with the distance you just traveled and add it to a running total (see Figure 5-5).

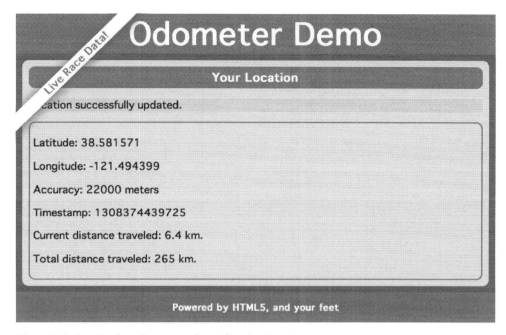

Figure 5-5. *Our Geolocation example application in action*

This sample works by using the `watchPosition()` capability we discussed in the last section. Every time a new position is sent to us, we will compare it to the last known position and calculate the distance traveled. This is accomplished using a well-known calculation known as the Haversine formula, which allows us to calculate distance between two longitude and latitude positions on a sphere. Listing 5-6 displays what the Haversine formula tells us.

Listing 5-6. *The Haversine Formula*

$$d = 2\arcsin\left(\sqrt{\sin^2\left(\frac{\phi_2 - \phi_1}{2}\right) + \cos_1 \cos_2 \sin^2\left(\frac{\lambda_2 - \lambda_1}{2}\right)}\right)$$

If you're hoping to learn how the Haversine formula works, you'll be sorely disappointed. Instead, we'll present you a JavaScript implementation of the formula, which allows anyone to use it to calculate the distance between two positions (see Listing 5-7).

Listing 5-7. A JavaScript Haversine Implementation

```
Number.prototype.toRadians = function() {
  return this * Math.PI / 180;
}

function distance(latitude1, longitude1, latitude2, longitude2) {
  // R is the radius of the earth in kilometers
  var R = 6371;

  var deltaLatitude = (latitude2-latitude1).toRadians();
  var deltaLongitude = (longitude2-longitude1).toRadians();
  latitude1 = latitude1.toRadians(), latitude2 = latitude2.toRadians();

  var a = Math.sin(deltaLatitude/2) *
          Math.sin(deltaLatitude/2) +
          Math.cos(latitude1) *
          Math.cos(latitude2) *
          Math.sin(deltaLongitude/2) *
          Math.sin(deltaLongitude/2);
  var c = 2 * Math.atan2(Math.sqrt(a),
                         Math.sqrt(1-a));
  var d = R * c;
  return d;
}
```

If you want to know why or how this formula works, consult a teenager's math textbook. For our purposes, we have written a conversion from degrees to radians, and we provided a distance() function to calculate the distance between two latitude and longitude position values.

If we check the user's position and calculate the distance traveled at frequent and regular intervals, it gives a reasonable approximation of distance traveled over time. This assumes that the user is moving in a straight direction during each interval, but we'll make that assumption for the sake of our example.

Writing the HTML Display

Let's start with the HTML display. We kept it quite simple for this exercise because the real interest is in the script driving the data. We display a page with the pertinent Geolocation data. In addition, we'll put a few status text indicators in place so that the user can see the summary of distance traveled (see Listing 5-8).

Listing 5-8. Code for the Distance Tracker HTML Page

```
<!DOCTYPE html>
<html>

<head>
  <meta charset="utf-8" >
  <title>Geolocation</title>
  <link rel="stylesheet" href="geo-html5.css" >
</head>
```

```
<body onload="loadDemo()">

  <header>
    <h1>Odometer Demo</h1>
    <h4>Live Race Data!</h4>
  </header>

  <div id="container">

  <section>
    <article>
      <header>
        <h1>Your Location</h1>
      </header>

        <p class="info" id="status">Geolocation is not supported in your browser.</p>

      <div class="geostatus">
        <p id="latitude">Latitude: </p>
        <p id="longitude">Longitude: </p>
        <p id="accuracy">Accuracy: </p>
        <p id="timestamp">Timestamp: </p>
        <p id="currDist">Current distance traveled: </p>
        <p id="totalDist">Total distance traveled: </p>
      </div>

    </article>
  </section>

  <footer>
    <h2>Powered by HTML5, and your feet!</h2>
  </footer>

  </div>
  .
  .
  .
  </body>
</html>
```

These values are all defaulted for now and are populated once data starts flowing into the application.

Processing the Geolocation Data

Our first JavaScript code section should look familiar. We've set a handler—loadDemo()—that will execute as soon as the page completes loading. This script will detect if Geolocation is supported in the browser and use a status update functions to change the status message at the top of the page to indicate what it finds. It will then request a watch of the user's position, as shown in Listing 5-9.

Listing 5-9. Adding the loadDemo() and Status Update Functions

```
 var totalDistance = 0.0;
 var lastLat;
var lastLong;

 function updateErrorStatus(message) {
   document.getElementById("status").style.background = "papayaWhip";
   document.getElementById("status").innerHTML = "<strong>Error</strong>: " + message;
 }

 function updateStatus(message) {
   document.getElementById("status").style.background = "paleGreen";
   document.getElementById("status").innerHTML = message;
 }

 function loadDemo() {
   if(navigator.geolocation) {
     document.getElementById("status").innerHTML = "HTML5 Geolocation is supported in your
browser.";
     navigator.geolocation.watchPosition(updateLocation, handleLocationError,
                                         {timeout:20000});
   }
 }
```

Note that we are setting a `maximumAge` option on our position watch: {`maximumAge:20000`}. This will tell the location service that we don't want any cached location values that are greater than 20 seconds (or 20,000 milliseconds) old. Setting this option will keep our page updating at regular intervals, but feel free to adjust this number and experiment with larger and smaller cache sizes.

For error handling, we'll use the same routine we identified earlier, as it is generic enough to work for our distance tracker. In it we'll check the error code of any error we receive and update the status message on the page accordingly as shown in Listing 5-10.

Listing 5-10. Adding the Error Handling Code

```
 function handleLocationError(error) {
   switch(error.code)
   {
   case 0:
     updateErrorStatus("There was an error while retrieving your location. Additional
details: " +
                                               error.message);
     break;
   case 1:
     updateErrorStatus("The user opted not to share his or her location.");
     break;
   case 2:
     updateErrorStatus("The browser was unable to determine your location. Additional
details: " +
                                               error.message);
     break;
```

```
  case 3:
    updateErrorStatus("The browser timed out before retrieving the location.");
    break;
  }
}
```

The bulk of our work will be done in our updateLocation() function. Here we will update the page with our most recent values and calculate the distance traveled, as shown in Listing 5-11.

Listing 5-11. Adding the updateLocation() Function

```
function updateLocation(position) {
  var latitude = position.coords.latitude;
  var longitude = position.coords.longitude;
  var accuracy = position.coords.accuracy;
  var timestamp = position.timestamp;

  document.getElementById("latitude").innerHTML = "Latitude: " + latitude;
  document.getElementById("longitude").innerHTML = "Longitude: " + longitude;
  document.getElementById("accuracy").innerHTML = "Accuracy: " + accuracy + " meters";
  document.getElementById("timestamp").innerHTML = "Timestamp: " + timestamp;
```

As you might expect, the first thing we will do when we receive an updated set of position coordinates is to record all the information. We gather the latitude, longitude, accuracy, and timestamp, and then update the table values with the new data.

You might not choose to display a timestamp in your own application. The timestamp number used here is in a form primarily useful to computers, which won't be meaningful to an end user. Feel free to replace it with a more user-friendly time indicator or remove it altogether.

The accuracy value is given to us in meters and might at first seem unnecessary. However, any data depends on its accuracy. Even if you don't present the user with the accuracy values, you should take them into account in your own code. Presenting inaccurate values could give the user a skewed idea of his or her location. Therefore, we will throw out any position updates with an unreasonably low accuracy, as shown in Listing 5-12.

Listing 5-12. Ignoring Inaccurate Accuracy Updates

```
// sanity test... don't calculate distance if accuracy
// value too large
if (accuracy >= 30000) {
  updateStatus("Need more accurate values to calculate distance.");
  return;
}
```

The Easiest Way to Travel

Brian says: "Keeping track of position accuracy is vital. As a developer, you won't have access to the methodologies a browser uses to calculate position, but you will have access to the accuracy attribute. Use it!

Sitting here in my backyard hammock on a lazy afternoon, I monitored my position on a geolocation–enabled cell phone browser. I was surprised to see that over the course of only a few minutes, my reclined body was reported to travel half a kilometer in distance at varying speeds. As exciting as this might sound, it is a reminder that data is only as accurate as its source permits."

Finally, we will calculate the distance traveled, assuming that we have already received at least one accurate position value before. We will update the totals of travel distance and display them for the user, and we will store the current values for future comparison. To keep our interface a little less cluttered, it is a good idea to round or truncate the calculated values, as shown in Listing 5-13.

Listing 5-13. Adding the Distance Calculation Code

```
// calculate distance
if ((lastLat != null) && (lastLong != null)) {
  var currentDistance = distance(latitude, longitude, lastLat, lastLong);
  document.getElementById("currDist").innerHTML =
          "Current distance traveled: " + currentDistance.toFixed(2) + " km";
  totalDistance += currentDistance;
  document.getElementById("totalDist").innerHTML =
          "Total distance traveled: " + currentDistance.toFixed(2) + " km";
  updateStatus("Location successfully updated.");

}
lastLat = latitude;
lastLong = longitude;

}
```

That's it. In fewer than 200 lines of HTML and script, we've created a sample application that monitors the viewer's position over time and demonstrated nearly the entire Geolocation API, complete with error handling. Although this example is inherently less interesting when viewed on a desktop computer, try it out on your favorite geolocation–enabled phone or device and see how mobile you truly are during the course of a day.

The Final Code

The full code sample is shown in Listing 5-14.

Listing 5-14. Complete Distance Tracker Code

```
<!DOCTYPE html>
<html>

<head>
  <meta charset="utf-8" >
  <title>Geolocation</title>
  <link rel="stylesheet" href="geo-html5.css" >
</head>
```

```
<body onload="loadDemo()">

  <header>
    <h1>Odometer Demo</h1>
    <h4>Live Race Data!</h4>
  </header>

  <div id="container">

  <section>
    <article>
      <header>
        <h1>Your Location</h1>
      </header>

        <p class="info" id="status">Geolocation is not supported in your browser.</p>

      <div class="geostatus">
        <p id="latitude">Latitude: </p>
        <p id="longitude">Longitude: </p>
        <p id="accuracy">Accuracy: </p>
        <p id="timestamp">Timestamp: </p>
        <p id="currDist">Current distance traveled: </p>
        <p id="totalDist">Total distance traveled: </p>
      </div>

    </article>
  </section>

  <footer>
    <h2>Powered by HTML5, and your feet!</h2>
  </footer>

  </div>

  <script>

    var totalDistance = 0.0;
    var lastLat;
    var lastLong;

    Number.prototype.toRadians = function() {
      return this * Math.PI / 180;
    }

    function distance(latitude1, longitude1, latitude2, longitude2) {
      // R is the radius of the earth in kilometers
      var R = 6371;

      var deltaLatitude = (latitude2-latitude1).toRadians();
      var deltaLongitude = (longitude2-longitude1).toRadians();
      latitude1 = latitude1.toRadians(), latitude2 = latitude2.toRadians();
```

```
  var a = Math.sin(deltaLatitude/2) *
          Math.sin(deltaLatitude/2) +
          Math.cos(latitude1) *
          Math.cos(latitude2) *
          Math.sin(deltaLongitude/2) *
          Math.sin(deltaLongitude/2);

  var c = 2 * Math.atan2(Math.sqrt(a),
                         Math.sqrt(1-a));
  var d = R * c;
  return d;
}

function updateErrorStatus(message) {
  document.getElementById("status").style.background = "papayaWhip";
  document.getElementById("status").innerHTML = "<strong>Error</strong>: " + message;
}

function updateStatus(message) {
  document.getElementById("status").style.background = "paleGreen";
  document.getElementById("status").innerHTML = message;
}

function loadDemo() {

if(navigator.geolocation) {
    document.getElementById("status").innerHTML = "HTML5 Geolocation is supported in your
    browser.";
    navigator.geolocation.watchPosition(updateLocation, handleLocationError,
                                        {timeout:10000});
  }
    }

function updateLocation(position) {
  var latitude = position.coords.latitude;
  var longitude = position.coords.longitude;
  var accuracy = position.coords.accuracy;
  var timestamp = position.timestamp;

  document.getElementById("latitude").innerHTML = "Latitude: " + latitude;
  document.getElementById("longitude").innerHTML = "Longitude: " + longitude;
  document.getElementById("accuracy").innerHTML = "Accuracy: " + accuracy + " meters";
  document.getElementById("timestamp").innerHTML = "Timestamp: " + timestamp;

  // sanity test... don't calculate distance if accuracy
  // value too large
  if (accuracy >= 30000) {
    updateStatus("Need more accurate values to calculate distance.");
    return;
  }
```

```
    // calculate distance
    if ((lastLat != null) && (lastLong != null)) {
      var currentDistance = distance(latitude, longitude, lastLat, lastLong);

      document.getElementById("currDist").innerHTML =
              "Current distance traveled: " + currentDistance.toFixed(2) + " km";

      totalDistance += currentDistance;
      document.getElementById("totalDist").innerHTML =
              "Total distance traveled: " + currentDistance.toFixed(2) + " km";
      updateStatus("Location successfully updated.");

    }

    lastLat = latitude;
    lastLong = longitude;

  }

  function handleLocationError(error) {
    switch(error.code)
    {
    case 0:
      updateErrorStatus("There was an error while retrieving your location. Additional
      details: " + error.message);
      break;
    case 1:
      updateErrorStatus("The user opted not to share his or her location.");
      break;
    case 2:
      updateErrorStatus("The browser was unable to determine your location. Additional
      details: " + error.message);
      break;
    case 3:
      updateErrorStatus("The browser timed out before retrieving the location.");
      break;
    }
  }

  </script>

</body>

</html>
```

Practical Extras

Sometimes there are techniques that don't fit into our regular examples, but which nonetheless apply to many types of HTML5 applications. We present to you some short, common, and practical extras here.

What's My Status?

You might have already noticed that a large portion of the Geolocation API pertains to timing values. This should not be too surprising. Techniques for determining location—cell phone triangulation, GPS, IP lookup, and so on—can take a notoriously long time to complete, if they complete at all. Fortunately, the API gives a developer plenty of information to create a reasonable status bar for the user.

If a developer sets the optional timeout value on a position lookup, she is requesting that the geolocation service notify her with an error if the lookup takes longer than the timeout value. The side effect of this is that it is entirely reasonable to show the user a status message in the user interface while the request is underway. The start of the status begins when the request is made, and the end of the status should correspond to the timeout value, whether or not it ends in success or failure.

In Listing 5-15, we'll kick off a JavaScript interval timer to regularly update the status display with a new progress indicator value.

Listing 5-15. Adding a Status Bar

```
function updateStatus(message) {
    document.getElementById("status").innerHTML = message;
}

function endRequest() {
  updateStatus("Done.");
}

function updateLocation(position) {
  endRequest();
  // handle the position data
}

function handleLocationError(error) {
  endRequest();

  // handle any errors
}

navigator.geolocation.getCurrentPosition(updateLocation,
                                         handleLocationError,
                                         {timeout:10000});
                                         // 10 second timeout value
```

updateStatus("Requesting Geolocation data…");

Let's break that example down a little. As before, we've got a function to update our status value on the page, as shown in the following example.

```
function updateStatus(message) {
  document.getElementById("status").innerHTML = message;
}
```

Our status here will be a simple text display, although this approach applies equally well for more compelling graphical status displays (see Listing 5-16).

Listing 5-16. Showing the Status

```
navigator.geolocation.getCurrentPosition(updateLocation,
                                         handleLocationError,
                                         {timeout:10000});
                                         // 10 second timeout value
```

updateStatus("Requesting location data…");

Once again, we use the Geolocation API to get the user's current position, but with a set timeout of ten seconds. Once ten seconds have elapsed, we should either have a success or failure due to the timeout option.

We immediately update the status text display to indicate that a position request is in progress. Then, once the request completes or ten seconds elapses—whichever comes first—you use the callback method to reset the status text, as shown in Listing 5-17.

Listing 5-17. Resetting the Status Text

```
function endRequest() {
  updateStatus("Done.");
}

function updateLocation(position) {
  endRequest();
  // handle the position data
}
```

A simple extra, but easy to extend.

This technique works well for one-shot position lookups because it is easy for the developer to determine when a position lookup request starts. The request starts as soon as the developer calls getCurrentPosition(), of course. However, in the case of a repeated position lookup via watchPosition(), the developer is not in control of when each individual position request begins.

Furthermore, the timeout does not begin until the user grants permission for the geolocation service to access position data. For this reason, it is impractical to implement a precise status display because the page is not informed during the instant when the user grants permission.

Show Me on a Google Map

One very common request for geolocation data is to show a user's position on a map, such as the popular Google Maps service. In fact, this is so popular that Google itself built support for Geolocation into its user interface. Simply press the Show My Location button (see Figure 5-6); Google Maps will use the Geolocation API (if it is available) to determine and display your location on the map.

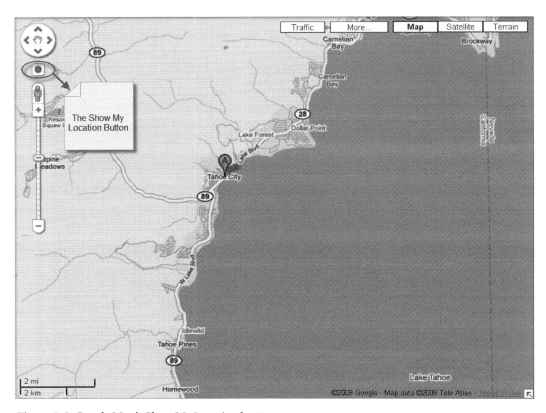

Figure 5-6. *Google Map's Show My Location button*

However, it is also possible to do this yourself. Although the Google Map API is beyond the scope of this book, it has (not coincidentally) been designed to take decimal latitude and longitude locations. Therefore, you can easily pass the results of your position lookup to the Google Map API, as shown in Listing 5-18. You can read more on this subject in *Beginning Google Maps Applications*, Second Edition (Apress, 2010).

Listing 5-18. *Passing a Position to the Google Map API*

```
//Include the Google maps library
<script src="http://maps.google.com/maps/api/js?sensor=false"></script>

// Create a Google Map... see Google API for more detail
var map = new google.maps.Map(document.getElementById("map"));

function updateLocation(position) {
  //pass the position to the Google Map and center it
```

```
map.setCenter(new google.maps.LatLng(
                       parseFloat(position.coords.latitude),
                       parseFloat(position.coords.longitude)));
navigator.geolocation.getCurrentPosition(updateLocation,
                       handleLocationError);
```

Summary

This chapter discussed Geolocation. You learned the Geolocation location information—latitude, longitude, and other attributes—and where they can come from. You also learned about the privacy concerns that accompany Geolocation and you've seen how the Geolocation API can be used to create compelling, location–aware web applications.

In the next chapter, we'll demonstrate how HTML5 lets you communicate between tabs and windows as well as between pages and servers with different domains.

CHAPTER 6

Using the Communication APIs

In this chapter, we'll explore what you can do with two of the important building blocks for real-time, cross-origin communication: *Cross Document Messaging* and *XMLHttpRequest Level 2* and we'll show you how they can be used to create compelling applications. Both of these building blocks add new communication options to HTML5 applications and allow applications served from different domains to safely communicate with each other.

First, we'll discuss the `postMessage` API and the origin security concept—two key elements of HTML5 communication—and then we'll show you how the `postMessage` API can be used to communicate between iframes, tabs, and windows.

Next, we'll discuss XMLHttpRequest Level 2—an improved version of XMLHttpRequest. We'll show you in which areas XMLHttpRequest has been improved. Specifically, we'll show you how you can use XMLHttpRequest to make cross-origin requests and how to use the new progress events.

Cross Document Messaging

Until recently, communications between frames, tabs, and windows in a running browser was entirely restricted due to security concerns. For instance, while it might be handy for certain sites to share information from inside the browser, it would also open up the possibility for malicious attacks. If browsers granted the ability to programmatically access the content loaded into other frames and tabs, sites would be able to steal whatever information they could get from another site's content using scripting. Wisely, the browser vendors restricted this access; attempting to retrieve or modify content loaded from another source raises a security exception and prevents the operation.

However, there are some legitimate cases for content from different sites to be able to communicate inside the browser. The classic example is the "mashup", a combination of different applications such as mapping, chat, and news from different sites, all combined together to form a new meta-application. In these cases, a well-coordinated set of applications would be served by direct communication channels inside the browser itself.

To meet this need, the browser vendors and standards bodies agreed to introduce a new feature: Cross Document Messaging. Cross Document Messaging enables secure cross-origin communication across iframes, tabs, and windows. It defines the `postMessage` API as a standard way to send messages. As shown in the following example, it is very simple to send a message with the `postMessage` API.

```
chatFrame.contentWindow.postMessage('Hello, world', 'http://www.example.com/');
```

To receive messages, you just have to add an event handler to your page. When a message arrives, you can check its origin and decide whether or not to do something with the message. Listing 6-1 shows an event listener that passes the message to a `messageHandler` function.

Listing 6-1. An Event Listener for Message Events

```
window.addEventListener("message", messageHandler, true);
function messageHandler(e) {
    switch(e.origin) {
      case "friend.example.com":
      // process message
      processMessage(e.data);
      break;
    default:
      // message origin not recognized
      // ignoring message
  }
}
```

A message event is a DOM event with `data` and `origin` properties. The `data` property is the actual message that the sender passed along and the `origin` property is the sender's origin. Using the `origin` property, it is easy for the receiving side to ignore messages from untrusted sources; the origin can simply be checked against a list of allowed origins.

As shown in Figure 6-1, the `postMessage` API provides a way to communicate between a chat widget iframe hosted at `http://chat.example.net` and an HTML page that contains the chat widget iframe hosted at `http://portal.example.com` (two different origins).

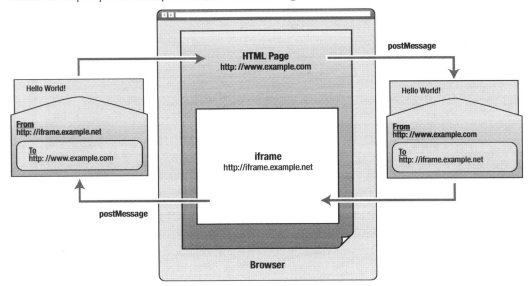

Figure 6-1. postMessage communication between an iframe and a main HTML page

In this example, the chat widget is contained in an iframe from another origin, so it does not have direct access to the parent window. When the chat widget receives a chat message, it can use `postMessage` to send a message to the main page so that the page can alert the user of the chat widget that a new message has been received. Similarly, the page can send messages about the user's status to the chat widget. Both the page and the widget can listen for messages from each other by adding the respective origins to a whitelist of allowed origins.

Figure 6-2 shows a real-life example of using the postMessage API in action. It is an HTML5 Slide viewer application called DZSlides, built by Firefox engineer and HTML5 evangelist Paul Rouget (http://paulrouget.com/dzslides). In this application, the presentation and its container communicate using the postMessage API.

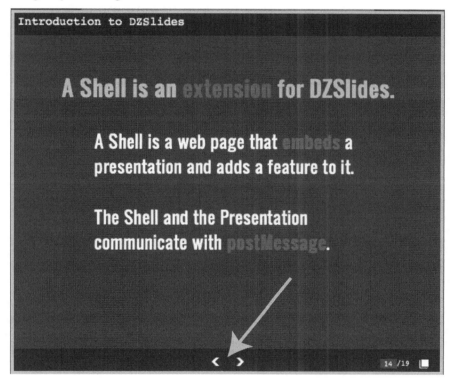

Figure 6-2. Real-life use of postMessage API in DZSlides application

Before the introduction of postMessage, communicating between iframes could sometimes be accomplished by direct scripting. A script running in one page would attempt to manipulate another document. This might not be allowed due to security restrictions. Instead of direct programmatic access, postMessage provides asynchronous message passing between JavaScript contexts. As shown in Figure 6-3, without postMessage, cross origin communication would result in security errors, enforced by browsers to prevent cross-site scripting attacks.

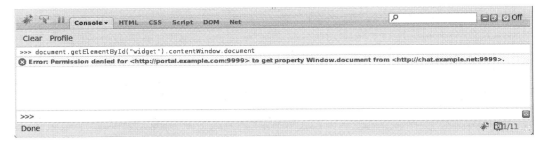

Figure 6-3. Cross-site scripting error in earlier version of Firefox and Firebug

The postMessage API can be used for communicating between documents with the same origin, but it is particularly useful when communication might otherwise be disallowed by the same-domain policy, which is enforced by browsers. However, there are reasons to use postMessage for messaging between same-origin documents as well because it provides a consistent, easy-to-use API. The postMessage API is used whenever there is communication between JavaScript contexts, such as with HTML5 Web Workers.

Understanding Origin Security

HTML5 clarifies and refines domain security by introducing the concept of an *origin*. An origin is a subset of an address used for modeling trust relationships on the Web. Origins are made up of a scheme, a host, and a port. For example, a page at https://www.example.com has a different origin than one at http://www.example.com because the scheme differs (https vs. http). The path is not considered in the origin value, so a page at http://www.example.com/index.html has the same origin as a page at http://www.example.com/page2.html because only the paths differ.

HTML5 defines the serialization of origins. In string form, origins can be referred to in APIs and protocols. This is essential for cross-origin HTTP requests using XMLHttpRequest, as well as for WebSockets.

Cross-origin communication identifies the sender by origin. This allows the receiver to ignore messages from origins it does not trust or does not expect to receive messages from. Furthermore, applications must opt-in to receiving messages by adding an event listener for message events. Because of this, there is no risk of messages interfering with an unsuspecting application.

Security rules for postMessage ensure that messages cannot be delivered to pages with unexpected—and possibly undesired—origins. When sending a message, the sender specifies the receiver's origin. If the window on which the sender is calling postMessage does not have that specific origin (for instance, if the user has navigated to another site) the browser will not transmit that message.

Likewise, when receiving a message, the sender's origin is included as part of the message. The message's origin is provided by the browser and cannot be spoofed. This allows the receiver to decide which messages to process and which to ignore. You can keep a white list and process only messages from documents with trusted origins.

Be careful with External input

Frank says: "Applications that process cross-origin messages should always verify the source origin of every message. Furthermore, message data should be treated with caution. Even if a message comes from a trusted source, it should be treated with the same caution as any other external input. The following two examples show a method of injecting content that can lead to trouble, as well as a safer alternative.

```
// Dangerous: e.data is evaluated as markup!
element.innerHTML = e.data;

// Better
element.textContent = e.data;
```

As a best practice, *never* evaluate strings received from third parties. Furthermore, avoid using eval with strings originating from your own application. Instead, you can use JSON with window.JSON or the json.org parser. JSON is a data language that is meant to be safely consumed by JavaScript, and the json.org parser is designed to be paranoid."

Browser Support for Cross Document Messaging

All major browsers, including Internet Explorer 8 and later, support the postMessage API. It is always a good idea to first test if HTML5 Cross Document Messaging is supported, before you use it. The section "Checking for Browser Support" later in this chapter will show you how you can programmatically check for browser support.

Using the postMessage API

In this section, we'll explore the use of the HTML5 postMessage API in more detail.

Checking for Browser Support

Before you call postMessage, it is a good idea to check if the browser supports it. The following example shows one way to check for postMessage support:

```
if (typeof window.postMessage === "undefined") {
    // postMessage not supported in this browser
}
```

Sending Messages

To send messages, invoke postMessage on the target window object, as shown in the following example:

```
window.postMessage("Hello, world", "portal.example.com");
```

The first argument contains the data to send, and the second argument contains the intended target. To send messages to iframes, you can invoke postMessage on the iframe's contentWindow, as shown in the following example:

```
document.getElementsByTagName("iframe")[0].contentWindow.postMessage("Hello, world",
"chat.example.net");
```

Listening for Message Events

A script receives messages by listening for events on the window object, as shown in Listing 6-2. In the event listener function, the receiving application can decide to accept or ignore the message.

Listing 6-2. Listening for Message Events and Comparing Origins Against a Whitelist

```
var originWhiteList = ["portal.example.com", "games.example.com", "www.example.com"];

function checkWhiteList(origin) {
    for (var i=0; i<originWhiteList.length; i++) {
        if (origin === originWhiteList[i]) {
          return true;
        }
    }
    return false;
}

function messageHandler(e) {
    if(checkWhiteList(e.origin)) {
        processMessage(e.data);
    } else {
        // ignore messages from unrecognized origins
    }
}
window.addEventListener("message", messageHandler, true);
```

■ **Note** The MessageEvent interface defined by HTML5 is also part of HTML5 WebSockets and HTML5 Web Workers. The communication features of HTML5 have consistent APIs for receiving messages. Other communication APIs, such as the EventSource API and Web Workers, also use MessageEvent to deliver messages.

Building an Application Using the postMessage API

Let's say that you wanted to build the aforementioned portal application with its cross-origin chat widget. You can use Cross Document Messaging to communicate between the portal page and the chat widget, as shown in Figure 6-4.

Cross-Origin Portal

Origin: http://portal.example.com:9999

Status [Out for a run!   ] [Change Status]

This uses postMessage to send a status update to the widget iframe contained in the portal page.

Widget iframe

Origin: http://chat.example.net:9999

Status set to: **Out for a run!** by containing portal.

[Runtime   ] [Send Notification]

This will ask the portal to notify the user. The portal does this by flashing the title. If the message comes from an origin other than http://chat.example.net:9999, the portal page will ignore it.

[Stop Blinking Title]

Figure 6-4. Portal page with cross-origin chat widget iframe

In this example, we show how a portal might embed widgets from third parties in iframes. Our example shows a single widget from chat.example.net. The portal page and widget then communicate using postMessage. In this case, the iframe represents a chat widget that wants to notify the user by blinking the title text. This is a common UI technique found in applications that receive events in the background. However, because the widget is isolated in an iframe served from a different origin than the parent page, changing the title would be a security violation. Instead, the widget uses postMessage to request that the parent page perform the notification on its behalf.

The example portal also sends messages to the iframe to inform the widget that the user has changed his or her status. Using postMessage in this way allows a portal such as this to coordinate with widgets across the combined application. Of course, because the target origin is checked when the message is sent, and the event origin is checked when it is received, there is no chance that data leaks out accidentally or is spoofed.

■ **Note** In this example application, the chat widget is not connected to a live chat system, and notifications are driven by the application's users clicking **Send Notification**. A working chat application could use Web Sockets, as described in Chapter 7.

For the sake of illustration, we created a few simple HTML pages: postMessagePortal.html and postMessageWidget.html. The following steps highlight the important parts of building the portal page and the chat widget page. The sample code for the following examples is located in the code/communication folder.

Building the Portal Page

First, add the chat widget iframe hosted at the different origin:

```
<iframe id="widget" src="http://chat.example.net:9999/postMessageWidget.html"></iframe>
```

Next, add an event listener messageHandler to listen for message events coming from the chat widget. As shown in the following example code, the widget will ask the portal to notify the user, which can be done by flashing the title. To make sure the message comes from the chat widget, the message's origin is verified; if it does not come from http://chat.example.net:9999, the portal page simply ignores it.

```
var trustedOrigin = "http://chat.example.net:9999";

function messageHandler(e) {
    if (e.origin == trustedOrigin) {
        notify(e.data);
    } else {
        // ignore messages from other origins
    }
}
```

Next, add a function to communicate with the chat widget. It uses postMessage to send a status update to the widget iframe contained in the portal page. In a live chat application, it could be used to communicate the user's status (available, away, and so on).

```
function sendString(s) {
    document.getElementById("widget").contentWindow.postMessage(s, targetOrigin);
}
```

Building the Chat Widget Page

First, add an event listener messageHandler to listen for message events coming from the portal page. As shown in the following example code, the chat widget listens for incoming status-change messages. To make sure the message comes from the portal page, the message's origin is verified; if it does not come from http://portal.example.com:9999, the widget simply ignores it.

```
var trustedOrigin = "http://portal.example.com:9999";
function messageHandler(e) {
    if (e.origin === trustedOrigin {
        document.getElementById("status").textContent = e.data;
    } else {
        // ignore messages from other origins
    }
```

```
}
```

Next, add a function to communicate with the portal page. The widget will ask the portal to notify the user on its behalf and uses `postMessage` to send a message to the portal page when a new chat message is received, as shown in the following example:

```
function sendString(s) {
    window.top.postMessage(s, trustedOrigin);
}
```

The Final Code

Listing 6-3 shows the complete code for the Portal page `postMessagePortal.html`.

Listing 6-3. Contents of postMessagePortal.html

```html
<!DOCTYPE html>
<title>Portal [http://portal.example.com:9999]</title>
<link rel="stylesheet" href="styles.css">
<style>
    iframe {
        height: 400px;
        width: 800px;
    }
</style>
<link rel="icon" href="http://apress.com/favicon.ico">
<script>

var defaultTitle = "Portal [http://portal.example.com:9999]";
var notificationTimer = null;

var trustedOrigin = "http://chat.example.net:9999";

function messageHandler(e) {
    if (e.origin == trustedOrigin) {
        notify(e.data);
    } else {
        // ignore messages from other origins
    }
}

function sendString(s) {
    document.getElementById("widget").contentWindow.postMessage(s, trustedOrigin);
}


function notify(message) {
    stopBlinking();
    blinkTitle(message, defaultTitle);
}
```

```
function stopBlinking() {
    if (notificationTimer !== null) {
        clearTimeout(notificationTimer);
    }
    document.title = defaultTitle;
}

function blinkTitle(m1, m2) {
    document.title = m1;
    notificationTimer = setTimeout(blinkTitle, 1000, m2, m1)
}

function sendStatus() {
var statusText = document.getElementById("statusText").value;
            sendString(statusText);
}

function loadDemo() {
    document.getElementById("sendButton").addEventListener("click", sendStatus, true);
    document.getElementById("stopButton").addEventListener("click", stopBlinking, true);
    sendStatus();
}
window.addEventListener("load", loadDemo, true);
window.addEventListener("message", messageHandler, true);

</script>

<h1>Cross-Origin Portal</h1>
<p><b>Origin</b>: http://portal.example.com:9999</p>
Status <input type="text" id="statusText" value="Online">
<button id="sendButton">Change Status</button>
<p>
This uses postMessage to send a status update to the widget iframe contained in the portal
page.
</p>
<iframe id="widget" src="http://chat.example.net:9999/postMessageWidget.html"></iframe>
<p>
    <button id="stopButton">Stop Blinking Title</button>
</p>
```

Listing 6-4 shows the code for the portal page postMessageWidget.html.

Listing 6-4. *Contents of postMessageWidget.html*

```
<!DOCTYPE html>
<title>widget</title>
<link rel="stylesheet" href="styles.css">
<script>

var trustedOrigin = "http://portal.example.com:9999";
```

```
function messageHandler(e) {
    if (e.origin === "http://portal.example.com:9999") {
        document.getElementById("status").textContent = e.data;
    } else {
        // ignore messages from other origins
    }
}

function sendString(s) {
    window.top.postMessage(s, trustedOrigin);
}

function loadDemo() {
    document.getElementById("actionButton").addEventListener("click",
        function() {
            var messageText = document.getElementById("messageText").value;
            sendString(messageText);
        }, true);

}
window.addEventListener("load", loadDemo, true);
window.addEventListener("message", messageHandler, true);

</script>
<h1>Widget iframe</h1>
<p><b>Origin</b>: http://chat.example.net:9999</p>
<p>Status set to: <strong id="status"></strong> by containing portal.<p>

<div>
    <input type="text" id="messageText" value="Widget notification.">
    <button id="actionButton">Send Notification</button>
</div>

<p>
This will ask the portal to notify the user. The portal does this by flashing the title. If
the message comes from an origin other than http://chat.example.net:9999, the portal page will
ignore it.
</p>
```

The Application in Action

To see this example in action, there are two prerequisites: the pages have to be served up by a web server and the pages have to be served up from two different domains. If you have access to multiple web servers (for example, two Apache HTTP servers) on separate domains, you can host the example files on those servers and run the demo. Another way to accomplish this on your local machine is to use Python SimpleHTTPServer, as shown in the following steps.

1. Update the path to the Windows hosts file
    (C:\Windows\system32\drivers\etc\hosts) and the Linux version (/etc/hosts)
    by adding two entries pointing to your localhost (IP address 127.0.0.1), as
    shown in the following example:

```
127.0.0.1 chat.example.net
127.0.0.1 portal.example.com
```

■ **Note** You must restart your browser after modifying the host file to ensure that the DNS entries take effect.

---

2. Install Python 2, which includes the lightweight SimpleHTTPServer web server.

3. Navigate to the directory that contains the two example files (postMessageParent.html and postMessageWidget.html).

4. Start Python as follows:

```
python -m SimpleHTTPServer 9999
```

5. Open a browser and navigate to http://portal.example.com:9999/postMessagePortal.html. You should now see the page shown in Figure 6-4.

XMLHttpRequest Level 2

XMLHttpRequest is the API that made Ajax possible. There are many books about XMLHttpRequest and Ajax. You can read more about XMLHttpRequest programming in John Resig's *Pro JavaScript Techniques*, (Apress, 2006).

XMLHttpRequest Level 2—the new version of XMLHttpRequest—has been significantly enhanced. In this chapter, we will be covering the improvements introduced in XMLHttpRequest Level 2. These improvements are centered on the following areas:

• Cross-origin XMLHttpRequests

• Progress events

• Binary Data

Cross-Origin XMLHttpRequest

In the past, XMLHttpRequest was limited to same-origin communication. XMLHttpRequest Level 2 allows for cross-origin XMLHttpRequests using Cross Origin Resource Sharing (CORS), which uses the *origin* concept discussed in the earlier *Cross Document Messaging* section.

Cross-origin HTTP requests have an Origin header. This header provides the server with the request's origin. This header is protected by the browser and cannot be changed from application code. In essence, it is the network equivalent of the origin property found on message events used in Cross Document Messaging. The origin header differs from the older referer [*sic*] header in that the referer is a complete URL including the path. Because the path may contain sensitive information, the referer is sometimes not sent by browsers attempting to protect user privacy. However, the browser will always send the required Origin headers when necessary.

Using cross-origin XMLHttpRequest, you can build web applications that use services hosted on different origins. For example, if you wanted to host a web application that used static content from one origin and Ajax services from another, you could use cross-origin XMLHttpRequest to communicate between the two. Without cross-origin XMLHttpRequest, you would be limited to same-origin communication. This would constrain your deployment options. For example, you might have to deploy the web application on a single domain or set up a subdomain.

As shown in Figure 6-5, cross-origin XMLHttpRequest allows you to aggregate content from different origins on the client side. Additionally, you can access secured content with the user's credentials if the target server allows it, providing users with direct access to personalized data. Server-side aggregation, on the other hand, forces all content to be funneled through a single server-side infrastructure, which can create a bottleneck.

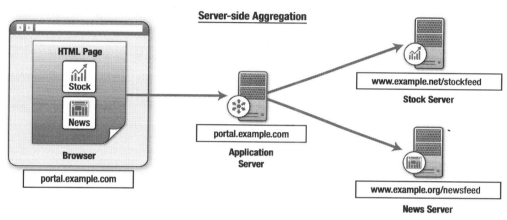

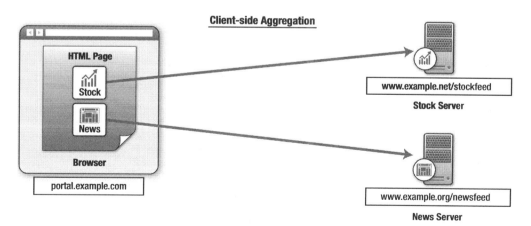

Figure 6-5. Difference between client-side and server-side aggregation

The CORS specification dictates that, for sensitive actions—for example, a request with credentials, or a request other than GET or POST—an OPTIONS preflight request must be sent to the server by the browser to see whether the action is supported and allowed. This means that successful communication may require a CORS-capable server. Listings 6-5 and 6-6 show the HTTP headers involved in a cross-origin exchange between a page hosted on www.example.com and a service hosted on www.example.net.

Listing 6-5. *Example Request Headers*

```
POST /main HTTP/1.1
Host: www.example.net
User-Agent: Mozilla/5.0 (X11; U; Linux x86_64; en-US; rv:1.9.1.3) Gecko/20090910 Ubuntu/9.04
(jaunty) Shiretoko/3.5.3
Accept: text/html,application/xhtml+xml,application/xml;q=0.9,*/*;q=0.8
Accept-Language: en-us,en;q=0.5
Accept-Encoding: gzip,deflate
Accept-Charset: ISO-8859-1,utf-8;q=0.7,*;q=0.7
Keep-Alive: 300
Connection: keep-alive
Referer: http://www.example.com/
Origin: http://www.example.com
Pragma: no-cache
Cache-Control: no-cache
Content-Length: 0
```

Listing 6-6. *Example Response Headers*

```
HTTP/1.1 201 Created
Transfer-Encoding: chunked
Server: Kaazing Gateway
Date: Mon, 02 Nov 2009 06:55:08 GMT
Content-Type: text/plain
Access-Control-Allow-Origin: http://www.example.com
Access-Control-Allow-Credentials: true
```

Progress Events

One of the most important API improvements in XMLHttpRequest has been the changes related to progressive responses. In the previous version of XMLHttpRequest, there was only a single readystatechange event. On top of that, it was inconsistently implemented across browsers. For example, readyState 3 (progress) never fires in Internet Explorer. Furthermore, the readyState change event lacked a way to communicate upload progress. Implementing an upload progress bar was not a trivial task and involved server-side participation.

XMLHttpRequest Level 2 introduces progress events with meaningful names. Table 6-2 shows the new progress event names. You can listen for each of these events by setting a callback function for the event handler attribute. For example, when the loadstart event fires, the callback for the onloadstart property is called.

Table 6-1. New XMLHttpRequest Level 2 Progress Event Names

Progress Event Name
loadstart
progress
abort
error
load
loadend

The old readyState property and readystatechange events will be retained for backward compatibility.

"Seemingly Arbitrary" Times

In the XMLHttpRequest Level 2 specification's description for the readystatechange event (maintained for backward compatibility), the readyState attribute is described as changing at, get this, "*some seemingly arbitrary times for historical reasons.*"

Browser Support for HTML5 XMLHttpRequest Level 2

HTML5 XMLHttpRequest is already supported in many browsers at the time of this writing. Due to the varying levels of support, it is a good idea to first test if HTML5 XMLHttpRequest is supported, before you use these elements. The section "Checking for Browser Support" later in this chapter will show you how you can programmatically check for browser support.

Using the XMLHttpRequest API

In this section, we'll explore the use of the XMLHttpRequest in more detail. For the sake of illustration, we've created a simple HTML page—crossOriginUpload.html. The sample code for the following examples is located in the code/communication folder.

Checking for Browser Support

Before you try to use XMLHttpRequest Level 2 functionality—such as cross-origin support—it is a good idea to check if it is supported. You can do this by checking whether the new withCredentials property is available on an XMLHttpRequest object as shown in Listing 6-7.

Listing 6-7. Checking if Cross-Origin Support Is Available in XMLHttpRequest

```
var xhr = new XMLHttpRequest()
if (typeof xhr.withCredentials === undefined) {
    document.getElementById("support").innerHTML =
        "Your browser <strong>does not</strong> support cross-origin XMLHttpRequest";
} else {
    document.getElementById("support").innerHTML =
        "Your browser <strong>does</strong>support cross-origin XMLHttpRequest";
}
```

Making Cross-Origin Requests

To make a cross-origin XMLHttpRequest, you must first create a new XMLHttpRequest object, as shown in the following example.

```
var crossOriginRequest = new XMLHttpRequest()
```

Next, make the cross-origin XMLHttpRequest by specifying an address on a different origin as shown in the following example.

```
crossOriginRequest.open("GET", "http://www.example.net/stockfeed", true);
```

Make sure, you listen for errors. There are many reasons why this request might not succeed. For example, network failure, access denied, and lack of CORS support on the target server.

WHY NOT JSONP?

Frank says: "One common way to fetch data from another origin is JSONP (JSON with padding). JSONP involves creating a script tag with the URL of a JSON resource. The URL has a query parameter containing the name of a function to invoke when the script loads. It is up to the remote server to wrap the JSON data with a call to the named function. This has serious security implications! When you use JSONP, you must completely trust the service providing the data. A malicious script could take over your application.

With XMLHttpRequest (XHR) and CORS, you receive data instead of code, which you can parse safely. It's far safer than evaluating external input."

Using Progress Events

Instead of numerical states representing different stages of the request and response, XMLHttpRequest Level 2 provides named progress events. You can listen for each of these events by setting a callback function for the event handler attribute.

Listing 6-8 shows how callback functions are used to handle progress events. Progress events have fields for the total amount of data to transfer, the amount that has already transferred, and a Boolean value indicating whether the total is known (it may not be in the case of streaming HTTP). XMLHttpRequest.upload dispatches events with the same fields.

Listing 6-8. Using the onprogress Event

```
crossOriginRequest.onprogress = function(e) {
    var total = e.total;
    var loaded = e.loaded;

    if (e.lengthComputable) {
        // do something with the progress information
    }
}
crossOriginRequest.upload.onprogress = function(e) {
    var total = e.total;
    var loaded = e.loaded;

    if (e.lengthComputable) {
        // do something with the progress information
    }
}
```

Binary Data

Browsers that support new binary APIs such as Typed Array (which is necessary for WebGL and programmable audio) may be able to send binary data with XMLHttpRequest. The XMLHttpRequest Level 2 specification includes support for calling the send() method with Blob and ArrayBuffer (aka Typed Array) objects (see Listing 6-9).

Listing 6-9. Sending a Typed Array of Bytes

```
var a = new Uint8Array([8,6,7,5,3,0,9]);
var xhr = new XMLHttpRequest();
xhr.open("POST", "/data/", true)
console.log(a)
xhr.send(a.buffer);
```

This makes an HTTP POST request with a binary content body. The content length is 7, and the body contains the bytes 8,6,7,5,3,0,9.

XMLHttpRequest Level 2 also exposes binary response data. Setting the responseType attribute to "text," "document," "arraybuffer," or "blob" controls the type of object returned by the response property. To see the raw bytes contained by the HTTP response body, set the responseType to "arraybuffer" or "blob."

In the next chapter, we'll see how WebSocket can be used to send and receive binary data using the same types.

Building an Application Using XMLHttpRequest

In this example, we'll look at uploading race geolocation coordinates to a web server hosted on a different origin. We use the new progress events to monitor the status of the HTTP request including the upload percentage. Figure 6-6 shows the application in action.

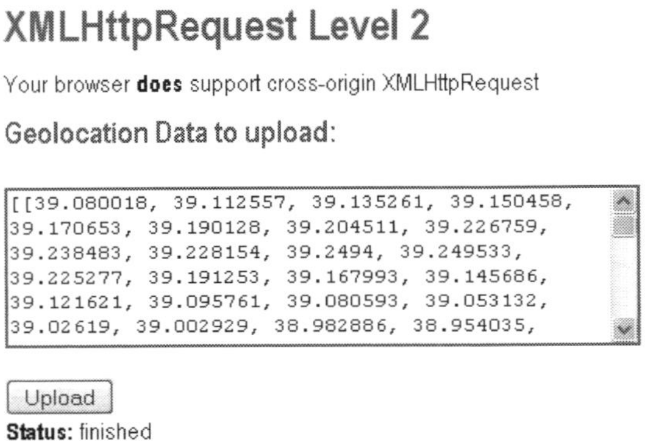

XMLHttpRequest Level 2

Your browser **does** support cross-origin XMLHttpRequest

Geolocation Data to upload:

```
[[39.080018, 39.112557, 39.135261, 39.150458,
39.170653, 39.190128, 39.204511, 39.226759,
39.238483, 39.228154, 39.2494, 39.249533,
39.225277, 39.191253, 39.167993, 39.145686,
39.121621, 39.095761, 39.080593, 39.053132,
39.02619, 39.002929, 38.982886, 38.954035,
```

Upload

Status: finished

Figure 6-6. A Web Application That Uploads Geolocation Data

For the sake of illustration, we've created the HTML file crossOrignUpload.html. The following steps highlight the important parts of building the cross-origin upload page shown in Figure 6-5. The sample code for the following examples is located in the code/communication folder.

First, create a new XMLHttpRequest object, as shown in the following example.

```
var xhr = new XMLHttpRequest();
```

Next, do check if cross-origin XMLHttpRequest is supported in the browser, as shown in the following example.

```
if (typeof xhr.withCredentials === undefined) {
  document.getElementById("support").innerHTML =
          "Your browser <strong>doesnot</strong> support cross-origin XMLHttpRequest";
} else {
    document.getElementById("support").innerHTML =
            "Your browser <strong>does</strong> support cross-origin XMLHttpRequest";
}
```

Next, set callback functions to handle the progress events and calculate the uploaded and downloaded ratios.

```
xhr.upload.onprogress = function(e) {
  var ratio = e.loaded / e.total;
  setProgress(ratio + "% uploaded");
}

xhr.onprogress = function(e) {
  var ratio = e.loaded / e.total;
  setProgress(ratio + "% downloaded");
}


xhr.onload = function(e) {
  setProgress("finished");
}
```

```
xhr.onerror = function(e) {
  setProgress("error");
}
```

Finally, open the request and send the string containing the encoded geolocation data. This will be a cross-origin request because the target location is a URL with a different origin than the page.

```
var targetLocation = "http://geodata.example.net:9999/upload";
xhr.open("POST", targetLocation, true);

geoDataString = dataElement.textContent;
xhr.send(geoDataString);
```

The Final Code

Listing 6-10 shows the complete application code—the contents of the crossOriginUpload.html file.

Listing 6-10. Contents of crossOriginUpload.html

```
<!DOCTYPE html>
<title>Upload Geolocation Data</title>
<link rel="stylesheet" href="styles.css">
<link rel="icon" href="http://apress.com/favicon.ico">
<script>

function loadDemo() {
    var dataElement = document.getElementById("geodata");
    dataElement.textContent = JSON.stringify(geoData).replace(",", ", ", "g");

    var xhr = new XMLHttpRequest()
    if (typeof xhr.withCredentials === undefined) {
        document.getElementById("support").innerHTML =
            "Your browser <strong>does not</strong> support cross-origin XMLHttpRequest";
    } else {
        document.getElementById("support").innerHTML =
            "Your browser <strong>does</strong> support cross-origin XMLHttpRequest";
    }

    var targetLocation = "http://geodata.example.net:9999/upload";

    function setProgress(s) {
        document.getElementById("progress").innerHTML = s;
    }

    document.getElementById("sendButton").addEventListener("click",
        function() {
            xhr.upload.onprogress = function(e) {
                var ratio = e.loaded / e.total;
                setProgress(ratio + "% uploaded");
            }
```

```
        xhr.onprogress = function(e) {
          var ratio = e.loaded / e.total;
          setProgress(ratio + "% downloaded");
        }

        xhr.onload = function(e) {
            setProgress("finished");
        }

        xhr.onerror = function(e) {
            setProgress("error");
        }

        xhr.open("POST", targetLocation, true);

        geoDataString = dataElement.textContent;
        xhr.send(geoDataString);
      }, true);

  }
  window.addEventListener("load", loadDemo, true);

</script>

<h1>XMLHttpRequest Level 2</h1>
<p id="support"></p>

<h4>Geolocation Data to upload:</h4>
<textarea id="geodata">
</textarea>
</div>

<button id="sendButton">Upload</button>

<script>
geoData = [[39.080018000000003, 39.112557000000002, 39.135261, 39.150458, 39.170653000000001,
39.190128000000001, 39.204510999999997, 39.226759000000001, 39.238483000000002,
39.228154000000004, 39.249400000000001, 39.249533, 39.225276999999998, 39.191253000000003,
39.167993000000003, 39.145685999999998, 39.121620999999998, 39.095761000000003, 39.080593,
39.053131999999998, 39.02619, 39.002929000000002, 38.982886000000001, 38.954034999999998,
38.944926000000002, 38.919960000000003, 38.925261999999996, 38.934922999999998,
38.949373000000001, 38.950133999999998, 38.952649000000001, 38.969692000000002,
38.988512999999998, 39.010652, 39.033088999999997, 39.053493000000003, 39.072752999999999], [-
120.15724399999999, -120.15818299999999, -120.15600400000001, -120.14564599999999, -
120.141285, -120.10889900000001, -120.09528500000002, -120.077596, -120.045428, -120.0119, -
119.98897100000002, -119.95124099999998, -119.93270099999998, -119.927131, -
119.92685999999999, -119.92636200000001, -119.92844600000001, -119.911036, -119.942834, -
119.94413000000002, -119.94555200000001, -119.95411000000001, -119.941327, -
119.94605900000001, -119.97527599999999, -119.99445, -120.028998, -120.066335, -
120.07867300000001, -120.089985, -120.112227, -120.09797000000001, -120.10881000000001, -
120.116692, -120.117847, -120.11727899999998, -120.14398199999999]]);
</script>
```

```
<p>
    <b>Status: </b> <span id="progress">ready</span>
</p>
```

The Application in Action

To see this example in action, there are two prerequisites: the pages have to be served up from different domains, and the target page has to be served up by a web server that understands CORS headers. A CORS-compliant Python script that can handle incoming cross-origin XMLHttpRequests is included in the example code for this chapter. You can run the demo on your local machine by performing the following steps:

1. Update your hosts file (C:\Windows\system32\drivers\etc\hosts on Windows or /etc/hosts on Unix/Linux) by adding two entries pointing to your localhost (IP address 127.0.0.1) as shown in the following example:

   ```
   127.0.0.1 geodata.example.net
   127.0.0.1 portal.example.com
   ```

   ■ **Note** You must restart your browser after modifying the host file to ensure the DNS entries take effect.

   ---

2. Install Python 2, which includes the lightweight SimpleHTTPServer web server, if you did not do so for the previous example.

3. Navigate to the directory that contains the example file (crossOrignUpload.html) and the Python CORS server script (CORSServer.py).

4. Start Python in this directory as follows:
   python CORSServer.py 9999

5. Open a browser and navigate to http://portal.example.com:9999/crossOriginUpload.html. You should now see the page shown in Figure 6-6.

Practical Extras

Sometimes there are techniques that don't fit into our regular examples, but that nonetheless apply to many types of HTML5 applications. We present to you some short, but common, practical extras here.

Structured Data

Early versions of postMessage only supported strings. Later revisions allowed other types of data including JavaScript objects, canvas imageData, and files. Support for different object types will vary by browser as the specification develops.

In some browsers, the limitations on JavaScript objects that can be sent with postMessage are the same as those for JSON data. In particular, data structures with cycles may not be allowed. An example of this is a list containing itself.

Framebusting

Framebusting is a technique for ensuring that your content is not loaded in an iframe. An application can detect that its window is not the outermost window (window.top) and subsequently break out of its containing frame, as shown in the following example.

```
if (window !== window.top) {
    window.top.location = location;
}
```

Browsers supporting the X-Frame-Options HTTP header will also prevent malicious framing for resources that set that header to DENY or SAMEORIGIN. However, there may be certain partner pages that you want to selectively allow to frame your content. One solution is to use postMessage to handshake between cooperating iframes and containing pages, as shown in the Listing 6-11.

Listing 6-11. Using postMessage in an iframe to Handshake with a Trusted Partner Page

```
var framebustTimer;
var timeout = 3000; // 3 second framebust timeout

if (window !== window.top) {
    framebustTimer = setTimeout(
        function() {
            window.top.location = location;
        }, timeout);
}

window.addEventListener("message", function(e) {
    switch(e.origin) {
        case trustedFramer:
            clearTimeout(framebustTimer);
            break;
    }
), true);
```

Summary

In this chapter, you have seen how HTML5 Cross Document Messaging and XMLHttpRequest Level 2 can be used to create compelling applications that can securely communicate cross-origin.

First, we discussed postMessage and the origin security concept—two key elements of HTML5 communication—and then we showed you how the postMessage API can be used to communicate between iframes, tabs, and windows.

Next, we discussed XMLHttpRequest Level 2—an improved version of XMLHttpRequest. We showed you in which areas XMLHttpRequest has been improved; most importantly in the readystatechange events area. We then showed you how you can use XMLHttpRequest to make cross-origin requests and how to use the new progress events.

Finally, we wrapped up the chapter with a few practical examples. In the next chapter, we'll demonstrate how HTML5 WebSockets enables you to stream real-time data to an application with incredible simplicity and minimal overhead.

## CHAPTER 7

Using the WebSocket API

In this chapter, we'll explore what you can do with the most powerful communication feature in the HTML5 specification: *WebSocket*, which defines a full-duplex communication channel that operates through a single socket over the web. WebSocket is not just another incremental enhancement to conventional HTTP communications; it represents a large advance, especially for real-time, event-driven web applications.

WebSocket provides such an improvement from the old, convoluted "hacks" that are used to simulate a full-duplex connection in a browser that it prompted Google's Ian Hickson—the HTML5 specification lead—to say:

> *"Reducing kilobytes of data to 2 bytes...and reducing latency from 150ms to 50ms is far more than marginal. In fact, these two factors alone are enough to make WebSocket seriously interesting to Google."*

> —www.ietf.org/mail-archive/web/hybi/current/msg00784.html

We'll show you in detail just why WebSocket provides such a dramatic improvement, and you'll see how—in one fell swoop—WebSocket makes all the old Comet and Ajax polling, long-polling, and streaming solutions obsolete.

Overview of WebSocket

Let's take a look at how WebSocket can offer a reduction of unnecessary network traffic and latency by comparing HTTP solutions to full duplex "real time" browser communication with WebSocket.

Real-Time and HTTP

Normally when a browser visits a web page, an HTTP request is sent to the web server that hosts that page. The web server acknowledges this request and sends back the response. In many cases—for example, for stock prices, news reports, ticket sales, traffic patterns, medical device readings, and so on—the response could be stale by the time the browser renders the page. If you want to get the most up-to-date real-time information, you can constantly refresh that page manually, but that's obviously not a great solution.

Current attempts to provide real-time web applications largely revolve around polling and other server-side push technologies, the most notable of which is "Comet", which delays the completion of an HTTP response to deliver messages to the client.

With polling, the browser sends HTTP requests at regular intervals and immediately receives a response. This technique was the first attempt for the browser to deliver real-time information. Obviously, this is a good solution if the exact interval of message delivery is known, because you can synchronize the client request to occur only when information is available on the server. However, real-time data is often not that predictable, making unnecessary requests inevitable and as a result, many connections are opened and closed needlessly in low-message-rate situations.

With long-polling, the browser sends a request to the server and the server keeps the request open for a set period of time. If a notification is received within that period, a response containing the message is sent to the client. If a notification is not received within the set time period, the server sends a response to terminate the open request. It is important to understand, however, that when you have a high message-volume, long-polling does not provide any substantial performance improvements over traditional polling.

With streaming, the browser sends a complete request, but the server sends and maintains an open response that is continuously updated and kept open indefinitely (or for a set period of time). The response is then updated whenever a message is ready to be sent, but the server never signals to complete the response, thus keeping the connection open to deliver future messages. However, since streaming is still encapsulated in HTTP, intervening firewalls and proxy servers may choose to buffer the response, increasing the latency of the message delivery. Therefore, many streaming solutions fall back to long-polling in case a buffering proxy server is detected. Alternatively, TLS (SSL) connections can be used to shield the response from being buffered, but in that case the setup and tear down of each connection taxes the available server resources more heavily.

Ultimately, all of these methods for providing real-time data involve HTTP request and response headers, which contain lots of additional, unnecessary header data and introduce latency. On top of that, full-duplex connectivity requires more than just the downstream connection from server to client. In an effort to simulate full-duplex communication over half-duplex HTTP, many of today's solutions use two connections: one for the downstream and one for the upstream. The maintenance and coordination of these two connections introduces significant overhead in terms of resource consumption and adds lots of complexity. Simply put, HTTP wasn't designed for real-time, full-duplex communication as you can see in the Figure 7-1, which shows the complexities associated with building a web application that displays real-time data from a back-end data source using a publish/subscribe model over half-duplex HTTP.

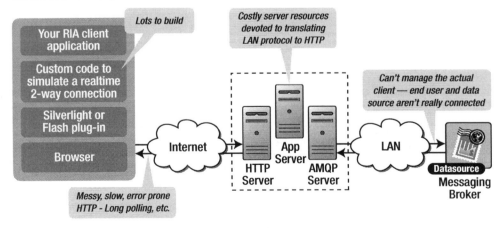

Figure 7-1. The complexity of real-time HTTP applications

It gets even worse when you try to scale out those solutions. Simulating bidirectional browser communication over HTTP is error-prone and complex and all that complexity does not scale. Even though your end users might be enjoying something that looks like a real-time web application, this "real-time" experience has a high price tag. It's a price that you will pay in additional latency, unnecessary network traffic and a drag on CPU performance.

Understanding WebSocket

WebSocket was first defined as "TCPConnection" in the Communications section of the HTML5 specification by Ian Hickson (lead writer of the HTML5 specification). The specification evolved and changed to WebSocket, which is now an independent specification (just like Geolocation, Web Workers and so on), to keep the discussion focused.

Both TCPConnection and WebSocket are names that refer to lower-level networking interfaces. TCP is a fundamental transport protocol for the Internet. WebSocket is a transport protocol for web applications. It provides a bidirectional stream of data that arrives in order, much like TCP. As with TCP, higher-level protocols can run over WebSocket. To be part of the Web, rather than connecting to an Internet host and port, WebSocket connects to URLs.

WHAT DO WEBSOCKET AND MODEL TRAINS HAVE IN COMMON?

Peter says: "Ian Hickson is quite the model train enthusiast; he has been planning ways to control trains from computers ever since 1984 when Marklin first came out with a digital controller, long before the web even existed.

At that time, Ian added TCPConnection to the HTML5 specification, he was working on a program to control a model train set from a browser and he was using the prevalent pre-WebSocket "hanging GET" and XHR techniques to achieve browser to train communication. The train-controller program would have been a lot easier to build if there was a way to have socket communication in a browser—much like traditional asynchronous client/server communication model that is found in "fat" clients. So, inspired by what *could* be possible, the (train) wheels had been set in motion and the WebSocket train had left the station. Next stop: the real-time web."

The WebSocket Handshake

To establish a WebSocket connection, the client and server upgrade from the HTTP protocol to the WebSocket protocol during their initial handshake, as shown in Figure 7-2. Note that this connection description represents draft 17 of the protocol.

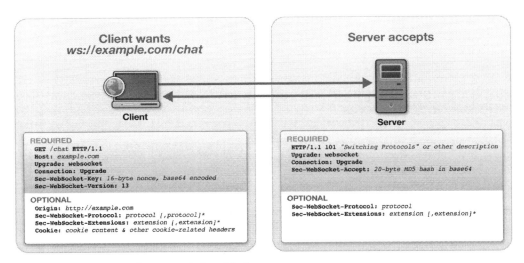

Figure 7-2. The WebSocket Upgrade handshake

Listing 7-1. The WebSocket Upgrade Handshake

From client to server:

```
GET /chat HTTP/1.1
Host: example.com
Connection: Upgrade
Sec-WebSocket-Protocol: sample
Upgrade: websocket
Sec-WebSocket-Version: 13
Sec-WebSocket-Key: 7cxQRnWs91xJW9TOQLSuVQ==
Origin: http://example.com

[8-byte security key]
```

From server to client:

```
HTTP/1.1 101 WebSocket Protocol Handshake
Upgrade: websocket
Connection: Upgrade
Sec-WebSocket-Accept: 7cxQRnWs91xJW9TOQLSuVQ==
WebSocket-Protocol: sample
```

Once established, WebSocket messages can be sent back and forth between the client and the server in full-duplex mode. This means that text-based messages can be sent full-duplex, in either direction at the same time. On the network each message starts with a 0x00 byte, ends with a 0xFF byte, and contains UTF-8 data in between.

The WebSocket Interface

Along with the definition of the WebSocket protocol, the specification also defines the WebSocket interface for use in JavaScript applications. Listing 7-2 shows the WebSocket interface.

Listing 7-2. The WebSocket Interface

```
[Constructor(DOMString url, optional DOMString protocols),
 Constructor(DOMString url, optional DOMString[] protocols)]
interface WebSocket : EventTarget {
  readonly attribute DOMString url;

  // ready state
  const unsigned short CONNECTING = 0;
  const unsigned short OPEN = 1;
  const unsigned short CLOSING = 2;
  const unsigned short CLOSED = 3;
  readonly attribute unsigned short readyState;
  readonly attribute unsigned long bufferedAmount;

  // networking
  [TreatNonCallableAsNull] attribute Function? onopen;
  [TreatNonCallableAsNull] attribute Function? onerror;
  [TreatNonCallableAsNull] attribute Function? onclose;
  readonly attribute DOMString extensions;
  readonly attribute DOMString protocol;
  void close([Clamp] optional unsigned short code, optional DOMString reason);

  // messaging
  [TreatNonCallableAsNull] attribute Function? onmessage;
           attribute DOMString binaryType;
  void send(DOMString data);
  void send(ArrayBuffer data);
  void send(Blob data);
};
```

Using the WebSocket interface is straightforward. To connect a remote host, just create a new WebSocket instance, providing the new object with a URL that represents the end-point to which you wish to connect. Note that a ws:// and wss:// prefix indicates a WebSocket and a secure WebSocket connection, respectively.

A WebSocket connection is established by upgrading from the HTTP protocol to the WebSocket protocol during the initial handshake between the client and the server, over the same underlying TCP/IP connection. Once established, WebSocket data frames can be sent back and forth between the client and the server in full-duplex mode. The connection itself is exposed via the message event and send method defined by the WebSocket interface. In your code, you use asynchronous event listeners to handle each phase of the connection life cycle.

```
myWebSocket.onopen = function(evt) { alert("Connection open ..."); };
myWebSocket.onmessage = function(evt) { alert( "Received Message:  " + evt.data); };
myWebSocket.onclose = function(evt) { alert("Connection closed."); };
```

A Dramatic Reduction in Unnecessary Network Traffic and Latency

So how efficient can WebSocket be? Let's compare a polling application and a WebSocket application side by side. To illustrate polling, we will examine a web application in which a web page requests real-time stock data from a web server using a traditional polling model. It does this by polling a Java Servlet that is hosted on a web server. A message broker receives data from a fictitious stock price feed with continuously updating prices. The web page connects and subscribes to a specific stock channel (a topic on the message broker) and uses an XMLHttpRequest to poll for updates once per second. When updates are received, some calculations are performed and the stock data is displayed as shown in Figure 7-3.

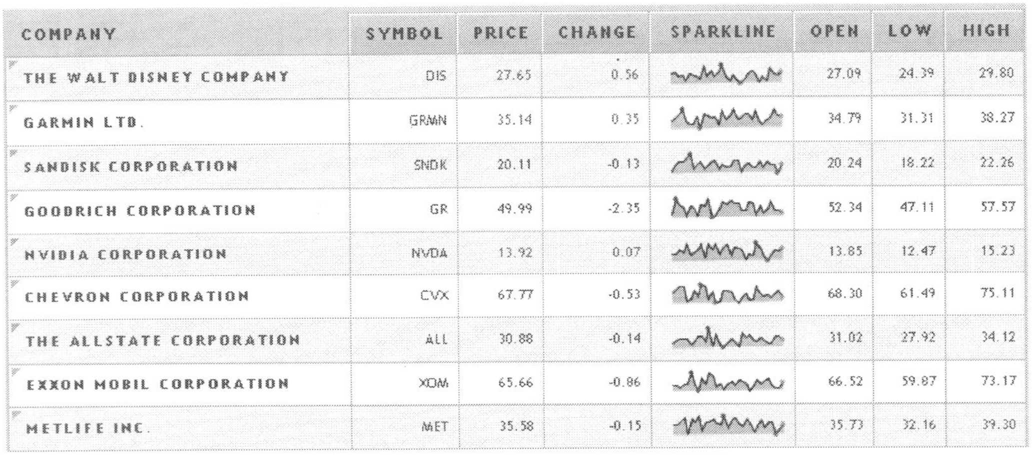

COMPANY	SYMBOL	PRICE	CHANGE	SPARKLINE	OPEN	LOW	HIGH
THE WALT DISNEY COMPANY	DIS	27.65	0.56		27.09	24.39	29.80
GARMIN LTD.	GRMN	35.14	0.35		34.79	31.31	38.27
SANDISK CORPORATION	SNDK	20.11	-0.13		20.24	18.22	22.26
GOODRICH CORPORATION	GR	49.99	-2.35		52.34	47.11	57.57
NVIDIA CORPORATION	NVDA	13.92	0.07		13.85	12.47	15.23
CHEVRON CORPORATION	CVX	67.77	-0.53		68.30	61.49	75.11
THE ALLSTATE CORPORATION	ALL	30.88	-0.14		31.02	27.92	34.12
EXXON MOBIL CORPORATION	XOM	65.66	-0.86		66.52	59.87	73.17
METLIFE INC.	MET	35.58	-0.15		35.73	32.16	39.30

Figure 7-3. Example JavaScript stock ticker application

It all sounds great, but a look under the hood reveals there are some serious issues with this application. For example, in Mozilla Firefox with Firebug, you can see that GET requests hammer the server at one-second intervals. Looking at the HTTP headers reveals the shocking amount of overhead that is associated with each request. Listings 7-3 and 7-4 show the HTTP header data for just a single request and response.

Listing 7-3. HTTP Request Header

```
GET /PollingStock//PollingStock HTTP/1.1
Host: localhost:8080
User-Agent: Mozilla/5.0 (Windows; U; Windows NT 5.1; en-US; rv:1.9.1.5) Gecko/20091102
 Firefox/3.5.5
Accept: text/html,application/xhtml+xml,application/xml;q=0.9,*/*;q=0.8
Accept-Language: en-us
Accept-Encoding: gzip,deflate
Accept-Charset: ISO-8859-1,utf-8;q=0.7,*;q=0.7
Keep-Alive: 300
Connection: keep-alive
Referer: http://www.example.com/PollingStock/
Cookie: showInheritedConstant=false; showInheritedProtectedConstant=false;
 showInheritedProperty=false; showInheritedProtectedProperty=false;
 showInheritedMethod=false; showInheritedProtectedMethod=false;
 showInheritedEvent=false; showInheritedStyle=false; showInheritedEffect=false
```

Listing 7-4. HTTP Response Header

```
HTTP/1.x 200 OK
X-Powered-By: Servlet/2.5
Server: Sun Java System Application Server 9.1_02
Content-Type: text/html;charset=UTF-8
Content-Length: 21
Date: Sat, 07 Nov 2009 00:32:46 GMT
```

Just for fun (ha!), we can count all the characters. The total HTTP request and response header information overhead contains 871 bytes and that does not even include any data. Of course, this is just an example and you can have less than 871 bytes of header data, but there are also common cases where the header data exceeded 2,000 bytes. In this example application, the data for a typical stock topic message is only about 20 characters long. As you can see, it is effectively drowned out by the excessive header information, which was not even required in the first place.

So, what happens when you deploy this application to a large number of users? Let's take a look at the network overhead for just the HTTP request and response header data associated with this polling application in three different use cases.

- **Use case A**: 1,000 clients polling every second: Network traffic is $(871 \times 1,000) =$ 871,000 bytes = 6,968,000 bits per second (6.6 Mbps)

- **Use case B**: 10,000 clients polling every second: Network traffic is $(871 \times 10,000) =$ 8,710,000 bytes = 69,680,000 bits per second (66 Mbps)

- **Use case C**: 100,000 clients polling every 1 second: Network traffic is $(871 \times 100,000) = 87,100,000$ bytes = 696,800,000 bits per second (665 Mbps)

That's an enormous amount of unnecessary network overhead. Consider if we rebuilt the application to use WebSocket, adding an event handler to the web page to asynchronously listen for stock update messages from the message broker (more on that in just a little bit). Each of these messages is a WebSocket frame that has as little as two bytes of overhead (instead of 871). Take a look at how that affects the network overhead in our three use cases.

- **Use case A**: 1,000 clients receive 1 message per second: Network traffic is $(2 \times 1,000) = 2,000$ bytes = 16,000 bits per second (0.015 Mbps)

- **Use case B**: 10,000 clients receive 1 message per second: Network traffic is $(2 \times 10,000) = 20,000$ bytes = 160,000 bits per second (0.153 Mbps)

- **Use case C**: 100,000 clients receive 1 message per second: Network traffic is $(2 \times 100,000) = 200,000$ bytes = 1,600,000 bits per second (1.526 Mbps)

As you can see in Figure 7-4, WebSocket provides a dramatic reduction of unnecessary network traffic compared to the polling solution.

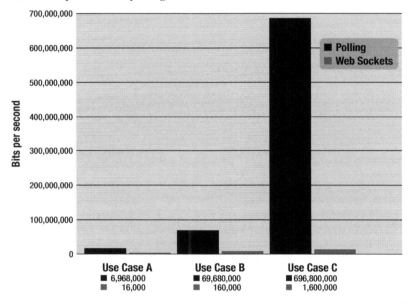

Figure 7-4. Comparison of the unnecessary network overhead between the polling WebSocket traffic

And what about the reduction in latency? Take a look at Figure 7-5. In the top half, you can see the latency of the half-duplex polling solution. If we assume, for this example, that it takes 50 milliseconds for a message to travel from the server to the browser, then the polling application introduces a lot of extra latency, because a new request has to be sent to the server when the response is complete. This new request takes another 50ms and during this time the server cannot send any messages to the browser, resulting in additional server memory consumption.

In the bottom half of the figure, you see the reduction in latency provided by the WebSocket solution. Once the connection is upgraded to WebSocket, messages can flow from the server to the browser the moment they arrive. It still takes 50 ms for messages to travel from the server to the browser, but the WebSocket connection remains open so there is no need to send another request to the server.

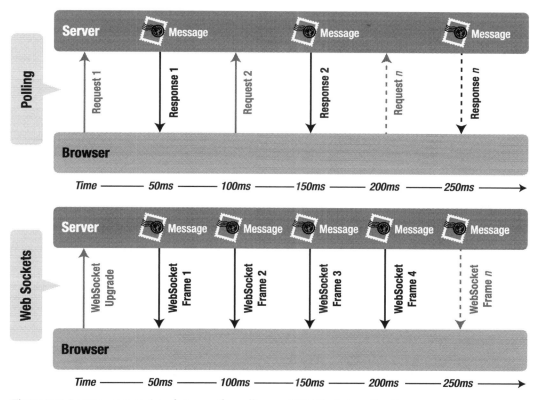

Figure 7-5. *Latency comparison between the polling and WebSocket applications*

WebSocket provides an enormous step forward in the scalability of the real-time web. As you have seen in this chapter, WebSocket can provide a 500:1 or—depending on the size of the HTTP headers— even a 1000:1 reduction in unnecessary HTTP header traffic and 3:1 reduction in latency.

Writing a Simple Echo WebSocket Server

Before you can use the WebSocket API, you need a server that supports WebSocket. In this section we'll take a look at how a simple WebSocket "echo" server is written. To run the examples for this chapter, we have included a simple WebSocket server written in Python. The sample code for the following examples is located in the WebSocket section of the book web site.

```
                    WEBSOCKET SERVERS
```

There are lots of WebSocket server implementations out there already and even more under development. The following are just a few of the existing WebSocket servers:

- **Kaazing WebSocket Gateway**—a Java-based WebSocket Gateway

- **mod_pywebsocket**—a Python-based extension for the Apache HTTP Server

- **Netty**—a Java network framework which includes WebSocket support

- **node.js**—a server-side JavaScript framework on which multiple WebSocket servers have been written

Kaazing's WebSocket Gateway includes full client-side WebSocket emulation support for browsers without native implementation of WebSocket, which allows you to code against the WebSocket API today and have your code work in all browsers.

To run the Python WebSocket echo server accepting connections at `ws://localhost:8000/echo`, open a command prompt, navigate to the folder that contains the file, and issue the following command:

```
python websocket.py
```

We have also included a *broadcast* server that accepts connections at `ws://localhost:8080/broadcast`. Contrary to the echo server, any WebSocket message sent to this particular server implementation will bounce back to *everyone* that is currently connected. It's a very simple way to broadcast messages to multiple listeners. To run the broadcast server, open a command prompt, navigate to the folder that contains the file, and issue the following command:

```
python broadcast.py
```

Both scripts make use of the example WebSocket protocol library in `websocket.py`. You can add handlers for other paths that implement additional server- side behavior.

▨ **Note** This is only a server for the WebSocket protocol, and it cannot respond to HTTP requests. The handshake parser is not fully HTTP compliant. However, because WebSocket connections begin with an HTTP request and rely on the Upgrade header, other servers can serve both WebSocket and HTTP on the same port.

Let's see what happens when a browser tries to communicate with this server. When the browser makes a request to the WebSocket URL, the server sends back the headers that finish the WebSocket handshake. A WebSocket handshake response must contain an `HTTP/1.1 101` status code and Upgrade connection headers. This informs the browser that the server is switching from the HTTP handshake to the WebSocket protocol for the remainder of the TCP session.

> ▓ **Note** If you are implementing a WebSocket server, you should refer to the protocol draft at the IETF at
> `http://tools.ietf.org/html/draft-ietf-hybi-thewebsocketprotocol` or the latest specification.

```
# write out response headers
self.send_bytes("HTTP/1.1 101 Switching Protocols\r\n")
self.send_bytes("Upgrade: WebSocket\r\n")
self.send_bytes("Connection: Upgrade\r\n")
self.send_bytes("Sec-WebSocket-Accept: %s\r\n" % self.hash_key(key))

if "Sec-WebSocket-Protocol" in headers:
    protocol = headers["Sec-WebSocket-Protocol"]
    self.send_bytes("Sec-WebSocket-Protocol: %s\r\n" % protocol)
```

WebSocket Framing

After the handshake, the client and server can send messages at any time. Each connection is represented in this server by a WebSocketConnection instance. The WebSocketConnection's send function, shown in Figure 7-6, writes out a message according to the WebSocket protocol. The bytes preceding the data payload mark the frame length and type. Text frames are UTF-8 encoded. In this server, each WebSocket connection is an asyncore.dispatcher_with_send, which is an asynchronous socket wrapper with support for buffered sends.

Data sent from the browser to the server is masked. Masking is an unusual feature of the WebSocket protocol. Every byte of payload data is XORed with a random mask to ensure that WebSocket traffic does not look like other protocols. Like the Sec-WebSocket-Key hash, this is meant to mitigate an arcane form of cross-protocol attack against non-compliant network infrastructure.

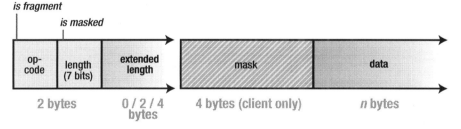

Figure 7-6. Components of a WebSocket frame

> ▓ **Note** There are many other asynchronous I/O frameworks for Python and other languages. Asyncore was chosen because it is included in the Python standard library. Note also that this implementation uses draft 10 of the protocol. This is a simple example designed for testing and illustration.

WebSocketConnection inherits from `asyncore.dispatcher_with_send` and overrides the send method in order to frame text and binary messages.

```
def send(self, s):
  if self.readystate == "open":
   self.send_bytes("\x00")
   self.send_bytes(s.encode("UTF8"))
   self.send_bytes("\xFF")
```

Handlers for `WebSocketConnections` in `websocket.py` follow a simplified dispatcher interface. The handler's `dispatch()` method is called with the payload of each frame the connection receives. The `EchoHandler` sends back each message to the sender.

```
class EchoHandler(object):
    """
    The EchoHandler repeats each incoming string to the same WebSocket.
    """

    def __init__(self, conn):
        self.conn = conn

    def dispatch(self, data):
        self.conn.send("echo: " + data)
```

The basic broadcast server `broadcast.py` works in much the same way, but in this case when the broadcast handler receives a frame, it sends it back on all connected WebSockets as shown in the following example:

```
class BroadcastHandler(object):
    """
    The BroadcastHandler repeats incoming strings to every connected
    WebSocket.
    """

    def __init__(self, conn):
        self.conn = conn

    def dispatch(self, data):
        for session in self.conn.server.sessions:
            session.send(data)
```

The handler in `broadcast.py` provides a lightweight message broadcaster that simply sends and receives any data. This is sufficient for the purposes of our example. Be aware that this broadcast service does not perform any input verification as would be desirable in a production message server. A production WebSocket server should, at the very least, verify the format of incoming data.

For completeness, Listings 7-5 and 7-6 provide the complete code for `websocket.py` and `broadcast.py`. Note that this is just an example server implementation; it is not suited for production deployment.

Listing 7-5. *Complete Code for websocket.py*

```
#!/usr/bin/env python

import asyncore
import socket
```

```python
import struct
import time
from hashlib import sha1
from base64 import encodestring


class WebSocketConnection(asyncore.dispatcher_with_send):

    TEXT = 0x01
    BINARY = 0x02

    def __init__(self, conn, server):
        asyncore.dispatcher_with_send.__init__(self, conn)

        self.server = server
        self.server.sessions.append(self)
        self.readystate = "connecting"
        self.buffer = ""

    def handle_read(self):
        data = self.recv(1024)
        self.buffer += data
        if self.readystate == "connecting":
            self.parse_connecting()
        elif self.readystate == "open":
            self.parse_frame()

    def handle_close(self):
        self.server.sessions.remove(self)
        self.close()

    def parse_connecting(self):
        """
        Parse a WebSocket handshake. This is not a full HTTP request parser!
        """
        header_end = self.buffer.find("\r\n\r\n")
        if header_end == -1:
            return
        else:
            header = self.buffer[:header_end]
            # remove header and four bytes of line endings from buffer
            self.buffer = self.buffer[header_end + 4:]
            header_lines = header.split("\r\n")
            headers = {}

            # validate HTTP request and construct location
            method, path, protocol = header_lines[0].split(" ")
            if method != "GET" or protocol != "HTTP/1.1" or path[0] != "/":
                self.terminate()
                return

            # parse headers
```

```python
    for line in header_lines[1:]:
      key, value = line.split(": ")
      headers[key] = value

    headers["Location"] = "ws://" + headers["Host"] + path

    self.readystate = "open"
    self.handler = self.server.handlers.get(path, None)(self)

    self.send_server_handshake_10(headers)

def terminate(self):
  self.ready_state = "closed"
  self.close()

def send_server_handshake_10(self, headers):
  """
  Send the WebSocket Protocol draft HyBi-10 handshake response
  """
  key = headers["Sec-WebSocket-Key"]

  # write out response headers
  self.send_bytes("HTTP/1.1 101 Switching Protocols\r\n")
  self.send_bytes("Upgrade: WebSocket\r\n")
  self.send_bytes("Connection: Upgrade\r\n")
  self.send_bytes("Sec-WebSocket-Accept: %s\r\n" % self.hash_key(key))

  if "Sec-WebSocket-Protocol" in headers:
    protocol = headers["Sec-WebSocket-Protocol"]
    self.send_bytes("Sec-WebSocket-Protocol: %s\r\n" % protocol)

def hash_key(self, key):
  guid = "258EAFA5-E914-47DA-95CA-C5AB0DC85B11"
  combined = key + guid
  hashed = sha1(combined).digest()
  return encodestring(hashed)

def parse_frame(self):
  """
  Parse a WebSocket frame. If there is not a complete frame in the
  buffer, return without modifying the buffer.
  """
  buf = self.buffer
  payload_start = 2

  # try to pull first two bytes
  if len(buf) < 3:
    return
  b = ord(buf[0])
  fin = b & 0x80     # 1st bit
  # next 3 bits reserved
  opcode = b & 0x0f   # low 4 bits
```

```
    b2 = ord(buf[1])
    mask = b2 & 0x80  # high bit of the second byte
    length = b2 & 0x7f  # low 7 bits of the second byte

    # check that enough bytes remain
    if len(buf) < payload_start + 4:
      return
    elif length == 126:
      length, = struct.unpack(">H", buf[2:4])
      payload_start += 2
    elif length == 127:
      length, = struct.unpack(">I", buf[2:6])
      payload_start += 4

    if mask:
      mask_bytes = [ord(b) for b in buf[payload_start:payload_start + 4]]
      payload_start += 4

    # is there a complete frame in the buffer?
    if len(buf) < payload_start + length:
      return

    # remove leading bytes, decode if necessary, dispatch
    payload = buf[payload_start:payload_start + length]
    self.buffer = buf[payload_start + length:]

    # use xor and mask bytes to unmask data
    if mask:
      unmasked = [mask_bytes[i % 4] ^ ord(b)
            for b, i in zip(payload, range(len(payload)))]
      payload = "".join([chr(c) for c in unmasked])

    if opcode == WebSocketConnection.TEXT:
      s = payload.decode("UTF8")
      self.handler.dispatch(s)
    if opcode == WebSocketConnection.BINARY:
      self.handler.dispatch(payload)
    return True

def send(self, s):
  """
  Encode and send a WebSocket message
  """

  message = ""
  # always send an entire message as one frame (fin)
  b1 = 0x80

  # in Python 2, strs are bytes and unicodes are strings
  if type(s) == unicode:
    b1 |= WebSocketConnection.TEXT
    payload = s.encode("UTF8")
```

```python
    elif type(s) == str:
      b1 |= WebSocketConnection.BINARY
      payload = s

    message += chr(b1)

    # never mask frames from the server to the client
    b2 = 0
    length = len(payload)
    if length < 126:
      b2 |= length
      message += chr(b2)
    elif length < (2 ** 16) - 1:
      b2 |= 126
      message += chr(b2)
      l = struct.pack(">H", length)
      message += l
    else:
      l = struct.pack(">Q", length)
      b2 |= 127
      message += chr(b2)
      message += l

    message += payload

    if self.readystate == "open":
      self.send_bytes(message)

  def send_bytes(self, bytes):
    try:
      asyncore.dispatcher_with_send.send(self, bytes)
    except:
      pass


class EchoHandler(object):
  """
  The EchoHandler repeats each incoming string to the same WebSocket.
  """

  def __init__(self, conn):
    self.conn = conn

  def dispatch(self, data):
    try:
      self.conn.send(data)
    except:
      pass


class WebSocketServer(asyncore.dispatcher):
```

```python
    def __init__(self, port=80, handlers=None):
        asyncore.dispatcher.__init__(self)
        self.handlers = handlers
        self.sessions = []
        self.port = port
        self.create_socket(socket.AF_INET, socket.SOCK_STREAM)
        self.set_reuse_addr()
        self.bind(("", port))
        self.listen(5)

    def handle_accept(self):
        conn, addr = self.accept()
        session = WebSocketConnection(conn, self)

if __name__ == "__main__":
    print "Starting WebSocket Server"
    WebSocketServer(port=8080, handlers={"/echo": EchoHandler})
    asyncore.loop()
```

You may have noticed an unusual key calculation in the WebSocket handshake. This is intended to prevent cross-protocol attacks. In short, this should stop malicious WebSocket client code from spoofing connections to non-WebSocket servers. Hashing a GUID and a random value is enough to positively identify that the responding server understands the WebSocket protocol.

Listing 7-6. Complete Code for broadcast.py

```python
#!/usr/bin/env python

import asyncore
from websocket import WebSocketServer


class BroadcastHandler(object):
    """
    The BroadcastHandler repeats incoming strings to every connected
    WebSocket.
    """

    def __init__(self, conn):
        self.conn = conn

    def dispatch(self, data):
        for session in self.conn.server.sessions:
            session.send(data)


if __name__ == "__main__":
    print "Starting WebSocket broadcast server"
    WebSocketServer(port=8080, handlers={"/broadcast": BroadcastHandler})
    asyncore.loop()
```

Now that we've got a working echo server, we need to write the client side. The web browsers implement the connecting half of the WebSocket Protocol. We can use the API from JavaScript to communicate with our simple server.

Using the WebSocket API

In this section, we'll explore the use of WebSocket in more detail.

Checking for Browser Support

Before you use the WebSocket API, you will want to make sure there is support in the browser for what you're about to do. This way, you can provide some alternate text, prompting the users of your application to upgrade to a more up-to-date browser. Listing 7-7 shows one way you can test for browser support.

Listing 7-7. Checking for Browser Support

```
function loadDemo() {

  if (window.WebSocket) {
    document.getElementById("support").innerHTML = "HTML5 WebSocket is supported in your
                                 browser.";
  } else {
     document.getElementById("support").innerHTML = "HTML5 WebSocket is not supported in
                                 your browser.";
  }
}
```

In this example, you test for browser support in the loadDemo function, which might be called when the application's page is loaded. A call to window.WebSocket will return the WebSocket object if it exists, or trigger the failure case if it does not. In this case, the page is updated to reflect whether there is browser support or not by updating a previously defined support element on the page with a suitable message.

Another way to see if WebSocket is supported in your browser, is to use the browser's console (Firebug or Chrome Developer Tools for example). Figure 7-7 shows how you can test whether WebSocket is supported natively in Google Chrome (if it is not, the window.WebSocket command returns "undefined.")

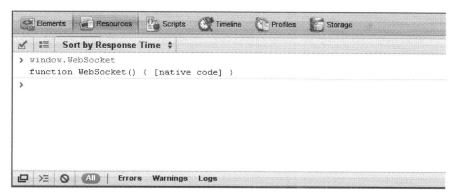

Figure 7-7. Testing WebSocket support in Google Chrome Developer Tools

Basic API Usage

The sample code for the following examples is located on the book web site in the WebSocket section. This folder contains a websocket.html file and a broadcast.html file (and a tracker.html file used in the following section) as well as the WebSocket server code shown previously that can be run in Python.

Creating a WebSocket object and Connecting to a WebSocket Server

Using the WebSocket interface is straight-forward. To connect to an end-point, just create a new WebSocket instance, providing the new object with a URL that represents the end-point to which you wish to connect. You can use the ws:// and wss:// prefixes to indicate a WebSocket and a WebSocket Secure connection, respectively.

```
url = "ws://localhost:8080/echo";
w = new WebSocket(url);
```

When connecting a WebSocket, you have the option of listing the protocols your application can speak. The second argument to the WebSocket constructor can be a string or array of strings with the names of the "subprotocols" that your application understands and wishes to use to communicate.

```
w = new WebSocket(url, protocol);
```

You can even list several protocols:

```
w = new WebSocket(url, ["proto1", "proto2"]);
```

Hypothetically, proto1 and proto2 are well defined, perhaps even registered and standardized, protocol names that both the client and server can understand. The server will select a preferred protocol from the list. When the socket opens, its protocol property will contain the protocol that the server chose.

```
onopen = function(e) {
  // determine which protocol the server selected
  log(e.target.protocol)
}
```

Protocols you might use include Extensible Messaging and Presence Protocol (XMPP, or Jabber), Advanced Message Queuing Protocol (AMQP), Remote Frame Buffer (RFB, or VNC) and Streaming Text Oriented Messaging Protocol (STOMP). These are real-world protocols spoken by many clients and servers. Using a standard protocol ensures interoperability between web applications and servers from different organizations. It also opens the door for public WebSocket services. You can speak to a server using a known protocol. Client applications that understand the same protocol can then connect and participate.

This example does not use a standard protocol. We aren't introducing external dependencies or taking the space to implement a complete standard protocol. As an example, it uses the WebSocket API directly, just as you would if you were starting to write code for a new protocol.

Adding Event Listeners

WebSocket programming follows an asynchronous programming model; once you have an open socket, you simply wait for events. You don't have to actively poll the server anymore. To do this, you add callback functions to the WebSocket object to listen for events.

A WebSocket object dispatches three events: open, close, and message. The open event fires when a connection is established, the message event fires when messages are received, and the close event fires when the WebSocket connection is closed. The error event fires in response to unexpected failure. As in most JavaScript APIs, there are corresponding callbacks (onopen, onmessage, onclose, and onerror) that are called when the events are dispatched.

```
w.onopen = function() {
  log("open");
  w.send("thank you for accepting this websocket request");
}
w.onmessage = function(e) {
  log(e.data);
}
w.onclose = function(e) {
  log("closed");
}
w.onerror = function(e) {
  log("error");
}
```

Let's have another look at that message handler. The data attribute on the message event is a string if the WebSocket protocol message was encoded as text. For binary messages, data can be either a Blob or an ArrayBuffer, depending on the value of the WebSocket's binaryType property.

```
w.binaryType = "arraybuffer";
w.onmessage = function(e) {
  // data can now be either a string or an ArrayBuffer
  log(e.data);
}
```

Sending Messages

While the socket is open (that is, after the onopen listener is called and before the onclose listener is called), you can use the send function to send messages. After sending one or more messages, you can also call close to terminate the connection, or you can also leave the connection open.

```
document.getElementById("sendButton").onclick = function() {
    w.send(document.getElementById("inputMessage").value);
}
```

That's it. Bidirectional browser communication made simple. For completeness, Listing 7-8 shows the entire HTML page with the WebSocket code.

In more advanced uses of WebSocket, you may want to measure how much data is backed up in the outgoing buffer before calling send(). The bufferedAmount attribute represents the number of bytes that have been sent on the WebSocket that have not yet been written onto the network. This could be useful for throttling the rate at which the application sends data.

```
document.getElementById("sendButton").onclick = function() {
  if (w.bufferedAmount < bufferThreshold) {
    w.send(document.getElementById("inputMessage").value);
  }
}
```

In addition to strings, WebSocket can send binary data. This is especially useful to implement binary protocols, such as the standard Internet protocols typically layered on top of TCP. The WebSocket API supports sending Blob and ArrayBuffer instances as binary data.

```
var a = new Uint8Array([8,6,7,5,3,0,9]);
w.send(a.buffer);
```

Listing 7-8. websocket.html Code

```
<!DOCTYPE html>
<title>WebSocket Test Page</title>

<script>
    var log = function(s) {
        if (document.readyState !== "complete") {
            log.buffer.push(s);
        } else {
            document.getElementById("output").textContent += (s + "\n")
        }
    }
    log.buffer = [];

    if (this.MozWebSocket) {
        WebSocket = MozWebSocket;
    }

    url = "ws://localhost:8080/echo";
    w = new WebSocket(url);
    w.onopen = function() {
```

```
        log("open");
        // set the type of binary data messages to ArrayBuffer
        w.binaryType = "arraybuffer";

        // send one string and one binary message when the socket opens
        w.send("thank you for accepting this WebSocket request");
        var a = new Uint8Array([8,6,7,5,3,0,9]);
        w.send(a.buffer);
    }
    w.onmessage = function(e) {
        log(e.data.toString());
    }
    w.onclose = function(e) {
        log("closed");
    }
    w.onerror = function(e) {
        log("error");
    }

    window.onload = function() {
        log(log.buffer.join("\n"));
        document.getElementById("sendButton").onclick = function() {
            w.send(document.getElementById("inputMessage").value);
        }
    }
}
</script>

<input type="text" id="inputMessage" value="Hello, WebSocket!"><button
id="sendButton">Send</button>
<pre id="output"></pre>
```

Running the WebSocket Page

To test the websocket.html page that contains the WebSocket code, open a command prompt, navigate to the folder that contains the WebSocket code, and issue the following command to host the HTML file:

```
python -m SimpleHTTPServer 9999
```

Next, open another command prompt, navigate to the folder that contains the WebSocket code, and issue the following command to run the Python WebSocket server:

```
python websocket.py
```

Finally, open a browser that supports WebSocket natively and navigate to http://localhost:9999/websocket.html.

Figure 7-8 shows the web page in action.

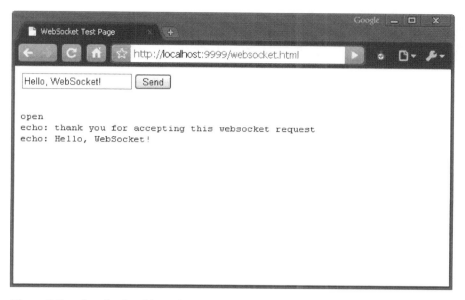

Figure 7-8. *websocket.html in action*

The example code folder also contains a web page that connects to the broadcast service that was created in the previous section. To see that action, close the command prompt that is running the WebSocket server and navigate to the folder that contains the WebSocket code, and issue the following command to run the python WebSocket server.

```
python broadcast.py
```

Open two separate browsers that supports WebSocket natively and navigate (in each browser) to `http://localhost:9999/broadcast.html`.

Figure 7-9 shows the broadcast WebSocket server in action on two separate web pages.

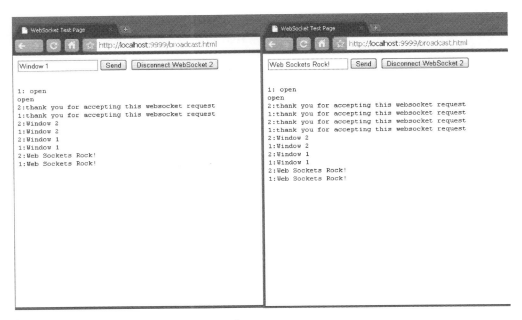

Figure 7-9. broadcast.html in action in two browsers

Building a WebSocket Application

Now that we've seen the basics of WebSocket, it's time to tackle something a little more substantial. Previously, we used the HTML5 Geolocation API to build an application that allowed us to calculate distance traveled directly inside our web page. We can utilize those same Geolocation techniques, mixed together with our new support for WebSocket, and create a simple application that keeps multiple participants connected: a location tracker.

■ **Note** We'll be using the broadcast WebSocket server described above, so if you aren't familiar with it you should consider taking some time to learn its basics.

In this application, we'll combine WebSocket and Geolocation by determining our location and broadcasting it to all available listeners. Everyone who loads this application and connects to the same broadcast server will regularly send their geographic location using the WebSocket. At the same time, the application will listen for any messages from the server and update in real-time display entries for everyone it hears about. In a race scenario, this sort of application could keep runners informed of the location of all their competitors and prompt them to run faster (or slow down).

This tiny application does not include any personal information other than latitude and longitude location. Name, date of birth, and favorite ice cream flavor are kept strictly confidential.

YOU WERE WARNED!

Brian says: "This application is all about sharing your personal information. Granted, only a location is shared. However, if you (or your users) didn't understand the browser warning that was offered when the Geolocation API was first accessed, this application should be a stark lesson in how easy it will be to transmit sensitive data to remote locations. Make sure your users understand the consequences of agreeing to submit location data.

When in doubt, go above and beyond in your application to let the user know how their sensitive data can be used. Make opting out the easiest path of action."

But that's enough warnings… Let's dig into the code. As always, the entire code sample is located online for your perusal. We'll focus on the most important parts here. The finished application will look like Figure 7-10. Although ideally, this would be enhanced by overlaying it on a map.

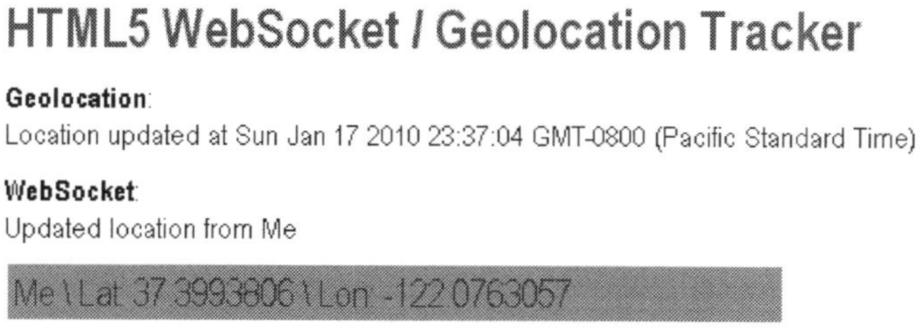

HTML5 WebSocket / Geolocation Tracker

Geolocation:
Location updated at Sun Jan 17 2010 23:37:04 GMT-0800 (Pacific Standard Time)

WebSocket:
Updated location from Me

Me \ Lat 37.3993806 \ Lon -122.0763057

Figure 7-10. The Location Tracker application

Coding the HTML File

The HTML markup for this application will be kept deliberately simple so that we can focus on the data at hand. How simple?

```
<body onload="loadDemo()">

<h1>HTML5 WebSocket / Geolocation Tracker</h1>

<div><strong>Geolocation</strong>: <p id="geoStatus">HTML5 Geolocation is
 <strong>not</strong> supported in your browser.</p></div>
<div><strong>WebSocket</strong>: <p id="socketStatus">WebSocket is <strong>not</strong>
 supported in your browser.</p></div>

</body>
```

Simple enough that we only include a title and a few status areas: one status area for Geolocation updates, and another to log any WebSocket activity. The actual visuals for location data will be inserted into the page as messages are received in real-time.

CHAPTER 7 ■ USING THE WEBSOCKET API

By default, our status messages indicate that a viewer's browser does not support either Geolocation or WebSocket. Once we detect support for the two HTML5 technologies, we'll update the status with something a little friendlier.

```
<script>

    // reference to the WebSocket
    var socket;

    // a semi-unique random ID for this session
    var myId = Math.floor(100000*Math.random());

    // number of rows of data presently displayed
    var rowCount = 0;
```

The meat of this application is once again accomplished via the script code. First, we will establish a few variables:

- A global reference to our socket so that any function can access it later.

- A random myId number between 0 and 100,000 to identify our location data online. This number is merely used to correlate changes in location over time back to the same source without using more personal information such as names. A sufficiently large pool of numbers makes it unlikely that more than one user will have the same identifier.

- A rowCount which holds how many unique users have transmitted their location data to us. This is largely used for visual formatting.

The next two functions should look familiar. As in other example applications, we've provided utilities to help us update our status message. This time, there are two status messages to update.

```
    function updateSocketStatus(message) {
        document.getElementById("socketStatus").innerHTML = message;
    }

    function updateGeolocationStatus(message) {
        document.getElementById("geoStatus").innerHTML = message;
    }
```

It is always helpful to include a user-friendly set of error messages whenever something goes wrong with location retrieval. If you need more information on the error handling associated with Geolocation, consult Chapter 5.

```
    function handleLocationError(error) {
        switch(error.code)
        {
        case 0:
          updateGeolocationStatus("There was an error while retrieving your location: " +
                      error.message);
          break;
        case 1:
          updateGeolocationStatus("The user prevented this page from retrieving a
                      location.");
          break;
```

```
    case 2:
      updateGeolocationStatus("The browser was unable to determine your location: " +
                    error.message);
      break;
    case 3:
      updateGeolocationStatus("The browser timed out before retrieving the location.");
      break;
    }
}
```

Adding the WebSocket Code

Now, let's examine something more substantial. The loadDemo function is called on the initial load of our page, making it the starting point of the application.

```
function loadDemo() {
    // test to make sure that sockets are supported
    if (window.WebSocket) {

        // the location of our broadcast WebSocket server
        url = "ws://localhost:8080";
        socket = new WebSocket(url);
        socket.onopen = function() {
            updateSocketStatus("Connected to WebSocket tracker server");
        }
        socket.onmessage = function(e) {
            updateSocketStatus("Updated location from " + dataReturned(e.data));
        }
    }
}
```

The first thing we do here is set up our WebSocket connection. As with any HTML5 technology, it is wise to check for support before jumping right in, so we test to make sure that window.WebSocket is a supported object in this browser.

Once that is verified, we make a connection to the remote broadcast server using the connect string format described above. The connection is stored in our globally declared socket variable.

Finally, we declare two handlers to take action when our WebSocket receives updates. The onopen handler will merely update the status message to let the user know that we made a successful connection. The onmessage will similarly update the status to let the user know that a message has arrived. It will also call our upcoming dataReturned function to show the arriving data in the page, but we'll tackle that later.

Adding the Geolocation Code

The next section should be familiar to you from Chapter 5. Here, we verify support for the Geolocation service and update the status message appropriately.

```
        var geolocation;
        if(navigator.geolocation) {
            geolocation = navigator.geolocation;
            updateGeolocationStatus("HTML5 Geolocation is supported in your browser.");
        }
```

```
// register for position updates using the Geolocation API
geolocation.watchPosition(updateLocation,
                          handleLocationError,
                          {maximumAge:20000});
}
```

As before, we watch our current location for changes and register that we want the updateLocation function called when they occur. Errors are sent to the handleLocationError function, and the location data is set to expire every twenty seconds.

The next section of code is the handler which is called by the browser whenever a new location is available.

```
function updateLocation(position) {
    var latitude = position.coords.latitude;
    var longitude = position.coords.longitude;
    var timestamp = position.timestamp;

    updateGeolocationStatus("Location updated at " + timestamp);

    // Send my location via WebSocket
    var toSend = JSON.stringify([myId, latitude, longitude]);
    sendMyLocation(toSend);
}
```

This section is similar to, but simpler than, the same handler in Chapter 5. Here, we grab the latitude, longitude, and timestamp from the position provided by the browser. Then, we update the status message to indicate that a new value has arrived.

Putting It All Together

The final section calculates a message string to send to the remote broadcast WebSocket server. The string here will be JSON encoded:

```
"[<id>, <latitude>, <longitude>]"
```

The ID will be the randomly calculated value already created to identify this user. The latitude and longitude are provided by the geolocation position object. We send the message directly to the server as a JSON encoded string.

The actual code to send the position to the server resides in the sendMyLocation() function.

```
function sendMyLocation(newLocation) {
    if (socket) {
        socket.send(newLocation);
    }
}
```

If a socket was successfully created—and stored for later access—then it is safe to send the message string passed into this function to the server. Once it arrives, the WebSocket message broadcast server will distribute the location string to every browser currently connected and listening for messages. Everyone will know where you are. Or, at least, a largely anonymous "you" identified only by a random number.

Now that we're sending messages, let's see how those same messages should be processed when they arrive at the browser. Recall that we registered an onmessage handler on the socket to pass any incoming data to a dataReturned() function. Next, we will look at that final function in more detail.

```
function dataReturned(locationData) {
    // break the data into ID, latitude, and longitude
    var allData = JSON.parse(locationData);
    var incomingId   = allData[1];
    var incomingLat  = allData[2];
    var incomingLong = allData[3];
```

The dataReturned function serves two purposes. It will create (or update) a display element in the page showing the position reflected in the incoming message string, and it will return a text representation of the user this message originated from. The user name will be used in the status message at the top of the page by the calling function, the socket.onmessage handler.

The first step taken by this data handler function is to break the incoming message back down into its component parts using JSON.parse. Although a more robust application would need to check for unexpected formatting, we will assume that all messages to our server are valid, and therefore our string separates cleanly into a random ID, a latitude, and a longitude.

```
    // locate the HTML element for this ID
    // if one doesn't exist, create it
    var incomingRow = document.getElementById(incomingId);
    if (!incomingRow) {
        incomingRow = document.createElement('div');
        incomingRow.setAttribute('id', incomingId);
```

Our demonstration user interface will create a visible <div> for every random ID for which it receives a message. This includes the user's ID itself; in other words, the user's own data will also be displayed only after it is sent and returned from the WebSocket broadcast server.

Accordingly, the first thing we do with the ID from our message string is use it to locate the display row element matching it. If one does not exist, we create one and set its id attribute to be the id returned from our socket server for future retrieval.

```
        incomingRow.userText = (incomingId == myId) ?
                                'Me'             :
                                'User ' + rowCount;

        rowCount++;
```

The user text to be displayed in the data row is easy to calculate. If the ID matches the user's ID, it is simply 'me'. Otherwise, the username is a combination of a common string and a count of rows, which we will increment.

```
        document.body.appendChild(incomingRow);
    }
```

Once the new display element is ready, it is inserted into the end of the page. Regardless of whether the display element is newly created or if it already existed—due to the fact that a location update was not the first for that particular user—the display row needs to be updated with the current text information.

```
    // update the row text with the new values
    incomingRow.innerHTML = incomingRow.userText + " \\ Lat: " +
                            incomingLat + " \\ Lon: " +
                            incomingLong;

    return incomingRow.userText;
```

```
      }
```

In our case, we will separate the user text name from the latitude and longitude values using a backslash (properly escaped, of course). Finally, the display name is returned to the calling function for updating the status row.

Our simple WebSocket and Geolocation mashup is now complete. Try it out, but keep in mind that unless there are multiple browsers accessing the application at the same time, you won't see many updates. As an exercise to the reader, consider updating this example to display the incoming locations on a global Google Map to get an idea of where HTML5 interest is flourishing at this very moment.

The Final Code

For completeness, the Listing 7-9 provides the entire tracker.html file.

Listing 7-9. The tracker.html Code

```
<!DOCTYPE html>
<html lang="en">

<head>
<title>HTML5 WebSocket / Geolocation Tracker</title>
<link rel="stylesheet" href="styles.css">
</head>

<body onload="loadDemo()">

<h1>HTML5 WebSocket / Geolocation Tracker</h1>

<div><strong>Geolocation</strong>: <p id="geoStatus">HTML5 Geolocation is
 <strong>not</strong> supported in your browser.</p></div>
<div><strong>WebSocket</strong>: <p id="socketStatus">WebSocket is <strong>not</strong>
 supported in your browser.</p></div>

<script>

    // reference to the WebSocket
    var socket;

    // a semi-unique random ID for this session
    var myId = Math.floor(100000*Math.random());

    // number of rows of data presently displayed
    var rowCount = 0;

    function updateSocketStatus(message) {
        document.getElementById("socketStatus").innerHTML = message;
    }

    function updateGeolocationStatus(message) {
        document.getElementById("geoStatus").innerHTML = message;
    }
```

```
function handleLocationError(error) {
    switch(error.code)
    {
    case 0:
      updateGeolocationStatus("There was an error while retrieving your location: " +
                              error.message);
      break;
    case 1:
      updateGeolocationStatus("The user prevented this page from retrieving a
                              location.");
      break;
    case 2:
      updateGeolocationStatus("The browser was unable to determine your location: " +
                              error.message);
      break;
    case 3:
      updateGeolocationStatus("The browser timed out before retrieving the location.");
      break;
    }
}

function loadDemo() {
    // test to make sure that sockets are supported
    if (window.WebSocket) {

        // the location where our broadcast WebSocket server is located
        url = "ws://localhost:8080";
        socket = new WebSocket(url);
        socket.onopen = function() {
            updateSocketStatus("Connected to WebSocket tracker server");
        }
        socket.onmessage = function(e) {
            updateSocketStatus("Updated location from " + dataReturned(e.data));
        }
    }

    var geolocation;
    if(navigator.geolocation) {
        geolocation = navigator.geolocation;
        updateGeolocationStatus("HTML5 Geolocation is supported in your browser.");

        // register for position updates using the Geolocation API
        geolocation.watchPosition(updateLocation,
                          handleLocationError,
                          {maximumAge:20000});
    }
}

function updateLocation(position) {
    var latitude = position.coords.latitude;
    var longitude = position.coords.longitude;
    var timestamp = position.timestamp;
```

```
        updateGeolocationStatus("Location updated at " + timestamp);

        // Send my location via WebSocket
        var toSend = JSON.stringify([myId, latitude, longitude]);
        sendMyLocation(toSend);
    }

    function sendMyLocation(newLocation) {
        if (socket) {
            socket.send(newLocation);
        }
    }

    function dataReturned(locationData) {
        // break the data into ID, latitude, and longitude
        var allData = JSON.parse(locationData)
        var incomingId   = allData[1];
        var incomingLat  = allData[2];
        var incomingLong = allData[3];

        // locate the HTML element for this ID
        // if one doesn't exist, create it
        var incomingRow = document.getElementById(incomingId);
        if (!incomingRow) {
            incomingRow = document.createElement('div');
            incomingRow.setAttribute('id', incomingId);

            incomingRow.userText = (incomingId == myId) ?
                                        'Me'              :
                                        'User ' + rowCount;

            rowCount++;

            document.body.appendChild(incomingRow);
        }

        // update the row text with the new values
        incomingRow.innerHTML = incomingRow.userText + " \\ Lat: " +
                                incomingLat + " \\ Lon: " +
                                incomingLong;

        return incomingRow.userText;
    }

</script>
</body>
</html>
```

Summary

In this chapter, you have seen how WebSocket provides a simple, yet powerful mechanism for creating compelling, real-time applications.

First we looked at the nature of the protocol itself, and how it interoperates with existing HTTP traffic. We compared the network overhead demands of current polling-based communication strategies versus the limited overhead of WebSocket.

To illustrate WebSocket in action, we explored a simple implementation of a WebSocket server to show how simple it is to implement this protocol in practice. Similarly, we examined the client-side WebSocket API, noting the ease of integration it provides with JavaScript.

Finally, we walked through a more complex sample application which combined the power of Geolocation with WebSocket to demonstrate how well the two technologies can work together.

Now that we've seen how HTML5 brings TCP-style network programming to the browser, we'll turn our attention to gathering more interesting data than just a user's current location. In the next chapter, we look at the enhancements made to form controls in HTML5.

## CHAPTER 8

Using the Forms API

In this chapter, we'll explore all the new capabilities at your command with a longstanding technology: HTML Forms. Forms have been the backbone of the explosion of the Web since they first appeared. Without form controls, web business transactions, social discussions, and efficient searches would simply not be possible.

Sadly, HTML5 Forms is one of the areas in greatest flux in both specification and implementation, in spite of having been in design for many years. There's good and bad news. The good news is that the progress in this area, while incremental, is increasing fairly rapidly. The bad news is that you'll need to tread carefully to find the subset of new form controls that will work in all your target browsers. The forms specification details a large set of APIs, and it is not uncommon to find that each major new release of an HTML5-compliant web browser adds support for one or more form controls and some of the helpful validation features.

Regardless, we'll use this chapter to help you navigate through the virtual sea of controls and find which ones are ready to use today, and which are nearing release.

Overview of HTML5 Forms

If you are already familiar with forms in HTML—and we assume you are if you are interested in pro HTML programming—then you will find the new additions in HTML5 to be a comfortable fit on a solid foundation. If you aren't yet familiar with the basics of form usage, we recommend any of the numerous books and tutorials on creating and handling form values. The topic is well covered at this point, and you will be happy to know that:

- Forms should still be encapsulated in a <form> element where the basic submission attributes are set.

- Forms still send the values of the controls to the server when the user or the application programmer submits the page.

- All of the familiar form controls—text fields, radio buttons, check boxes, and so on—are still present and working as before (albeit with some new features).

- Form controls are still fully scriptable for those who wish to write their own modifiers and handlers.

HTML Forms Versus XForms

You may have heard references to XForms in the last few years, long before the HTML5 effort gained much traction. XForms is an XML-centric, powerful, and somewhat complex, standard for specifying client-side form behavior that has been developed in its own W3C working group for nearly ten years. XForms harnesses the full power of XML Schema to define precise rules for validation and formatting. Unfortunately, no current major browser supports XForms without additional plug-ins.

HTML5 Forms are not XForms.

Functional Forms

HTML5 Forms has instead focused on evolving the existing, simple HTML Forms to encompass more types of controls and address the practical limitations that web developers face today. There is an important note to keep in mind, especially as you compare form implementations across different browsers.

▓ **Note** The most important concept to grasp about HTML5 Forms is that the specification deals with functional behavior and semantics, not appearances or displays.

For example, while the specification details the functional APIs for elements such as color and date pickers, number selectors, and email address entry, the specification does not state how browsers should render these elements to end users. This is a great choice on multiple levels. It allows browsers to compete on innovate ways to provide user interaction; it separates styling from semantics; and it allows future or specialized user input devices to interact in ways that are natural to their operation. However, until your targeted browser platforms support all the form controls in your application, make sure you provide enough contextual information for the user to know how to interact with a fallback rendering. With the right tips and descriptions, users will have no trouble with your application, even if it falls back to alternate content when presented with unknown input types.

HTML5 Forms encompasses a great number of new APIs and elements types, and support for them is all over the map now. In order to wrap our heads around all the new functionality, we will address it by breaking it into two categories

- New input types
- New functions and attributes

However, before we even start with that, let's take a quick assessment of how the HTML5 Form specifications are supported in today's browsers.

Browser Support for HTML5 Forms

Browser support for HTML5 Forms is growing, but still limited. The major browser vendors all support many of the form controls, with Opera taking the lead in early implementations. However, the specification is stable.

Checking for browser support is less useful in the context of the new Forms, as they have been designed to degrade gracefully in older browsers. Largely, this means that it is safe for you to use the new elements today, because older browsers will fall back to simple text field displays for any input types that they do not understand. However, as we'll see later in this chapter, this raises the importance of multi-tier form validation, as it is not sufficient to rely on the presence of browser validators to enforce the data types for your form controls, even if you assume full modern-browser support.

Now that we have surveyed the browser landscape, let's take a look at the new form controls added in the HTML5 specification.

An Input Catalog

One of the best places to get a catalog of all the new and changed elements in HTML5 is the markup list maintained at the W3C site itself. The W3C keeps a catalog page file at `http://dev.w3.org/html5/markup/`

This page denotes all the current and future elements in an HTML page. New and changed elements are noted in the catalog list. However, "new" in this list only means that the element has been added since the HTML4 specification—not that the element is implemented in browsers or in a final specification yet. With that warning in place, let's take a look at the new form elements arriving with HTML5, starting with the ones that are being implemented today. Table 8-1 lists the new `type` attributes. For example, many HTML developers will be intimately familiar with `<input type="text">` and `<input type="checkbox">`. The new input types follow a similar model to the existing ones.

Table 8-1. New HTML5 Form Elements Appearing in Browsers

Type	Purpose
tel	Telephone number
email	Email address text field
url	Web location URL
search	Term to supply to a search engine. For example, the search bar atop a browser.
range	Numeric selector within a range of values, typically visualized as a slider
number	A field containing a numeric value only

What do these new input types provide? In terms of programmatic APIs... not a lot. In fact, in the case of the types for `tel`, `email`, `url`, and `search`, there are no attributes distinguishing them from the simplest input type of `text`.

So, what do you get exactly by specifying that an input is of a specialized type? You get specialized input controls. (Restrictions may apply. Offer void in many desktop browsers.)

Let's illustrate with an example. By specifying that an input is of type `email`

```
<input type="email">
```

rather than using the conventional standard, which states that a field is merely of type text

```
<input type="text">
```

you provide a hint to the browser to present a different user interface or input where applicable. You also provide the browser the ability to further validate the field before submission, but we'll cover that topic later in this chapter.

Mobile device browsers have been some of the quickest to take up support for these new form input types. On a phone, every key press or tap is a higher burden on a user who may not have a full keyboard. Consequently, the mobile device browsers support these new input types by displaying a different input interface based on the type declared. In the Apple iPhone, the standard onscreen keyboard display for an input with type text appears as it does in Figure 8-1.

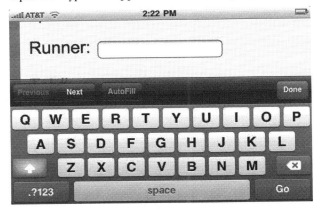

Figure 8-1. Onscreen keyboard display for an input with type text

However, when an input field is marked as being of type e-mail, the iPhone presents a different keyboard layout customized for e-mail entry, as shown in Figure 8-2.

Figure 8-2. Onscreen keyboard display for an input with type e-mail

Note the subtle tweaks to the space bar area of the keyboard to allow for the @ symbol and easy access to the period. Similar tweaks to the keyboard layout are done for type URL and type search. However, in the desktop version of the Safari browser—and in any browser that does not explicitly support the types for e-mail, URL, search, and tel—only the normal text input field will be displayed. Future browsers, even the desktop versions, may provide visual hints or cues to the user to indicate that the field is of a certain subtype. Opera, for example, will display a small envelope icon next to a field to indicate that it is expecting an e-mail address. However, it is safe to use these types in your web applications today, as any browser will either optimize for the type or simply do nothing at all.

Another specialized type that is gaining traction in browsers now is the `<input type="range">`. This specialized input control is designed to let users pick from within a range of numbers. For example, a range control could be used in a form to select an age from a range that limits access to minors under the age of, say, 18. By creating a range input and setting its special min and max values, a developer can request that a page display a constrained numerical picker that only operates within the specified bounds. In the Opera browser, for example, the control:

```
<input type="range" min="18" max="120">
```

gives a convenient way to pick a suitable value for age-restricted material. In the Opera browser, it displays as follows:

Unfortunately, the range input itself doesn't display a numerical representation of the browser. Moreover, without one, it is practically impossible for the user to know what the currently selected value happens to be. To fix this, one can easily add an `onchange` handler to update a display field based on changes to the current range value as shown in Listing 8-1.

■ **Note** Why don't `range` elements contain visual displays by default? Perhaps it is so that user interface designers can customize the exact position and appearance of displays. Making the display optional adds a bit of work, but much more flexibility.

The new form controls now include a simple `output` element, which is designed just for this type of operation. An `output` is a form element, which simply holds a value. As such, we can use it to display the value of our `range` control.

Listing 8-1. onchange Handler to Update an output

```
<label for="age">Age</label>
<input id="age" type="range" min="18" max="120" value="18" onchange="ageDisplay.value=value">
<output id="ageDisplay">18</output>
```

This gives a nice display to our range input, as follows:

Age ⬚ 44

Opera and the WebKit-based browsers—Safari and Chrome—have now added support for the type `range` element. Firefox support is planned, but not yet scheduled as of this writing. Firefox will fall back to a simple text element when presented with a `range` input type.

Another of the new form elements that has gained widespread support is the **progress** element. The **progress** element does exactly what you might expect; it displays the percentage of a task that is completed in a handy visual format.

Progress can be either determinate or indeterminate. Think of indeterminate progress as a task that takes an unknown amount of time, yet one where you want to assure the user that some progress is being made. To show an indeterminate progress element, simply include one with no attributes:

```
<progress></progress>
```

An indeterminate progress bar usually displays a bar in motion, but with no indicator of the overall percentage complete.

A determinate progress bar, on the other hand, shows an actual percentage-style display of the completed work. To trigger a determinate progress bar display, set the **value** and **max** attributes on the element. The percentage of the bar displayed as completed is calculated by dividing the **value** you set by the **max** you set. They can be any values you choose, to make calculation easier. For example, to show 30% completion, we can create a progress element such as:

```
<progress value="30" max="100"></progress>
```

With these values set, the user can quickly see how much of your long-running operation or multi-step process is complete. Using script to change the **value** attribute, it is easy to update the display to indicate progress toward a final goal.

Here Be Dragons

Brian says: "The phrase 'Here be dragons' is said to have been used in history to denote dangerous areas on maps where unknown perils lurk. The same could be said for the following form elements. Although they are specified, and have been for lengths of time now, most are lacking in actual implementation.

As such, expect large changes between now and the time that browser developers have had a chance to play with the designs, smooth the rough edges, and respond with feedback and changes. Rather than rely on the following components as inevitable, take them as a sign of the direction in which HTML5 forms are moving. If you attempt to use them today, the risk you take is your own..."

Additional form elements that are planned but not widely supported yet include the ones listed in Table 8-2.

Table 8-2. *Future HTML5 Form Elements*

Type	Purpose
color	Color selector, which could be represented by a wheel or swatch picker
datetime	Full date and time display, including a time zone, as shown in Figure 8-3
datetime-local	Date and time display, with no setting or indication for time zones
time	Time indicator and selector, with no time zone information
date	Selector for calendar date
week	Selector for a week within a given year
month	Selector for a month within a given year

Although some early implementations of these elements are beginning to appear in leading edge browsers (for example, the datetime display in Opera as shown in Figure 8-3), we won't focus on them in this chapter as they are likely to undergo significant change. Stay tuned to future revisions!

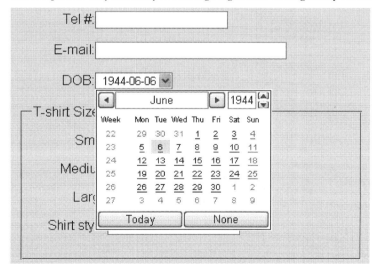

Figure 8-3. *Display for an input of type datetime*

Using the HTML5 Forms APIs

Now that we've spent some time familiarizing ourselves with the new form element types, let's turn to the attributes and APIs that are present on both the old and new form controls. Many of them are designed to reduce the amount of scripting needed to create a powerful web application user interface. You may find that the new attributes give you the power to enhance your user interface in ways that you had not considered. Or, at the very least, you may be able to remove blocks of script in your existing pages.

New Form Attributes and Functions

First, we'll consider new attributes, functions, and a few elements that did not previously exist in earlier versions of HTML. Like the new input types, it is generally safe to use these attributes today, whether or not your target browser supports them. This is because the attributes will be safely ignored by any browser on the market today if the browser does not understand them.

The placeholder Attribute

The `placeholder` attribute gives input controls an easy way to provide descriptive, alternate hint text which is shown only when the user has not yet entered any values. This is common in many modern user interface frameworks, and popular JavaScript frameworks have also provided emulation of this feature. However, modern browsers have it built-in.

To use this attribute, simply add it to an input with a text representation. This includes the basic text type, as well as the semantic types such as `email`, `number`, `url`, etc.

```
<label>Runner: <input name="name" placeholder="First and last name"></label>
```

In a modern browser, this causes the field to display a faint version of the placeholder text which will disappear whenever the user or application puts focus into the field, or whenever there is a value present.

Runner: `First and last name`

The same attribute, when running in a non-supporting browser, will just be ignored, causing the default field behavior to display.

Runner: `                    `

Similarly, whenever a value is entered in the field, the placeholder text will not appear.

Runner: `Racer Ecks`

The autocomplete Attribute

The autocomplete attribute, introduced in Internet Explorer 5.5, has finally been standardized. Hooray! (Browsers have been supporting the attribute for nearly as long as its inception, but having a specified behavior helps everyone.)

The autocomplete attribute tells the browser whether or not the value of this input should be saved for future. For example:

```
<input type="text" name="creditcard" autocomplete="off">
```

The autocomplete attribute should be used to protect sensitive user data from insecure storage in the local browser files. Table 8-3 shows the different behavior types.

Table 8-3. Autocomplete Behavior in Input Controls

Type	Purpose
on	The field is not secure, and its value can be saved and restored.
off	The field is secure, and its value should not be saved.
unspecified	Default to the setting on the containing <form>. If not contained in a form, or no value is set on the form, then behave as if on.

The autofocus Attribute

The autofocus attribute lets a developer specify that a given form element should take input focus immediately when the page loads. Only one attribute per page should specify the autofocus attribute. Behavior is undefined if more than one control is set to autofocus.

※ **Note** Only one autofocus control per page is difficult to achieve if your content is being rendered into a portal or shared content page. Do not rely on autofocus if you are not in complete control of the page.

To set the focus automatically to a control such as a search text field, simply set the autofocus attribute on that element alone:

```
<input type="search" name="criteria" autofocus>
```

Like other boolean attributes, no value needs to be specified for the true case.

■ **Note** Autofocus can annoy users if they are not expecting a focus change. Many users utilize keystrokes for navigation, and switching focus to a form control subverts that ability. Use it only when it is a given that a form control should take all default keys.

The spellcheck Attribute

The `spellcheck` attribute can be set on input controls with text content, as well as the **textarea**. When set, it suggests to the browser whether or not spelling feedback should be given. A normal representation of this element is to draw a red dotted line under text that does not map any entry in the currently set dictionary. This hints to the user to double-check the spelling or to get a suggestion from the browser itself.

Note that the `spellcheck` attribute needs a value. You can't just set the attribute alone on the element.

```
<textarea id="myTextArea" spellcheck="true">
```

Also note that most browsers will default to leaving the spellcheck on, so unless the element (or one of its parent elements) turns off spellchecking, it will display by default.

The list Attribute and the datalist Element

The `list` attribute and `datalist` element combine to let a developer specify a list of possible values for an input. To use this combination:

1. Create a datalist element in your document with its id set to a unique value. The datalist can be located anywhere in the document.

2. Populate the datalist with as many option elements as needed to represent the full set of suggestions for values of a control. For example, a datalist representing e-mail contacts should contain all of the contact e-mail addresses as individual option children.

   ```
   <datalist id="contactList">
       <option value="x@example.com" label="Racer X">
       <option value="peter@example.com" label="Peter">
   </datalist>
   ```

3. Link the input element to the datalist by setting the list attribute to a value which is the id of the associated datalist.

   ```
   <input type="email" id="contacts" list="contactList">
   ```

On a supporting browser this produces a customized list control like the following:

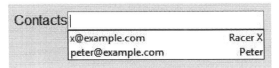

The min and max Attributes

As seen before in our example for `<input type="range">`, the `min` and `max` attributes allow a numerical input to be constrained to minimum and maximum values. One, both, or neither of these attributes can be provided as necessary, and the input control should adjust accordingly to increase or decrease the range of acceptable values. For example, to create a range control representing a level of confidence in ability from zero% to 100%, the following code could be used as follows:

```
<input id="confidence" name="level" type="range" min="0" max="100" value="0">
```

This would create a range control with a minimum zero value and maximum of 100, which, coincidentally, are the default values for the same.

The step Attribute

Also, for input types which expect numerical values, the `step` attribute specifies the granularity of increments or decrements in value as the range is adjusted. For example, our confidence level range control listed above can be set up with a `step` attribute of five as follows:

```
<input id="confidence" name="level" type="range" min="0" max="100" step="5" value="0">
```

This would limit the acceptable values to be increments of five from the starting value. In other words, only 0, 5, 10, 15, … 100 would be allowed either through typed input or through a slider control, depending on the browser representation of the input.

The default `step` value is dependent on the type of control to which it is applied. For a `range` input, the default step is one. To accompany the `step` attribute, HTML5 introduces two functions on the input element that allow the value to be controlled: `stepUp` and `stepDown`.

As you might expect, these functions increment or decrement the current value, respectively. As you might also expect, the amount by which the value is increased or decreased is the value of the step. As such, the value of a numeric input control can be tweaked without direct input from the user.

The valueAsNumber Function

The new `valueAsNumber` function is a handy way to convert the value of a control from text to number… and back! That is the case because the `valueAsNumber` is both a getter and a setter function. When called as a getter, the `valueAsNumber` function converts the text value of an input field into a number type upon which calculations are allowed. If the text value does not cleanly convert into a `number` type, then the `NaN` value (Not-a-Number) is returned.

The `valueAsNumber` can also be used to set the value of an input to a numeric type. For example, our confidence range could be set using a call such as:

```
document.getElementById("confidence").valueAsNumber(65);
```

Make sure the number meets the requirements of the `min`, `max`, and `step`, or an error will be thrown.

The required Attribute

If any input control has the `required` attribute set, then a value must be set on it before its form can be submitted. For example, to set a text input field as required, simply add the attribute as shown here:

```
<input type="text" id="firstname" name="first" required>
```

If no value is set on this field, either programmatically or by the user, the ability to submit this form is blocked. The `required` attribute is the simplest type of form validation, but the capabilities of validation are vast. Let's discuss form validation in more detail now.

Checking Forms with Validation

Before we get too deep into specifics, let's review what form validation really entails. At its core, form validation is a system for detecting invalid control data and flagging those errors for end users. In other words, form validation is a series of checks and notifications that let a user correct the controls of a form before submitting it to the server.

But what is form validation, really?

It is an optimization.

Form validation is an optimization because it alone is not sufficient to guarantee that forms submitted to the server are correct and valid. It is an optimization because it is designed to help a web application fail fast. In other words, it is better to notify a user that a page contains invalid form controls right inside the page, using the browser's built-in processing. Why bother with the expense of a network round trip just so the server can inform a user that there was a typo in the data entry? If the browser has all the knowledge and capability to catch errors before they leave the client, we should take advantage of that.

However, browser form checking is not sufficient to handle all errors.

Malicious or Misunderstood?

Brian says: "Even though the HTML5 specification goes a long way in improving the ability to check forms within the browser, it is still not a replacement for server validation. It may never be.

Obviously, there are many error conditions that require server interaction to verify, such as whether or not a credit card is authorized to make a purchase, or even basic authentication. However, even mundane validation cannot rely solely on clients. Some users may be using browsers that don't support the form validation features. A few may turn off scripting altogether, which can end up disabling all but the simplest attribute-based validators. Yet other users can utilize an assortment of tools such as the Greasemonkey browser add-on to modify a page's content to their…. err, content. This could include removing all form validation checks. Ultimately, it is not sufficient to rely on client-side validation as the sole means of checking any important data. If it exists on the client, it can be manipulated.

HTML5 Form validation lets users get important feedback fast, but don't rely on it for absolute correctness!"

That being said, HTML5 does introduce eight handy ways to enforce correctness on form control entry. Let's examine them in turn, starting with the object that gives us access to their status: the `ValidityState`.

The `ValidityState` can be accessed from any form control in a browser that supports HTML5 Form validation:

```
var valCheck = document.myForm.myInput.validity;
```

This simple command grabs a reference to the `ValidityState` object of a form element conspicuously named `myInput`. This object contains handy references to each of the eight possible validity statuses, as well as an overall validity summary check. You can get the overall state of this form by calling:

`valCheck.valid`

This call will provide a Boolean value which informs us whether or not all validity constraints are currently met on this particular form control. Think of the `valid` flag as a summary: if all eight constraints are passing, the `valid` flag will be true. Otherwise, if any of the validity constraints fail, the `valid` attribute will be false.

≋ **Note** The `ValidityState` object is a live object. Once you grab a reference to it, you can keep a hold of it and the validity checks it returns will update as needed when changes occur.

As mentioned before, there are eight possible validity constraints on any given form element. Each can be accessed from the `ValidityState` by accessing the field with the appropriate name. Let's look at what they mean, how they can be enforced on a form control, and how you can use the `ValidityState` to check for them:

valueMissing

Purpose: Ensure that some value is set on this form control
Usage: Set the `required` attribute on the form control to true
Usage example: `<input type="text" name="myText" required>`
Details: If the `required` attribute is set on a form control, the control will be in an invalid state unless the user or a programmatic call sets some value to the field. For example, a blank text field will fail a required check, but will pass as soon as any text is entered. When blank, the `valueMissing` will return true.

typeMismatch

Purpose: Guarantee that the type of the value matches expectations (number, email, URL, and so on)
Usage: Specify one of the appropriate `type` attributes on the form control
Usage example: `<input type="email" name="myEmail">`
Details: Special form control types aren't just for customized phone keyboards! If your browser can determine that the value entered into a form control doesn't conform to the rules for that type—for example, an email address without an @ symbol—the browser can flag this control as having a type mismatch. Another example would be a number field that cannot parse to a valid number. In either case, the `typeMismatch` will return `true`.

patternMismatch

Purpose: Enforce any pattern rule set on a form control which details specific valid formats
Usage: Set the `pattern` attribute on the form control with the appropriate pattern
Usage example: `<input type="number" name="creditcardnumber" pattern="[0-9]{16}" title="A credit card number is 16 digits with no spaces or dashes">`

Details: The `pattern` attribute gives developers a powerful and flexible way of enforcing a regular expression pattern on the value of a form control. When a pattern is set on a control, the `patternMismatch` will return true whenever the value does not conform to the rules of the pattern. To assist users and assistive technology, you should set the `title` on any pattern-controlled field to describe the rules of the format.

tooLong

Purpose: Make sure that a value does not contain too many characters
Usage: Put a `maxLength` attribute on the form control
Usage example: `<input type="text" name="limitedText" maxLength="140">`
Details: This humorously-named constraint will return true if the value length exceeds the `maxLength`. While form controls will generally try to enforce the maximum length during user entry, certain situations including programmatic settings can cause the value to exceed the maximum.

rangeUnderflow

Purpose: Enforce the minimum value of a numeric control
Usage: Set a `min` attribute with the minimum allowed value
Usage example: `<input type="range" name="ageCheck" min="18">`
Details: In any form controls that do numeric-range checking, it is possible for the value to get temporarily set below the allowable range. In these cases, the `ValidityState` will return true for the `rangeUnderflow` field.

rangeOverflow

Purpose: Enforce the maximum value of a numeric control
Usage: Set a `max` attribute with the maximum allowed value
Usage example: `<input type="range" name="kidAgeCheck" max="12">`
Details: Similar to its counterpart `rangeUnderflow`, this validity constraint will return `true` if the value of a form control becomes greater than the `max` attribute.

stepMismatch

Purpose: Guarantee that a value conforms to the combination of `min`, `max`, and `step`
Usage: Set a step attribute to specify the granular steps of a numeric value
Usage example: `<input type="range" name="confidenceLevel" min="0" max="100" step="5">`
Details: This constraint enforces the sanity of the combinations of `min`, `max`, and `step`. Specifically, the current value must be a multiple of the step added to the minimum value. For example, a range from 0 to 100 with steps at every 5 would not allow a value of 17 without `stepMismatch` returning true.

customError

Purpose: Handle errors explicitly calculated and set by the application code
Usage: Call `setCustomValidity(message)` to put a form control into the `customError` state
Usage example: `passwordConfirmationField.setCustomValidity("Password values do not match.");`
Details: For those cases where the built-in validity checks don't apply, the custom validity errors can suffice. Application code should set a custom validity message whenever a field does not conform to semantic rules.

One common use case for custom validity is when consistency between controls is not achieved, for example if password confirmation fields don't match. (We'll delve into this specific example in the

"Practical Extras" section.) Whenever a custom validity message is set, the control will be invalid and return the `customError` constraint as `true`. To clear the error, simply call `setCustomValidity("")` on the control with an empty string value.

Validation Fields and Functions

Together, these eight constraints allow a developer to find out exactly why a given form control is failing a validation check. Or, if you don't care which specific reason is causing the failure, simply access the Boolean value `valid` on the `ValidityState`; it is an aggregate of the other eight constraints. If all eight constraints return `false`, then the `valid` field will return `true`. There are a few other helpful fields and functions on the form controls which can assist you in programming for validation checking.

The willValidate Attribute

The `willValidate` attribute simply indicates whether validation will be checked on this form control at all. If any of the above constraints—e.g. the `required` attribute, `pattern` attribute, etc.—are set on the control, the `willValidate` field will let you know that validation checking is going to be enforced.

The checkValidity Function

The `checkValidity` function allows you to check validation on the form without any explicit user input. Normally, a form's validation is checked whenever the user or script code submits the form. This function allows validation to be done at any time.

▨ **Note** Calling `checkValidity` on a form control doesn't just check validation, it causes all resulting events and UI triggers to occur just as if the form had been submitted.

The validationMessage Attribute

This attribute isn't yet supported by any current browser versions, but it might be by the time you read this. The `validationMessage` attribute lets you query programmatically a localized error message that the browser would display based on the current state of validation. For example, if a `required` field has no value, the browser might present an error message to the user that "This field requires a value." Once supported, this is the text string that would be returned by the `validationMessage` field, and it would adjust according to the current state of validation on the control.

Validation Feedback

On the subject of validation feedback… one topic we've avoided thus far is how and when the browser should present the user with feedback on a validation error. The specification does not dictate the terms of how the user interface is updated to present an error message, and existing implementations differ fairly significantly. Consider the case for Opera. In Opera 10.5, the browser indicates that a validation error has occurred by marking the field in error with a popup message and a flashing red field:

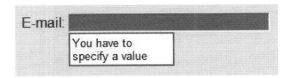

In contrast, at the time of this writing the Google Chrome 13 browser only navigates to the offending field and puts the focus there when an error is found. What is the correct behavior?

Neither is specified. However, if you would like to take control of the feedback shown to the user when a validation error occurs, there is an appropriate handler for you to do so: the invalid event.

Whenever a form is checked for validity—either due to the form being submitted, or due to the checkValidity function being called directly—any form in an invalid state will be delivered an invalid event. This event can be ignored, observed, or even cancelled. To add an event handler to a field which will receive this notification, add some code similar to Listing 8-2.

Listing 8-2. Adding Event Handlers for Invalid Events

```
// event handler for "invalid" events
function invalidHandler(evt) {
  var validity = evt.srcElement.validity;

  // check the validity to see if a particular constraint failed
  if (validity.valueMissing) {
    // present a UI to the user indicating that the field is missing a value
  }

  // perhaps check additional constraints here…

  // If you do not want the browser to provide default validation feedback,
  // cancel the event as shown here
  evt.preventDefault();
}

// register an event listener for "invalid" events
myField.addEventListener("invalid", invalidHandler, false);
```

Let's break that code snippet down a bit.

First, we declare a handler to receive invalid events. The first thing we do inside that handler is check the source of the event. Recall that the invalid event is fired on the form control with a validation error. Therefore, the srcElement of the event will be the misbehaving form control.

From the source, we grab the validity object. Using this ValidityState instance, we can check its individual constraint fields to determine exactly what went wrong. In this case, since we know that our field has a required attribute on it, we first check to see if the valueMissing constraint has been violated.

If our check succeeds, we can modify the user interface on the page to inform the user that a value needs to be entered for the field in error. Perhaps an alert or an informative error region could be displayed? This is up to you to decide.

Once we've told the user what the error is and how to correct it, we need to decide if we want the browser itself to display its built-in feedback. By default, the browser will do just that. To prevent the browser from showing its own error message, we can call evt.preventDefault() to stop the default handling and take care of the matter entirely ourselves.

Once again, the choice here is yours. The HTML5 Forms API provides you with the flexibility to achieve a customized API or to fall back to default browser behavior.

Turning Off Validation

In spite of the power behind the validation API, there are… (ahem) valid reasons why you might want to turn off validation on a control or an entire form. The most common reason is that you might choose to submit the temporary contents of a form to be saved or retrieved for later, even if the contents aren't quite valid yet.

Imagine the case of a user who is entering a complex order entry form, but needs to run an errand midway through the process. Ideally, you might present the user with a "save" button which stores the values of the form by submitting them to the server. However, if the form was only partially completed, validation rules might prevent the content from being submitted. The user would be very displeased if she had to complete or abandon the form due to an unexpected interruption.

To handle this, a form itself can be programmatically set with the attribute `noValidate`, which will cause it to forego any validation logic otherwise present and simply submit the form. Naturally, this attribute can be set either via script or original markup.

A more useful way to turn off validation is to set a `formNoValidate` attribute on a control such as a form submit button. Take the following submit button, set up as a "save" button, for example:

```
<input type="submit" formnovalidate name="save" value="Save current progress">
<input type="submit" name="process" value="Process order">
```

This snippet will create a two normal looking submit buttons. The second will submit the form, as usual. However, the first button is marked with the `noValidate` attribute, causing all validation to be bypassed when it is used. This allows the data to be submitted to the server without checking for correctness. Of course, your server will need to be set up to handle unvalidated data, but best practices dictate that this should be the case at all times.

Building an Application with HTML5 Forms

Now, let's use the tools we've described in this chapter to create a simple signup page which showcases new features in HTML5 Forms. Turning back to our familiar Happy Trails Running Club, we'll create a page for race registration that incorporates new form elements and validation.

As always, the source code for the demo files we show here is available in the code/forms folder. Therefore, we'll spend less attention on the CSS and peripheral markup, and more on the core of the page itself. That being said, let's start with a look at the finished page shown in Figure 8-4, then break it down into sections to tackle one-by-one.

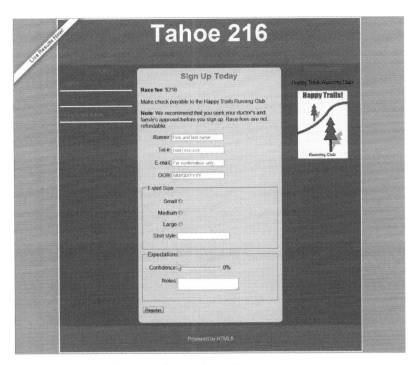

Figure 8-4. Example page with race signup form

This signup page demonstrates many of the elements and APIs we've explored in this chapter, including validation. Although the actual display may look somewhat different on your browser, it should degrade gracefully even if the browser does not support a particular feature.

On to the code!

The header, navigation, and footer have all been seen before on our previous examples. The page now contains a `<form>` element.

```
<form name="register">
  <p><label for="runnername">Runner:</label>
    <input id="runnername" name="runnername" type="text"
           placeholder="First and last name" required></p>
  <p><label for="phone">Tel #:</label>
    <input id="phone" name="phone" type="tel"
           placeholder="(xxx) xxx-xxx"></p>
  <p><label for="emailaddress">E-mail:</label>
    <input id="emailaddress" name="emailaddress" type="email"
           placeholder="For confirmation only"></p>
  <p><label for="dob">DOB:</label>
    <input id="dob" name="dob" type="date"
           placeholder="MM/DD/YYYY"></p>
```

In this first section, we see the markup for the four primary inputs: name, phone, email, and birthday. For each, we've set a `<label>` with descriptive text and tied it to the actual control using the `for` attribute. We've also set placeholder text to show a description to the user of just what type of content belongs there.

For the runner name text field, we've made it a required value by setting the `required` attribute. This will cause form validation to kick in with a `valueMissing` constraint if nothing is entered. On the phone input, we've declared it to be of type `tel`. Your browser may or may not display this field differently or provide optimized keyboards.

Similarly, the e-mail field has been marked of type `e-mail`. Any specific handling is up to the browser. Some browsers will throw a `typeMismatch` constraint if they detect that the entered value is not a valid email.

Finally, the date-of-birth field is declared as type `date`. Not many browsers support this yet, but when they do, they will automatically render a date picking control on this input.

```
<fieldset>
  <legend>T-shirt Size: </legend>
  <p><input id="small" type="radio" name="tshirt" value="small">
    <label for="small">Small</label></p>
  <p><input id="medium" type="radio" name="tshirt" value="medium">
    <label for="medium">Medium</label></p>
  <p><input id="large" type="radio" name="tshirt" value="large">
    <label for="large">Large</label></p>
  <p><label for="style">Shirt style:</label>
    <input id="style" name="style" type="text" list="stylelist" title="Years of
        participation"></p>
  <datalist id="stylelist">
   <option value="White" label="1st Year">
   <option value="Gray" label="2nd - 4th Year">
   <option value="Navy" label="Veteran (5+ Years)">
  </datalist>
</fieldset>
```

In our next section, we set out the controls to be used to T-shirt selection. The first few controls are a standard set of radio buttons for selecting a shirt size.

The next section is more interesting. Here, we exercise the `list` attribute and its corresponding `<datalist>` element. In the `<datalist>,` we declare a set of types that should be displayed for this list with distinct values and labels, representing the types of T-shirts available based on veteran status. Although this list is quite simple, the same technique can be used for lengthy lists of dynamic elements.

```
<fieldset>
  <legend>Expectations:</legend>
  <p>
  <label for="confidence">Confidence:</label>
  <input id="confidence" name="level" type="range"
      onchange="confidenceDisplay.value=(value +'%')"
      min="0" max="100" step="5" value="0">
  <output id="confidenceDisplay">0%</output></p>
  <p><label for="notes">Notes:</label>
    <textarea id="notes" name="notes" maxLength="140"></textarea></p>
</fieldset>
```

In our final section of controls, we create a slider for the user to express his or her confidence in completing the race. For this, we use an input of type `range`. Since our confidence is measured in percentages, we set a `minimum`, a `maximum`, and `step` value on the input. These force a constraint within normal percentage ranges. Additionally, we constrain the movement of the value to 5% step increments, which you will be able to observe if your browser supports a range slider interface control. Although it should not be possible to trigger them through simple control interactions, there are possible validation constraints on this control for `rangeUnderflow`, `rangeOverflow`, and `stepMismatch`.

Because a range control does not show a textual representation of its value by default, we will add an `<output>` to our application for that purpose. The `confidenceDisplay` will be manipulated through the `onchange` handler of the range control, but we'll see that in action in just a minute.

Finally, we add a `<textarea>` to contain any extra notes from the registrant. By setting a `maxLength` constraint on the notes control, we allow it to achieve a `tooLong` constraint, perhaps if a lengthy value is pasted into the field.

```
<p><input type="submit" name="register" value="Register"></p>
</form>
```

We finish off our control section with a submit button that will send in our form registration. In this default example, the registration is not actually being sent to any server.

There are a few scripts we still need to describe: how we will override the browser's built-in form validation feedback and how we will listen for events. Although you might find the browser's default handling of form errors to be acceptable, it is always good to know your options.

```
<script type="text/javascript">

    function invalidHandler(evt) {
        // find the label for this form control
        var label = evt.srcElement.parentElement.getElementsByTagName("label")[0];

        // set the label's text color to red
        label.style.color = 'red';

        // stop the event from propagating higher
        evt.stopPropagation();

        // stop the browser's default handling of the validation error
        evt.preventDefault();
    }

    function loadDemo() {
        // register an event handler on the form to
        // handle all invalid control notifications
        document.register.addEventListener("invalid", invalidHandler, true);
    }

    window.addEventListener("load", loadDemo, false);

</script>
```

This script shows how we override the handling of validation errors. We start by registering event listeners for the special event type `invalid`. In order to capture `invalid` events on all form controls, we register the handler on the form itself, making sure to register for event capture so that events will arrive at our handler.

```
// register an event handler on the form to
```

```
// handle all invalid control notifications
document.register.addEventListener("invalid", invalidHandler, true);
```

Now, whenever any of our form elements triggers a validation constraint, our `invalidHandler` will be called. In order to provide more subtle feedback than some of the prominent browsers do by default, we will color the label of the offending form field red. To do so, first we locate the `<label>` by traversing to the parent.

```
// find the label for this form control
var label = evt.srcElement.parentElement.getElementsByTagName("label")[0];
```

```
// set the label's text color to red
label.style.color = 'red';
```

After setting the label to be a lovely red color, we want to stop the browser or any other handler from double handling our invalid event. Using the power of DOM, we call `preventDefault()` to stop any browser default handling of the event, and `stopPropagation()` to keep other handlers from getting access.

```
// stop the event from propagating higher
evt.stopPropagation();
```

```
// stop the browser's default handling of the validation error
evt.preventDefault();
```

And with just a few simple steps, we've provided a validated form with our own special interface validation code!

Practical Extras

Sometimes there are techniques that don't fit into our regular examples, but which nonetheless apply to many types of HTML5 applications. We present to you some short, but common, practical extras here.

The Password Is: Validation!

One handy way to use the HTML5 Form validation support for custom validators is to implement the common technique of verifying passwords during a password change. The standard technique is to provide two password fields which must match before the form is submitted successfully. Here, we provide a way to utilize the `setCustomValidation` call to make sure that two password fields are matched before the form submits.

Recall that the `customError` validation constraint gives you a chance to set an error on a form control whenever the standard constraint rules do not apply. Specifically, one good reason to trigger the `customError` constraint is when the validation depends on the concurrent state of multiple controls, such as the two password fields here.

Because the `ValidityState` object is assumed to be live once a reference to it is obtained, it is a good idea to set the custom error on the `ValidityState` whenever the password fields are mismatched and immediately clear the error whenever the fields match again. A good approach for achieving this is to use the onchange event handler for the password fields.

```
<form name="passwordChange">
    <p><label for="password1">New Password:</label>
    <input type="password" id="password1" onchange="checkPasswords()"></p>
```

213

```
<p><label for="password2">Confirm Password:</label>
<input type="password" id="password2" onchange="checkPasswords()"></p>
</form>
```

As you can see here, on a trivial form with two password fields, we can register a function to execute every time the value of one of the passwords changes.

```
function checkPasswords() {
  var pass1 = document.getElementById("password1");
  var pass2 = document.getElementById("password2");

  if (pass1.value != pass2.value)
    pass1.setCustomValidity("Your passwords do not match. Please recheck that your
        new password is entered identically in the two fields.");
  else
    pass1.setCustomValidity("");
}
```

Here is one way to handle the password matching. Simply grab the values of the two password fields, and if they do not match, set a custom error. For the sake of a validation routine, it is probably acceptable just to set the error on one of the two password fields. If they do match, set the empty string as the custom error to clear it; this is the specified way for removing a custom error.

Once you've got the error set on the field, you can use the approaches described earlier in this chapter to show feedback to the user and let her change the passwords to match, as expected.

Forms Are Stylin'

In order to help developers distinguish among form controls that have specific validation characteristics, the developers of CSS have helpfully added a set of pseudo-classes that can be used to set styles on form controls based on the state of their validity. In other words, if you desire form elements on your page to change style automatically based on whether or not they are currently complying with validation (or not), you can set these style pseudo-classes in your rules. These functions are very similar to long-standing pseudo classes such as :visited and :hover on links. Table 8-4 shows the new pseudo-classes proposed for the CSS Selectors Level 4 specification can be used to select form elements.

Table 8-4. CSS Pseudoclasses for HTML5 Form Validation

Type	Purpose
valid	This pseudo-class selects any form element that passes all validity rules. In other words, this form element has state that is ready to be submitted.
invalid	This pseudo-class selects any form element that has errors or problems preventing it from being submitted. Selectors with this class are useful for showing users errors on the page.
in-range	This pseudo-class only selects elements such as inputs of type range where the current value is safely between the minimum and maximum values.
out-of-	This pseudo-class selects elements with inputs that have values outside of the accepted

range	range.
required	Any elements that have been marked as required will be selected by this pseudo-class.
optional	Form elements that are not marked as required fall into this pseudo-class. Only form elements fit this category.

With these pseudo-classes, it is easy to mark form controls in a page with visual styling that changes as the form elements themselves adjust. For example, to show all invalid form elements with a red background, you can simply use the CSS rule:

```
:invalid {
    background-color:red;
}
```

These pseudo-classes will adjust automatically as the user enters input. No code is required!

Summary

In this chapter, you have seen how to take something old—HTML forms—and make it into something new by using new elements, attributes, and APIs available in HTML5. We've seen new controls for advanced input types, with even more to come. We've seen how client validation can be integrated directly into form controls in order to prevent unnecessary server round trips to process bad data. Overall, we've seen ways to reduce the amount of scripting you need to create full-featured applications user interfaces.

In the next chapter, we'll investigate how browsers give you the ability to spawn independent execution environments to handle long-running tasks: HTML5 Web Workers.

CHAPTER 9

Working with Drag-and-Drop

Traditional drag-and-drop has been popular with users since the days of the original Apple Macintosh. But today's computers and mobile devices have much more sophisticated drag-and-drop behavior. Drag-and-drop is used in file management, transferring data, diagramming, and many other operations where moving an object is more naturally envisioned with a gesture than a key command. Ask developers on the street what drag-and-drop encompasses, and you are likely to get a myriad of different answers depending on their favorite programs and current work assignments. Ask non-technical users about drag-and-drop, and they may stare at you blankly; the feature is now so ingrained into computing that it does not often get called out by name anymore.

And yet, HTML has not had drag-and-drop as a core feature in its many years of existence. Although some developers have used the built-in ability to handle low-level mouse events as a way to hack up primitive drag-and-drop, those efforts paled in comparison to the type of drag-and-drop features that have been available in desktop applications for decades. With the arrival of a well-specified set of drag-and-drop functionality, HTML applications have advanced one step closer to matching the capabilities of their desktop counterparts.

Web Drag-and-Drop: The Story So Far

You may have seen examples of drag-and-drop on the Web already and are wondering if these are uses of HTML5 drag-and-drop. The answer? Probably not.

The reason is that HTML and DOM have exposed low-level mouse events since the early days of DOM events, and that has been sufficient for creative developers to craft a rudimentary drag-and-drop capability. When coupled with CSS positioning, it is possible to approximate a drag-and-drop system through the creation of complex JavaScript libraries and a firm knowledge of DOM events.

For example, by handling the following DOM events, it is possible to move items around in a web page if you code a set of logical steps (and some caveats):

- mousedown: The user is starting some mouse operation. (Is it a drag or just a click?)

- mousemove: If the mouse is not up yet, a move operation is starting. (Is it a drag or a select?)

- mouseover: The mouse has moved over an element. (Is it one of the ones I want to drop on?)

- mouseout: The mouse has left an element that will no longer be a possible place to drop. (Do I need to draw feedback?)

- mouseup: The mouse has released, possibly triggering a drop operation. (Should the drop complete on this location based on where it started from?)

Although modeling a crude drag-and-drop system using low-level events is possible, it suffers from some notable drawbacks. First, the logic necessary to handle the mouse events is more complex than you might imagine, as each of the listed events has many edge cases that must be accounted for. Although some were in the previous list, the reality is that there are enough of them to warrant their own chapter. During these events, CSS must be carefully updated to provide feedback to the user about the possibility of dragging or dropping at any particular location.

However, an even more serious drawback is that this type of ad hoc drag-and-drop implementation relies on total control of the system. If you try mixing your app content with other content in the same page, things quickly spiral out of control when different developers start using events for their own means. Similarly, if you try to drag-and-drop content from someone else's code, you may have trouble unless the two codebases are carefully coordinated beforehand. Also, ad hoc drag-and-drop does not interact with the user's desktop or work across windows.

The new HTML5 drag-and-drop API has been designed to address these limitations, borrowing from the way drag-and-drop has been provided in other user interface frameworks.

■ **Note** Even when properly implemented, beware of the limitations of drag-and-drop in any application. Mobile devices that use drag gestures to navigate might not function correctly if drag behavior is overridden. Also, drag-and-drop can interfere with drag selection. Take care to use it sparingly and appropriately.

Overview of HTML5 Drag-and-Drop

If you have used the drag-and-drop APIs in programming technologies such as Java or Microsoft MFC, then you're in luck. The new HTML5 drag-and-drop API is closely modeled on the concepts of these environments. Getting started is easy, but mastering the new functionality means that you will need to become acquainted with a new set of DOM events, though this time at a higher level of abstraction.

The Big Picture

The easiest way to learn the new API is to map it to the concepts with which you are already familiar. If you are reading a book on pro HTML5 programming, we'll make a bold assumption that you are experienced with using drag-and-drop in your day-to-day computing. Nonetheless, we can start by putting some standard terms on the major concepts.

As shown in Figure 9-1, when you (as a user) start a drag-and-drop operation, you start by clicking and dragging the pointer. The item or region where you began the drag is known as the **drag source**. When you release the pointer and complete the operation, the region or item you are targeting at the end is known as the **drop target**. As the mouse moves across the page, you may traverse a series of drop targets before you actually release the mouse.

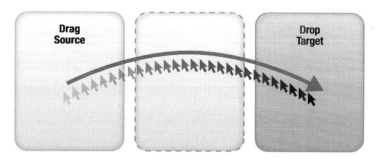

Figure 9-1. *Drag sources and drop targets*

So far, so good. But simply holding down the mouse and moving it to another part of an application is not what constitutes a drag-and-drop. Rather, it is the feedback during the operation that makes for a successful interaction. Consider your own uses of drag-and-drop in past experiences; the ones that are the most intuitive are those where the system is giving constant updates to let you know what will happen if you release at this point in time:

- Does the cursor indicate that the current position is a valid drop target, or does it imply a rejection with a "forbidden" cursor indicator?

- Does the cursor imply to the user that the operation will be a move, link, or a copy, such as with a "plus" sign indicator on the cursor?

- Does the area or target you are hovering over change its appearance in any way to indicate that it is currently selected as a drop if you release right now?

In order to give similar feedback to users over the course of an HTML drag-and-drop operation, the browsers will emit a whole slew of events over the course of a single drag. This proves quite handy, as during these events we will have full power to change the DOM and style of the page elements to give just the type of feedback that users will be expecting.

Beyond the drag source and drop target, there is one more key concept to learn in the new API: the *data transfer*. The specification describes the data transfer as the set of objects used to expose the drag data store that underlies a drag-and-drop operation. However, it may be easier just to think of the data transfer as being the central control of drag-and-drop. The operation type (e.g., move, copy, or link), the image to use as feedback during the drag, and the retrieval of the data itself are all managed here.

Regarding the data itself, the dataTransfer mechanism for completing the drop directly addresses one of the limitations of the old ad hoc drag-and-drop techniques described previously. Instead of forcing all drag sources and drop targets to be aware of each other, the data transfer mechanism works similar to a network protocol negotiation. In this case, the negotiation is performed via Multipurpose Internet Mail Exchange (MIME) types.

■ **Note** MIME types are the same types used to attach files to e-mail. They are an Internet standard that is used pervasively in all types of Web traffic, and they are very common in HTML5. In short, MIME types are standardized text strings used to classify the type of unknown content, such as "text/plain" for plain text and "image/png" for PNG images.

The purpose of using MIME types is to allow the source and target to negotiate on which format best suits the needs of the drop target. As shown in Figure 9-2, during a drag start, the dataTransfer object is loaded up with data representing all reasonable types, or "flavors," by which the data can be transferred. Then, when the drop completes, the drop handler code can scan the available types of data and decide which MIME type format best suits its needs.

For example, imagine a list item in a web page representing a person. There are many different ways to represent the data for a person; some are standard, some are not. When a drag starts on a particular person's list item, the drag start handler can declare that the person's data is available in a few formats, as shown in Table 9-1.

***Table 9-1.** Examples of MIME Types in Data Transfer of a Person*

MIME Type	Result
text/plain	A standard MIME type for unformatted text. We can use it as the most common representation, such as the person's name.
image/png	A standard MIME type for PNG images. Here, it could represent the person's picture in PNG format.
image/jpeg	The standard MIME type for JPEG images. It could be used to transfer the person's picture in that format.
text/x-age	A non-standard MIME type (as indicated by the x- prefix). We could use this format to transfer our own types of information, such as the person's age.

When the drop completes, the drop handler can query for a list of available data types. From the provided list, the handler can choose which type is most appropriate. A text list drop target may choose to grab the text/plain "flavor" of data to retrieve the person's name, while a more advanced control might choose to retrieve and display the person's PNG image as a result of the drop. And, if the source and target have coordinated on non-standard types, the target could also retrieve the person's age at the time of the drop.

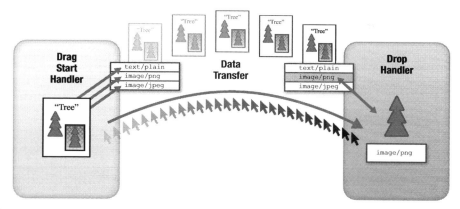

Figure 9-2. Drag and drop negotiation of data "flavors"

It is this negotiation process that allows for drag sources and drop targets to be decoupled. As long as the drag sources provide data in a choice of MIME types, the drop target can choose which format suits its operation the best, even if the two came from different developers. In later sections of this chapter, we'll explore how even more unusual MIME types, such as files, can be used.

Events to Remember

Now that we've explored the key concepts of the drag-and-drop API, let's focus on the events that can be used throughout the process. As you'll see, the events operate at a higher level than the mouse events previously utilized to mock up a drag-and-drop system. However, drag-and-drop events extend the DOM mouse event. Therefore, you still have access to the low-level mouse information, such as coordinates, if you need it.

Propagation and Prevention

But before we focus on drag and-drop-itself, let's refresh on two DOM event functions that have been around since the browsers standardized on DOM Level 3 events: the stopPropagation and preventDefault functions.

Consider the case where one element in a page is nested inside another element. We will refer to them as the child and parent elements, respectively. The child takes up some, but not all, of the visible space of the parent. Although we are only referring to two elements in our example, in practice a web page often has many levels of nesting.

When a user clicks a mouse on the child, which element should actually receive the event: the child, the parent, or both? And if both, in which order? The answer to this question was settled by the World Wide Web Consortium (W3C) in the DOM events specification. Events flow from a parent, through intermediaries, and down to the most specific child first in a process known as "event capture." Once the child has had access to the event, the event flows back up the element hierarchy via a process known as "event bubbling." Together, these two flows allow developers to catch and process the event in the way that is most suitable to their page architecture. Only elements with handlers actually registered will process the event, which keeps the system lightweight. The overall approach is a compromise among different behaviors from multiple browser vendors, and it is consistent with other native development frameworks, some of which capture and some of which bubble.

However, at any time a handler can call the stopPropagation function on the event, which will stop it from further traversing down the event capture chain or up through the bubbling phase.

■ **Note** Microsoft has provided a great interactive demo of event models at
http://ie.microsoft.com/testdrive/HTML5/ComparingEventModels

Browsers also have default implementations for how some events will be handled. For example, when a user clicks on a page link, the default behavior is to navigate the browser to the destination specified by the link. Developers can prevent this by intercepting the event in a handler and calling preventDefault on it. This allows code to override the default behaviors of some built-in events. It is also how a developer can cancel a drag-and-drop operation in an event handler.

Both stopPropagation and preventDefault will be handy in our examples of the drag-and-drop API.

Drag-and-Drop Event Flow

When a user initiates a drag-and-drop operation in an HTML5-ready browser, a series of events trigger at the start and continue throughout the course of the whole operation. We will examine them in turn here.

dragstart

The dragstart event is fired on an element in the page when the user begins to drag on it. In other words, once the mouse is down and the user moves the mouse, the dragstart is initiated. The dragstart event is of key importance, as it is the only event where the dataTransfer can have data set on it using the setData call. This means that in a dragStart handler, the possible data types need to be set up so that they can be queried at the end of the drop, as described previously.

Interception!

Brian says: "If you are wondering why the data types can only be set during the dragStart event, there's actually a very good reason for that.

Because drag-and-drop has been designed to work across windows and across content from various sources, it would be a security risk if drag event listeners were able to insert or replace data when the drag passed over them. Imagine a malicious section of code with event listeners inserted that queried and replaced drag data of any drag travelling by. This would misrepresent the intentions of the drag source, and as such any data replacements after the start are forbidden."

---

drag

The drag event can be thought of as the continuous event of a drag operation. As the user moves the mouse cursor around the page, the drag event is called repeatedly on the drag *source*. The drag event will fire a few times each second during the operation. Although the visuals of the drag feedback can be modified during a drag event, the data on the dataTransfer is off-limits.

dragenter

When the drag crosses into a new element on the page, a dragenter event fires on that element. This event is a good time to set drop feedback on the element based on whether or not it can receive the drop.

dragleave

Conversely, the browser will fire a dragleave event whenever the user moves the drag out of the element where dragenter was previously called. Drop feedback can be restored at this time, as the mouse is no longer over this target.

dragover

The dragover event is called at frequent intervals as the mouse moves over an element during a drag operation. Unlike its counterpart drag event, which is called on the drag source, this event is called on the current target of the mouse.

drop

The drop event is called on the current mouse target when the user releases the mouse. Based on the result of the dataTransfer object, this is where the code to handle the drop should be executed.

dragend

The final event in the chain, dragend fires on the drag source, indicating that the drag completed. It is particularly suitable for cleaning up the state used during the drag, as it is called regardless of whether or not the drop completes.

Altogether, there are plenty of ways for you to intercept the drag-and-drop operations and take action. The drag-and-drop event chain is summarized in Figure 9-3.

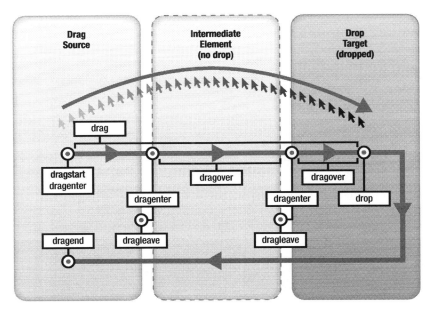

Figure 9-3. *Drag-and-drop event flow*

Drag Participation

Now that you've seen the different events that can be triggered during a drag-and-drop operation, you might be wondering what it takes to mark elements in your web application as draggable. That's easy!

Aside from a few elements—such as text controls—elements in a page are not draggable by default. In order to mark a specific element as draggable, however, all you need to do is add one attribute: draggable.

```
<div id="myDragSource" draggable="true">
```

Simply by adding that attribute, you cause the browser to fire the aforementioned events. Then, you only need to add the event handlers to manage them.

Transfer and Control

Before we move into our example, let's assess the dataTransfer object in more detail. The dataTransfer is available from every drag-and-drop event, as shown in Listing 9-1.

Listing 9-1. *Retrieving the dataTransfer Object*

```
Function handleDrag(evt) {
    var transfer = evt.dataTransfer;
    // …
}
```

As discussed in Listing 9-1, the dataTransfer is used to get and set the actual drop data during the negotiation between source and target. This is done using the following functions and properties:

- setData(format, data): Calling this function during dragStart allows you to register one transfer item under a MIME type format.

- getData(format): This function allows the registered data item for a given type to be retrieved.

- types: This property returns an array of all currently registered formats.

- items: This property returns a list of all items and their associated formats together.

- files: This property returns any files associated with the drop. This is discussed in more detail in a later section.

- clearData(): Calling this function with no argument clears out all registered data. Calling it with a format argument removes only that specific registration.

Two more functions can be used to alter the feedback during a drag operation:

- setDragImage(element, x, y): Tells the browser to use an existing image element as the drag image, which will display alongside the cursor to hint to the user about the drag operation effects. If x and y coordinates are provided, then those coordinates will be considered as the drop point for the mouse.

- addElement(element): By calling this function with a provided page element, you tell the browser to draw that element as a drag feedback image.

A final set of properties allows the developer to set and/or query the types of drag operations that are allowed:

- effectAllowed: Setting this property to one of none, copy, copyLink, copyMove, link, linkMove, move, or all tells the browser that only the type(s) of operations listed here are to be allowed for the user. For example, if copy is set, only copy operations will be allowed, and move or link operations will be prevented.

- dropEffect: This property can be used to determine which type of operation is currently underway or set to force a particular operation type. The types of operations are copy, link, and move. Or, the value none can be set to prevent any drop from happening at that point in time.

Together, these operations give a fine level of control over drag-and-drop. Now, let's see them in action.

Building an Application with Drag-and-Drop

Using the concepts we've already learned, we'll build a simple drag-and-drop page in the theme of our Happy Trails Running Club. This page lets the club race organizers drag members of the club into one of two lists: racers and volunteers. In order to sort them into competitive groups, racers will be sorted by their age. Volunteers, on the other hand, are only sorted by their names, as their ages don't matter when they are not competing.

The sorting of the lists is done automatically. The application itself will show feedback indicating where proper drop areas are for members into the two lists as shown in Figure 9-4.

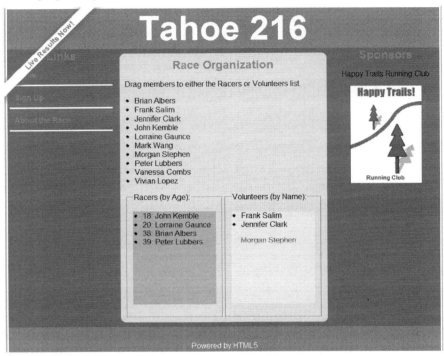

Figure 9-4. *Example page showing racers sorted into lists*

All of the code for this example is included with the book's samples in the code/draganddrop directory. We'll step through the page and explain how it works in practice.

First, let's look at the markup for the page. At the top, we've declared the data on our club members (see Listing 9-2).

Listing 9-2. *Markup Displaying Draggable Member Names and Ages*

```
<p>Drag members to either the Racers or Volunteers list.</p>

<ul id="members">
  <li draggable="true" data-age="38">Brian Albers</li>
  <li draggable="true" data-age="25">Frank Salim</li>
  <li draggable="true" data-age="47">Jennifer Clark</li>
  <li draggable="true" data-age="18">John Kemble</li>
  <li draggable="true" data-age="20">Lorraine Gaunce</li>
  <li draggable="true" data-age="30">Mark Wang</li>
  <li draggable="true" data-age="41">Morgan Stephen</li>
  <li draggable="true" data-age="39">Peter Lubbers</li>
```

```
<li draggable="true" data-age="33">Vanessa Combs</li>
<li draggable="true" data-age="54">Vivian Lopez</li>
</ul>
```

As you can see, each of the member list elements is marked as draggable. This tells the browser to let drags start on each of them. The next thing you'll notice is that the age of a given member is encoded as a data attribute. The data- notation is a standard way to store non-standard attributes on an HTML element.

Our next section contains the target lists (see Listing 9-3).

Listing 9-3. Markup for Drop List Targets

```
<div class="dropList">
<fieldset id="racersField">
<legend>Racers (by Age):</legend>
<ul id="racers"></ul>
</fieldset>
</div>

<div class="dropList">
<fieldset id="volunteersField">
<legend>Volunteers (by Name):</legend>
<ul id="volunteers"></ul>
</fieldset>
</div>
```

The unordered lists identified as racers and volunteers are the ultimate destinations where our members will be inserted. The fieldsets surrounding them serve as functional equivalents of a moat around a castle. When the user drags into the fieldset, we'll know that they have exited the contained list and we'll update our visual feedback accordingly.

Speaking of feedback, there are a few CSS styles in our page that are important to note (see Listing 9-4).

Listing 9-4. Styles for Drag-and-Drop Demo

```
#members li {
    cursor: move;
}

.highlighted {
    background-color: yellow;
}

.validtarget {
    background-color: lightblue;
}
```

First, we make sure that every member in our source list shows a move cursor. This gives a hint to the user that the items are draggable.

Next, we define two style classes: highlighted and validtarget. These are used to draw background colors on our lists as the drag-and-drop is in progress. The validtarget background will be displayed on our destination lists during the entire drag to hint that they are valid drop targets. When the user actually

227

moves a member over a target list it will change to the highlighted style, indicating that the user is actually over a drop target.

To keep track of the state on our page, we'll declare a few variables (see Listing 9-5).

Listing 9-5. List Item Declarations

```
// these arrays hold the names of the members who are
// chosen to be racers and volunteers, respectively
var racers = [];
var volunteers = [];

// these variables store references to the visible
// elements for displaying who is a racer or volunteer
var racersList;
var volunteersList;
```

The first two variables will serve as internal arrays, which keep track of which members are in the racers and volunteers lists. The second two variables are only going to be used as handy references to the unordered lists containing the visual display of members in the respective lists.

Now, let's set all of our page items up to handle drag-and-drop (see Listing 9-6).

Listing 9-6. Event Handler Registration

```
function loadDemo() {

    racersList = document.getElementById("racers");
    volunteersList = document.getElementById("volunteers");

    // our target lists get handlers for drag enter, leave, and drop
    var lists = [racersList, volunteersList];
    [].forEach.call(lists, function(list) {
        list.addEventListener("dragenter", handleDragEnter, false);
        list.addEventListener("dragleave", handleDragLeave, false);
        list.addEventListener("drop", handleDrop, false);
    });

    // each target list gets a particular dragover handler
    racersList.addEventListener("dragover", handleDragOverRacers, false);
    volunteersList.addEventListener("dragover", handleDragOverVolunteers, false);

    // the fieldsets around our lists serve as buffers for resetting
    // the style during drag over
    var fieldsets = document.querySelectorAll("#racersField, #volunteersField");
    [].forEach.call(fieldsets, function(fieldset) {
        fieldset.addEventListener("dragover", handleDragOverOuter, false);
    });

    // each draggable member gets a handler for drag start and end
    var members = document.querySelectorAll("#members li");
    [].forEach.call(members, function(member) {
        member.addEventListener("dragstart", handleDragStart, false);
        member.addEventListener("dragend", handleDragEnd, false);
```

```
    });

}

window.addEventListener("load", loadDemo, false);
```

When the window initially loads, we call a loadDemo function to set up all of our drag-and-drop event handlers. Most of them don't need event capture, and we will set the capture argument accordingly. Both the racersList and the volunteersList will receive handlers for dragenter, dragleave, and drop events, as these are fired on drop targets. Each list will receive a separate dragover event listener, as that will allow us to easily update the drag feedback based on the target the user is currently dragging over.

As mentioned previously, we are also adding dragover handlers on the fieldsets surrounding the target lists. Why do we do this? To make it easier to detect when a drag has exited our target lists. Although it is easy for us to detect that a user has dragged an item over our list, it is not so easy to determine when the user has dragged an item *out* of our list. This is because the dragleave events fire both when an item is dragged out of our list *and* when the item is dragged over a child already in the destination list. Essentially, when you drag from a parent element over one of its contained children, the drag exits the parent and enters the child. Although this provides a lot of information, it actually makes it tricky to know when a drag is leaving the outer boundaries of a parent element. Therefore, we will use a notification that we are dragging over an element *surrounding* our list to inform us that we have exited the list. More information on this will be provided later.

This Way to the eGRESS

Brian says: "One of the more counter-intuitive aspects of the drag-and-drop specification is the order of events. Although you might expect that a dragged item would exit one target before it entered another, you'd be wrong!

The order of events fired during a drag from element A into element B is that a dragenter event is fired on element B before the dragleave is fired on element A. This maintains consistency with the HTML mouse event specification, but it is one of the odder aspects of the design. There are more of these quirks ahead, to be sure."

Our final set of handlers registers dragstart and dragend listeners on every draggable club member in our initial list. We will use them to initialize and clean up any drag. You might notice that we don't add handlers for the drag event, which fires periodically on the drag source. As we will not be updating the appearance of the dragged item, it will be unnecessary for our example.

Now, we'll go through the actual event handlers in turn, based on the order in which they generally fire (see Listing 9-7).

Listing 9-7. dragstart Event Handler

```
// called at the beginning of any drag
function handleDragStart(evt) {

    // our drag only allows copy operations
    evt.effectAllowed = "copy";

    // the target of a drag start is one of our members
    // the data for a member is either their name or age
    evt.dataTransfer.setData("text/plain", evt.target.textContent);
    evt.dataTransfer.setData("text/html", evt.target.dataset.age);

    // highlight the potential drop targets
    racersList.className = "validtarget";
    volunteersList.className = "validtarget";

    return true;
}
```

The handler for dragstart is called on the draggable item where the users begin the operation. It is a somewhat special handler, as it sets up the capabilities of the entire process. First, we set the effectAllowed, which tells the browser that only copies are allowed when dragging from this element—no moves or links.

Next, we preload all of the possible flavors of data that might be requested at the end of a successful drop. Naturally, we want to support a text version of our element, so we set the MIME type text/plain to return the text inside our draggable node, (i.e., the club member's name).

For our second data flavor, we would like the drop operation to transfer another type of data about the drag source; in our case, it is the age of the club member. Unfortunately, due to bugs, not all browsers support user-defined MIME types such as application/x-age yet, which would be the best fit for such an arbitrary flavor. Instead, we will reuse another commonly supported MIME format—text/html—to stand in for an age flavor for now. Hopefully the WebKit browsers will address this limitation soon.

Don't forget that the dragstart handler is the only handler where data transfer values can be set. Attempting to do so in other handlers will fail in order to prevent rogue code from changing the data mid-drag.

Our final action in the start handler is purely for demo purposes. We will change the background color of our potential drop target lists to give the user a hint about what is possible. Our next handlers will process events as the dragged item enters and leaves elements on the page (see Listing 9-8).

Listing 9-8. dragenter and dragleave Event Handlers

```
// stop propagation and prevent default drag behavior
// to show that our target lists are valid drop targets
function handleDragEnter(evt) {
    evt.stopPropagation();
    evt.preventDefault();
    return false;
}

function handleDragLeave(evt) {
```

```
        return false;
    }
```

The `dragleave` event is not used by our demo, and we handle it purely for illustrative purposes.

The `dragenter` event, however, can be handled and canceled by calling `preventDefault` on it when it is fired over a valid drop target. This informs the browser that the current target is a valid drop target, as the *default* behavior is to assume that any target is not a valid drop target.

Next, we will look at the `dragover` handlers (see Listing 9-9). Recall that these fire at regular intervals whenever the drag hovers over the elements in question.

Listing 9-9. dragover Handler for Outer Container

```
// for better drop feedback, we use an event for dragging
// over the surrounding control as a flag to turn off
// drop highlighting
function handleDragOverOuter(evt) {

    // due to Mozilla firing drag over events to
    // parents from nested children, we check the id
    // before handling
    if (evt.target.id == "racersField")
      racersList.className = "validtarget";

    else if (evt.target.id == "volunteersField")
      volunteersList.className = "validtarget";

    evt.stopPropagation();
    return false;
}
```

Our first of three `dragover` handlers will be used only to adjust the drag feedback. Recall that it is difficult to detect when a drag has left a target, such as our intended racers and volunteers lists. Therefore, we use a drag movement over the fieldsets surrounding the lists to indicate that the drag has exited the vicinity of the lists. This allows us to turn off the drop highlighting on the lists accordingly.

Note that our simple code, as listed, will change the CSS `className` repeatedly if the user hovers in the fieldset area. For optimization purposes, it is good practice to only change the `className` once, as it may cause the browser to do more work than necessary.

Finally, we stop propagation of the event to any other handlers in the page. We don't want any other handlers to override our logic. In the next two `dragover` handlers, we take a different approach (see Listing 9-10).

Listing 9-10. dragover Handler for Target Lists

```
// if the user drags over our list, show
// that it allows copy and highlight for better feedback
function handleDragOverRacers(evt) {
    evt.dataTransfer.dropEffect = "copy";
    evt.stopPropagation();
    evt.preventDefault();

    racersList.className = "highlighted";
    return false;
```

```
}

function handleDragOverVolunteers(evt) {
    evt.dataTransfer.dropEffect = "copy";
    evt.stopPropagation();
    evt.preventDefault();

    volunteersList.className = "highlighted";
    return false;
}
```

These two handlers, while somewhat verbose, are listed in full to clarify our demo. The first handles dragover events in the racers list, and the second handles dragover events identically in the volunteers list.

The first action we take is to set the dropEffect to indicate that only copies are allowed on this node, not moves or links. This is a good practice, even though our original dragstart handler already limited the drag-and-drop operation to be copy-only.

Next we prevent other handlers from accessing the event and cancel it. Canceling a dragover event has an important function: it tells the browser that the default operation—*not* allowing a drop here—is not valid. Essentially, we are telling the browser that it should not not allow a drop; and so, the drop is allowed. Although this may seem counter-intuitive, recall that preventDefault is used to tell the browser not to do its normal built-in operation for an event. For example, calling preventDefault on a click on a link tells the browser to not navigate to the link's reference. The specification designers could have created a new event or API for this dragover, but they opted to keep to the API patterns that were already used throughout HTML.

We will also give the user visual feedback by changing the background color to yellow via the highlighted CSS class whenever the user drags over our lists. The main work of the drag-and-drop is done in the drop handler, which we examine next in Listing 9-11.

Listing 9-11. Drop Handler for Target Lists

```
// when the user drops on a target list, transfer the data
function handleDrop(evt) {
    evt.preventDefault();
    evt.stopPropagation();

    var dropTarget = evt.target;

    // use the text flavor to get the name of the dragged item
    var text  = evt.dataTransfer.getData("text/plain");

    var group = volunteers;
    var list  = volunteersList;


    // if the drop target list was the racer list, grab an extra
    // flavor of data representing the member age and prepend it
    if ((dropTarget.id != "volunteers") &&
        (dropTarget.parentNode.id != "volunteers")) {
        text = evt.dataTransfer.getData("text/html") + ": " + text;
        group = racers;
        list  = racersList;
```

```
    }

    // for simplicity, fully clear the old list and reset it
    if (group.indexOf(text) == -1) {
        group.push(text);
        group.sort();

        // remove all old children
        while (list.hasChildNodes()) {
            list.removeChild(list.lastChild);
        }

        // push in all new children
        [].forEach.call(group, function(person) {
            var newChild = document.createElement("li");
            newChild.textContent = person;
            list.appendChild(newChild);
        });
    }

    return false;
}
```

Once again, we start by preventing the default drop behavior and preventing the control from propagating to other handlers. The default drop event depends on the location and type of element dropped. For example, dropping an image dragged in from another source displays it in the browser window, and dropping a link into a window navigates to it by default. We want total control of drop behavior in our demo, so we cancel any default behaviors.

Recall that our demo shows how multiple data flavors set up in the dragstart can be retrieved from a dropped element. Here, we see how that retrieval completes. By default, we get the plain text data representing the club member's name by using the text/plain MIME format. If the user drops into the volunteers list, this is sufficient.

However, if the user is dropping the club member into the racers list, we take one additional step to fetch the age of the club member, which we previously set using the text/html flavor during dragstart. We prepend it to the club member's name to display both age and name in the racers list.

Our final block of code is a simple, albeit unoptimized, routine to clear out all previous members of the target list, add our new member (if he didn't exist already), sort, and refill the list. The end result is a sorted list containing the old members and the newly dropped member, if he was not present before.

Regardless of whether or not the user completed the drag-and-drop, we need a dragend handler to clean up (see Listing 9-12).

Listing 9-12. *dragend Handler for Clean Up*

```
// make sure to clean up any drag operation
function handleDragEnd(evt) {

    // restore the potential drop target styles
    racersList.className = null;
    volunteersList.className = null;
    return false;
}
```

A dragend handler is called at the end of the drag, whether or not a drop actually occurred. If the user canceled the drag or completed it, the dragend handler is still called. This gives us a good place to clean up any state we changed at the beginning of the process. Not surprisingly, we reset the CSS classes of our lists to their default, unstyled state.

Sharing Is Caring

Brian says: "If you are wondering whether or not the drag-and-drop functionality is worth all of the event handler code, don't forget one of the key benefits of the API: sharing drags across windows and even across browsers.

Because the design of HTML5 drag-and-drop was built to mirror that of desktop capabilities, it is not surprising that it also supports sharing across applications. You can try this out by loading our example in multiple browser windows and dragging members from one source list to the racers and volunteers lists of another window. Although our simple highlighting feedback was not designed for this case, the actual drop capability works across windows and even across browsers if they support the API." Our drag-and-drop example is a simple one, but it illustrates the full capability of the API.

Getting Into the dropzone

If you're thinking that handling all of the drag-and-drop events is complicated, you're not alone. The authors of the specification have designed an alternative, shorthand mechanism to support drop events: the dropzone attribute.

The dropzone provides developers with a compact way to register that an element is willing to accept drops without coding up lengthy event handlers. The attribute consists of a few space-separated patterns that, when provided, allow the browser to automatically wire up the drop behavior for you (see Table 9-2).

Table 9-2.Tokens of the dropzone Attribute

Token	Result
copy, move, link	Only one of the three operation types is allowed. If none is specified, copy is assumed.
s:<mime>	Using the characters s: followed by a MIME type indicates that data of that MIME type is allowed to be dropped on the element.
f:<mime>	Using the characters f: followed by a MIME type indicates that files of that MIME type are allowed to be dropped on the element.

Borrowing from our example application, the racers list element could be specified as having the following attribute:

```
<ul id="racers" dropzone="copy s:text/plain s:text/html" ondrop="handleDrop(event)">
```

This provides a quick way of telling the browser that copy operations for elements that support either the plain text or HTML data format are allowed to drop on our list.

The `dropzone` is not supported by most major browser vendors at the time of writing, but support for it is likely forthcoming.

Handling Drag-and-Drop for Files

If you've ever wanted an easier way to add files to your web application, or you've wondered how some of the newest sites allow you to drag files directly into a page and upload them, the answer is the HTML5 File API. Although the size and status of the entire W3C File API is out of scope for this discussion, many browsers already support a subset of the standard, which allows files to be dragged into an application.

▓ **Note** The W3C File API is documented online at `www.w3.org/TR/FileAPI`.

The File API contains functionality for asynchronously reading files in a web page, uploading them to servers while tracking process, and turning files into page elements. However, affiliated specifications such as drag-and-drop use a subset of the File API, and that is the area where we will focus our attention in this chapter.

Recall that we've already alluded to file drag-and-drop twice in this chapter. First, the `dataTransfer` object contains a property named `files`, which will contain a list of files attached to the drag, if appropriate. For example, if a user drags a file or set of files in from the desktop into your application's web page, the browser will fire drag-and-drop events where the `dataTransfer.files` object has a value. Additionally, browsers that support the previously mentioned `dropzone` attribute allow files of specific MIME types to be valid drops on an element by using the `f:` MIME type prefix.

▓ **Note** Currently, the Safari browser only supports drag-and-drop operations for files. Drags initiated inside a page will fire most drag-and-drop events, but `drop` events only occur if the type of drag is a file.

As usual, you cannot access the files during most drag-and-drop events, because they are protected for security reasons. Although some browsers might let you get access to the list of files during drag events, no browser will let you get access to the file data. In addition, the `dragstart`, `drag`, and `dragend` events that are fired at the drag source element are not triggered in a file drag-and-drop, as the source is the file system itself.

The file items in our file list support the following properties:

- **name**: The full filename with extension

- **type**: The MIME type of the file

- **size**: The size of the file in bytes

- **lastModifiedDate**: The timestamp for when the file contents were last modified

Let's walk through a simple example of file drag-and-drop where we will show the characteristics of any file dropped onto our page, shown in Figure 9-5. This code is contained in the fileDrag.html example included with the book.

There were 2 files dropped.

1. **organizer.html** (*text/html*) : size: 8366 bytes - modified: Sat Oct 01 2011 11:16:54 GMT-0700 (Pacific Daylight Time)
2. **fileDrag.html** (*text/html*) : size: 3466 bytes - modified: Sun Oct 02 2011 13:46:55 GMT-0700 (Pacific Daylight Time)

Figure 9-5. Demo page displaying the characteristics of dropped files

The HTML for our demo is actually quite simple (see Listing 9-13).

Listing 9-13. Markup for File Drop Demo

```
<body>
<div id="droptarget">
<div id="status"></div>
</div>
</body>
```

We have only two elements in the page. A drop target where files will be dropped and a status display area.

As with our last example, we will register drag-and-drop event handlers during page load (see Listing 9-14).

Listing 9-14. Loading and Initialization Code for File Drop Demo

```
var droptarget;

// set the status text in our display
function setStatus(text) {
    document.getElementById("status").innerHTML = text;
}

// ...


function loadDemo() {

    droptarget = document.getElementById("droptarget");
    droptarget.className = "validtarget";

    droptarget.addEventListener("dragenter", handleDragEnter, false);
    droptarget.addEventListener("dragover", handleDragOver, false);
    droptarget.addEventListener("dragleave", handleDragLeave, false);
    droptarget.addEventListener("drop", handleDrop, false);

    setStatus("Drag files into this area.");
}

window.addEventListener("load", loadDemo, false);
```

This time, the drop target receives all of the event handlers. Only a subset of handlers is needed, and we can ignore events that take place at the drag source.

When the user drags files into our drop target, we will display what we know about the drop candidates (see Listing 9-15).

Listing 9-15. File Drop Drag Enter Handler

```
// handle drag events in the drop target
function handleDragEnter(evt) {

    // if the browser supports accessing the file
    // list during drag, we display the file count
    var files = evt.dataTransfer.files;

    if (files)
        setStatus("There are " + evt.dataTransfer.files.length +
            " files in this drag.");
    else
        setStatus("There are unknown items in this drag.");

    droptarget.className = "highlighted";

    evt.stopPropagation();
    evt.preventDefault();
```

```
    return false;
}
```

Although some browsers allow access to the `dataTransfer` files mid-drag, we will handle the case where that information is off-limits. When the count is known, we will display it in the status.

Handling `dragover` and `dragleave` events is straightforward (see Listing 9-16).

Listing 9-16. File drop dragover and dragleave Handlers

```
// preventing the default dragover behavior
// is necessary for successful drops
function handleDragOver(evt) {
    evt.stopPropagation();
    evt.preventDefault();

    return false;
}

// reset the text and status when drags leave
function handleDragLeave(evt) {
    setStatus("Drag files into this area.");

    droptarget.className = "validtarget";

    return false;
}
```

As always, we must cancel `dragover` events to allow drops to be handled by our own code rather than the browser's default behavior, which is usually to display them inline. For a `dragleave`, we only set the status text and style to indicate that drops are no longer valid when the mouse leaves. The bulk of our work is done in the drop handler (see Listing 9-17).

Listing 9-17. File Drop Handler

```
// handle the drop of files
function handleDrop(evt) {
    // cancel the event to prevent viewing the file
    evt.preventDefault();
    evt.stopPropagation();

    var filelist = evt.dataTransfer.files;

    var message = "There were " + filelist.length + " files dropped.";

    // show a detail list for each file in the drag
    message += "<ol>";

    [].forEach.call(filelist, function(file) {
        message += "<li>";
        message += "<strong>" + file.name + "</strong> ";
        message += "(<em>" + file.type + "</em>) : ";
```

```
        message += "size: " + file.size + " bytes - ";
        message += "modified: " + file.lastModifiedDate;
        message += "</li>";
    });

    message += "</ol>";

    setStatus(message);
    droptarget.className = "validtarget";

    return false;
}
```

As discussed previously, it is necessary to cancel the event using preventDefault so that the browser's default drop code is never triggered.

Then, because we have more access to data in the drop handler than during the drag, we can inspect the files attached to the dataTransfer and discover the characteristics of the dropped files. In our example, we will merely display the properties of the files, but with full use of the HTML5 File API, you can read in the contents for local display or upload them to the server powering your application.

Practical Extras

Sometimes there are techniques that don't fit into our regular examples but which nonetheless apply to many types of HTML5 applications. We present to you a short, but common, practical extra here.

Customizing the Drag Display

Usually, the browser will default the visual cursor indicator for a drag operation. An image or link will move with the cursor (sometimes sized down for practical viewing), or a ghosted image of the dragged element will hover at the drag position.

However, if you need to change the default drag image display, the API provides you with a simple API for doing just that. It is only possible to change the drag image during the dragstart handler—once again due to security concerns—but you can do so easily by simply passing the element that represents the appearance of the cursor to the dataTransfer.

```
        var dragImage = document.getElementById("happyTrails");
        evt.dataTransfer.setDragImage(dragImage, 5, 10);
```

Note the offset coordinates passed to the setDragImage call. These x and y coordinates tell the browser which pixel inside the image to use as the point underneath the mouse cursor. For example, by passing in the values 5 and 10 for x and y, respectively, the image will be positioned such that the cursor is 5 pixels from the left and 10 pixels from the top, as shown in Figure 9-6.

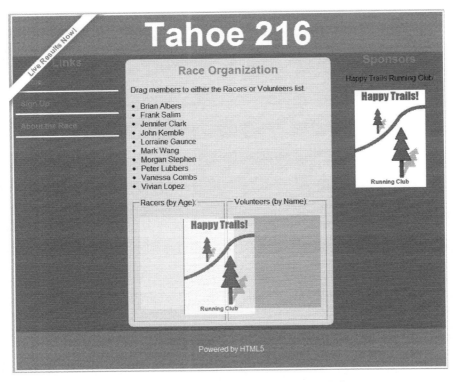

Figure 9-6. *Demo page with a drag image set to the Happy Trails logo*

The drag image does not need to be an image, however. Any element can be set as the drag image; if it is not an image, the browser will create a visual snapshot of it to serve as the cursor display.

Summary

The drag-and-drop API can be a tricky one to master. It involves the correct handling of many events, some of which may be hard to manage if your drop target layout is complex. However, if you are looking for drag operations that cross windows or browsers, or even interact with the desktop, you will need to learn the subtleties of the API. By design, it combines the power of native application drag-and-drop while still working inside the security restrictions of an environment where data must be protected from third-party code.

For more information on using dropped files as application data, make sure to check out the W3C File API. In the next chapter, we will examine the Web Workers API, which will allow you to spawn background scripts outside of your main page to speed up execution and improve the user experience.

CHAPTER 10

Using the Web Workers API

JavaScript is single-threaded. As a result, long-lasting computations (not necessarily due to poorly written code) will block the UI thread and make it impossible to add text to text boxes, click buttons, use CSS effects, and, in most browsers, open new tabs until control has returned. As an answer to that problem, HTML5 Web Workers provide background-processing capabilities to web applications and typically run on separate threads so that JavaScript applications using Web Workers can take advantage of multicore CPUs. Separating long-running tasks into Web Workers also avoids the dreaded slow-script warnings, shown in Figure 10-1, that display when JavaScript loops continue for several seconds.

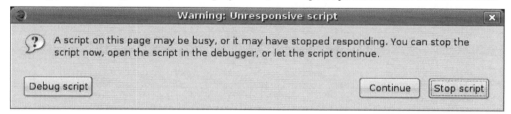

Figure 10-1. Slow script warning in Firefox

As powerful as Web Workers are, there are also certain things they cannot do. For example, when a script is executing inside a Web Worker it cannot access the web page's window object (window.document), which means that Web Workers don't have direct access to the web page and the DOM API. Although Web Workers cannot block the browser UI, they can still consume CPU cycles and make the system less responsive.

Let's say you want to create a web application that has to perform some background number crunching, but you do not want those tasks to interfere with the interactivity of the web page itself. Using Web Workers, you can spawn a Web Worker to perform the tasks and add an event listener to listen to messages from the Web Worker as they are sent.

Another use case for Web Workers could be an application that listens for broadcast news messages from a back-end server, posting messages to the main web page as they are received from the back-end server. This Web Worker might use Web Sockets or Server-Sent Events to talk to the back-end server.

In this chapter, we'll explore what you can do with Web Workers. First, we'll discuss how Web Workers work and the level of browser support available at the time of this writing. Then, we'll discuss how you can use the APIs to create new workers and how to communicate between a worker and the context that spawned it. Finally, we'll show you how you can build an application with Web Workers.

Browser Support for Web Workers

The majority of the modern web browsers support Web Workers. Check the web site http://caniuse.com (search for Web Workers) for the most up-to-date support matrix. While there are polyfill (emulation) libraries available for most other APIs—for example, for HTML5 Canvas there are libraries such as excanvas.js and flashcanvas.js that provide an emulation of the Canvas APIs (using Flash under the covers)—an emulation for Web Workers does not make a lot of sense, however. You can either call your worker code as a worker, or run the same code inline in your page, blocking the UI thread. The improved responsiveness of the worker-based page may just be enough to have people upgrade to a more modern browser (at least we hope it will).

Using the Web Workers API

In this section, we'll explore the use of the Web Workers API in more detail. For the sake of illustration, we've created a simple browser page: echo.html. Using Web Workers is fairly straightforward—you create a Web Worker object and pass in a JavaScript file to be executed. Inside the page you set up an event listener to listen to incoming messages and errors that are posted by the Web Worker and if you want to communicate from the page to the Web Worker, you call postMessage to pass in the required data. The same is true for the code in the Web Worker JavaScript file—event handlers must be set up to process incoming messages and errors, and communication with the page is handled with a call to postMessage.

Checking for Browser Support

Before you call the Web Workers API functions, you will want to make sure there is support in the browser for what you're about to do. This way, you can provide some alternate text, prompting the users of your application to use a more up-to-date browser. Listing 10-1 shows the code you can use to test for browser support.

Listing 10-1. Checking for Browser Support

```
function loadDemo() {
  if (typeof(Worker) !== "undefined") {
    document.getElementById("support").innerHTML =
            "Excellent! Your browser supports Web Workers";
  }
}
```

In this example, you test for browser support in the loadDemo function, which might be called when the page is loaded. A call to typeof(Worker) will return the window's global Worker property, which will be undefined if the browser doesn't support the Web Workers API. In this example, the page is updated to reflect whether there is browser support by updating a previously defined support element on the page with a suitable message, as shown at the top of Figure 10-2.

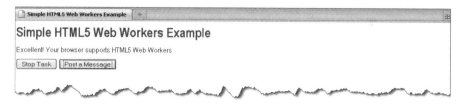

Figure 10-2. Example of showing whether Web Workers is supported

Creating Web Workers

Web Workers are initialized with the URL of a JavaScript file, which contains the code the worker will execute. This code sets event listeners and communicates with the script that spawned it. The URL for the JavaScript file can be a relative or absolute URL with the same origin (the same scheme, host, and port) as the main page:

```
worker = new Worker("echoWorker.js");
```

Inline Workers

To start a worker you need to point to a file. You may have seen some examples of script elements that have the type javascript/worker, as shown in the following example:

```
<script id="myWorker" type="javascript/worker">
```

Don't let this fool you into thinking that you can simply set the type of a script element to run the JavaScript code as a Web Worker. In this case, the type information is used to signal the browser and its JavaScript engine *not* to parse and run the script. In fact, the type may as well have been *anything* other than text/javascript. The script example shown is a building block for *inline Web Workers*—a feature that can be used only if your browser also supports the File System API (Blob Builder or File Writer). In that case you can programmatically find the script block (in the previous case, the element with the myWorker id) and write the Web Worker JavaScript file to disk. After that, you can call the inline Web Worker in your code.

Shared Workers

There is yet another type of worker, which is not widely supported at the time of this writing: the shared Web Worker. A shared Web Worker is like a normal Web Worker, but it can be shared across multiple pages on the same origin. Shared Web Workers introduce the notion of *ports* that are used for PostMessage communication. Shared Web Workers can be useful for data synchronization among multiple pages (or tabs) on the same origin or to share a long-lived resource (like a WebSocket) among several tabs.

The syntax for starting a shared Web Worker is as follows:

```
sharedWorker = new SharedWorker(sharedEchoWorker.js');
```

243

Loading and Executing Additional JavaScript

An application composed of several JavaScript files can contain `<script>` elements that synchronously load JavaScript files as the page loads. However, because Web Workers do not have access to the document object, there is an alternative mechanism for synchronously importing additional JavaScript files from within workers—`importScripts`:

```
importScripts("helper.js");
```

Importing a JavaScript file simply loads and executes JavaScript into an existing worker. Multiple scripts can be imported by the same call to `importScripts`. They are executed in the order specified:

```
importScripts("helper.js", "anotherHelper.js");
```

Communicating with Web Workers

Once the Web Worker is spawned, you can use the `postMessage` API to send data to and from Web Workers. This is the same `postMessage` API that is used for cross-frame and cross-window communication. `postMessage` can be used to send most JavaScript objects, but not functions or objects with cyclic references.

Let's say that you want to build a simple Web Worker example that allows users to send a message to a worker, which in turn echoes back the message. This example may not be very useful in real life, but it's useful enough to explain the concepts you need to build more complex examples. Figure 10-3 shows this example web page and its Web Worker in action. The code for this simple page is listed at the end of this section.

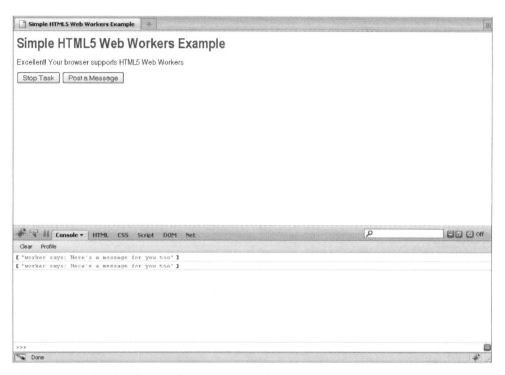

Figure 10-3. *A simple web page that uses Web Workers*

To set up proper communication with your Web Worker, code has to be added to the *main page* (the page that calls the Web Worker) as well as the worker JavaScript file.

Coding the Main Page

To communicate from the page to the Web Worker, you call postMessage to pass in the required data. To listen to incoming messages and errors that are sent by the Web Worker to the page, you set up an event listener.

To set up communication between the main page and the Web Worker, first add the call to postMessage to the main page, as follows:

```
document.getElementById("helloButton").onclick = function() {
    worker.postMessage("Here's a message for you");
}
```

In the preceding example, a message is sent to the Web Worker when the user clicks the **Post a Message** button. Next, add an event listener to the page that listens for messages from the Web Worker:

```
worker.addEventListener("message", messageHandler, true);
```

```
function messageHandler(e) {
    // process message from worker
}
```

Coding the Web Worker JavaScript File

You must now add similar code to the Web Worker JavaScript file—event handlers must be set up to process incoming messages and errors, and communication with the page is handled with a call to postMessage.

To complete the communication between the page and the Web Worker, first, add the call to postMessage; for example, inside a messageHandler function:

```
function messageHandler(e) {
    postMessage("worker says: " + e.data + " too");
}
```

Next, add an event listener to the Web Worker JavaScript file that handles messages coming from the main page:

```
addEventListener("message", messageHandler, true);
```

In this example, the messageHandler function is called immediately when the message is received so that the message can be echoed back.

Note that if this was a shared worker, you would use a slightly different syntax (using a port):

```
sharedWorker.port.addEventListener("message", messageHandler, true);
sharedWorker.port.postMessage("Hello HTML5");
```

In addition, the worker can listen to a connect event for incoming connections. You can use this to count active connections.

Handling Errors

Unhandled errors in a Web Worker script fire error events on the Web Worker object. Listening for these error events is especially important when you are debugging scripts that make use of Web Workers. The following shows an example of an error handling function in a Web Worker JavaScript file that logs errors to the console:

```
function errorHandler(e) {
    console.log(e.message, e);
}
```

To handle the errors, you must add an event listener to the main page:

```
worker.addEventListener("error", errorHandler, true);
```

Most browsers don't have a great way to step through Web Worker code yet, but Google Chrome offers Web Worker debugging capabilities in its Chrome Developer Tools (in the Scripts tab, look for Worker inspectors), as shown in Figure 10-4.

Figure 10-4. Web Worker debugging options in Chrome Developer Tools

Stopping Web Workers

Web Workers don't stop by themselves; but the page that started them can stop them. If the page is closed, Web Workers will be garbage-collected, so rest assured you won't have any zombie workers hanging around performing background tasks. However, you may want to reclaim resources when a Web Worker is no longer needed—perhaps when the main page is notified that the Web Worker has finished its tasks. You may also wish to cancel a long-running task in response to user actions. Calling terminate stops the Web Worker. A terminated Web Worker will no longer respond to messages or perform any additional computations. You cannot restart a worker; instead, you can create a new worker using the same URL:

```
worker.terminate();
```

Using Web Workers within Web Workers

The Worker API can be used inside Web Worker scripts to create subworkers:

```
var subWorker = new Worker("subWorker.js");
```

Lots of Workers

Peter says: "If you spawn a Worker that *recursively* spawns subworker with the same JavaScript source file, you will see some interesting results, to say the least."

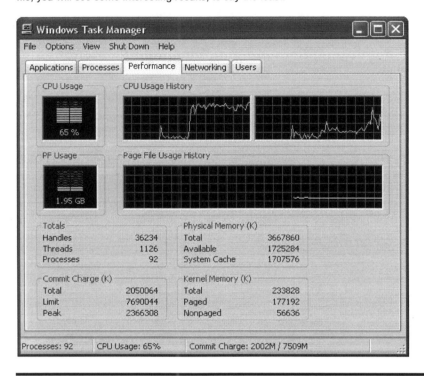

Using Timers

Although Web Workers cannot access the window object, they can make use of the full JavaScript timing API, typically found on the global window:

```
var t = setTimeout(postMessage, 2000, "delayed message");
```

Example Code

For completeness, Listings 10-2 and 10-3 show the code for the simple page and the Web Worker JavaScript file.

Listing 10-2. Simple HTML Page That Calls a Web Worker

```html
<!DOCTYPE html>
<title>Simple Web Workers Example</title>
<link rel="stylesheet" href="styles.css">

<h1>Simple Web Workers Example</h1>
<p id="support">Your browser does not support Web Workers.</p>

<button id="stopButton" >Stop Task</button>
<button id="helloButton" >Post a Message</button>

<script>
    function stopWorker() {
        worker.terminate();
    }

    function messageHandler(e) {
        console.log(e.data);
    }

    function errorHandler(e) {
        console.warn(e.message, e);
    }

    function loadDemo() {
        if (typeof(Worker) !== "undefined") {
            document.getElementById("support").innerHTML =
                "Excellent! Your browser supports Web Workers";

            worker = new Worker("echoWorker.js");
            worker.addEventListener("message", messageHandler, true);
            worker.addEventListener("error", errorHandler, true);

            document.getElementById("helloButton").onclick = function() {
                worker.postMessage("Here's a message for you");
        }

            document.getElementById("stopButton").onclick = stopWorker;
        }
}

window.addEventListener("load", loadDemo, true);
</script>
```

Listing 10-3. Simple Web Worker JavaScript File

```javascript
function messageHandler(e) {
    postMessage("worker says: " + e.data + " too");
}
addEventListener("message", messageHandler, true);
```

Building an Application with Web Workers

So far, we've focused on using the different Web Worker APIs. Let's see how powerful the Web Workers API can really be by building an application: a web page with an image-blurring filter, parallelized to run on multiple Web Workers. Figure 10-5 shows what this application looks like when you start it.

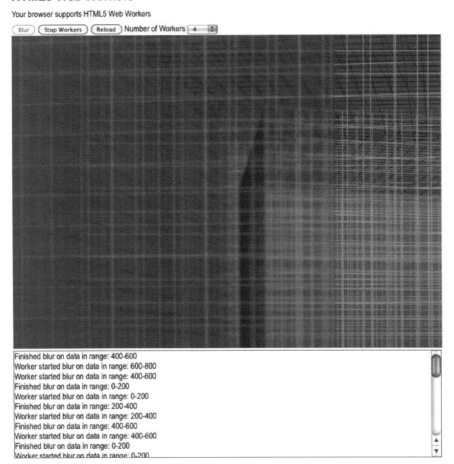

Figure 10-5. Web Worker–based web page with image-blurring filter

This application sends image data from a canvas to several Web Workers (you can specify how many). The Web Workers then process the image with a simple box-blur filter. This may take several seconds, depending on the size of the image and the computational resources available (even machines with fast CPUs may have load from other processes, causing JavaScript execution to take more wall-clock time to complete). Figure 10-6 shows the same page after running the blur filtering process for a while.

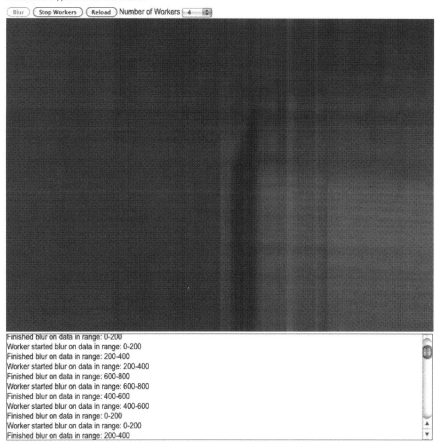

Figure 10-6. *Image-blurring web page after running for a while*

However, because the heavy lifting takes place in Web Workers, there is no danger of slow-script warnings and, therefore, no need to manually partition the task into scheduled slices—something you would have to consider if you could not use Web Workers.

Coding the blur.js Helper Script

Inside the blur.js application page, we can use a straightforward implementation of a blur filter that loops until it has completely processed its input, as shown in Listing 10-4.

Listing 10-4. A JavaScript Box-blur Implementation in the File blur.js

```
function inRange(i, width, height) {
    return ((i>=0) && (i < width*height*4));
}

function averageNeighbors(imageData, width, height, i) {
    var v = imageData[i];

    // cardinal directions
    var north = inRange(i-width*4, width, height) ? imageData[i-width*4] : v;
    var south = inRange(i+width*4, width, height) ? imageData[i+width*4] : v;
    var west = inRange(i-4, width, height) ? imageData[i-4] : v;
    var east = inRange(i+4, width, height) ? imageData[i+4] : v;

    // diagonal neighbors
    var ne = inRange(i-width*4+4, width, height) ? imageData[i-width*4+4] : v;
    var nw = inRange(i-width*4-4, width, height) ? imageData[i-width*4-4] : v;
    var se = inRange(i+width*4+4, width, height) ? imageData[i+width*4+4] : v;
    var sw = inRange(i+width*4-4, width, height) ? imageData[i+width*4-4] : v;

    // average
    var newVal = Math.floor((north + south + east + west + se + sw + ne + nw + v)/9);

    if (isNaN(newVal)) {
        sendStatus("bad value " + i + " for height " + height);
        throw new Error("NaN");
    }
    return newVal;
}

function boxBlur(imageData, width, height) {
    var data = [];
    var val = 0;
    for (var i=0; i<width*height*4; i++) {
        val = averageNeighbors(imageData, width, height, i);
        data[i] = val;
    }

    return data;
}
```

In brief, this algorithm blurs an image by averaging nearby pixel values. For a large image with millions of pixels, this takes a substantial amount of time. It is very undesirable to run a loop such as this in the UI thread. Even if a slow-script warning did not appear, the page UI would be unresponsive until the loop terminated. For this reason, it makes a good example of background computation in Web Workers.

Coding the blur.html Application Page

Listing 10-5 shows the code for the HTML page that calls the Web Worker. The HTML for this example is kept simple for reasons of clarity. The purpose here is not to build a beautiful interface, but to provide a simple skeleton that can control the Web Workers and demonstrate them in action. In this application, a canvas element that displays the input image is injected into the page. We have buttons to start blurring the image, stop blurring, reset the image, and specify the number of workers to spawn.

Listing 10-5. *Code for the Page blur.html*

```
<!DOCTYPE html>
<title>Web Workers</title>
<link rel="stylesheet" href = "styles.css">

<h1>Web Workers</h1>

<p id="status">Your browser does not support Web Workers.</p>


<button id="startBlurButton" disabled>Blur</button>
<button id="stopButton" disabled>Stop Workers</button>
<button onclick="document.location = document.location;">Reload</button>

<label for="workerCount">Number of Workers</label>
<select id="workerCount">
    <option>1</option>
    <option selected>2</option>
    <option>4</option>
    <option>8</option>
    <option>16</option>
</select>

<div id="imageContainer"></div>
<div id="logOutput"></div>
```

Next, let's add the code to create workers to the file blur.html. We instantiate a worker object, passing in a URL of a JavaScript file. Each instantiated worker will run the same code but be responsible for processing different parts of the input image:

```
function initWorker(src) {
    var worker = new Worker(src);
    worker.addEventListener("message", messageHandler, true);
    worker.addEventListener("error", errorHandler, true);
    return worker;
}
```

Let's add the error handling code to the file blur.html, as follows. In the event of an error in the worker, the page will be able to display an error message instead of continuing unaware. Our example shouldn't encounter any trouble, but listening for error events is generally a good practice and is invaluable for debugging.

```
function errorHandler(e) {
```

```
        log("error: " + e.message);
}
```

Coding the blurWorker.js Web Worker Script

Next, we add the code that our workers use to communicate with the page to the file blurWorker.js (see Listing 10-6). As the Web Workers finish blocks of computation, they can use postMessage to inform the page that they have made progress. We will use this information to update the image displayed on the main page. After creation, our Web Workers wait for a message containing image data and the instruction to commence blurring. This message is a JavaScript object containing the type of message and the image data represented as an array of Numbers.

Listing 10-6. Sending and Handling Image Data in the File blurWorker.js

```javascript
function sendStatus(statusText) {
    postMessage({"type" : "status",
                 "statusText" : statusText}
               );
}

function messageHandler(e) {
    var messageType = e.data.type;
    switch (messageType) {
        case ("blur"):
            sendStatus("Worker started blur on data in range: " +
                           e.data.startX + "-" + (e.data.startX+e.data.width));
            var imageData = e.data.imageData;
            imageData = boxBlur(imageData, e.data.width, e.data.height, e.data.startX);

            postMessage({"type" : "progress",
                         "imageData" : imageData,
                         "width" : e.data.width,
                         "height" : e.data.height,
                         "startX" : e.data.startX
                        });
            sendStatus("Finished blur on data in range: " +
                           e.data.startX + "-" + (e.data.width+e.data.startX));
            break;
        default:
            sendStatus("Worker got message: " + e.data);
    }
}
addEventListener("message", messageHandler, true);
```

Communicating with the Web Workers

In the file blur.html, we can use our workers by sending them some data and arguments that represent a blur task. This is done by using postMessage to send a JavaScript object containing the Array of RGBA image data, the dimensions of the source image, and the range of pixels for which the worker is responsible. Each worker processes a different section of the image based on the message it receives:

```
function sendBlurTask(worker, i, chunkWidth) {
      var chunkHeight = image.height;
      var chunkStartX = i * chunkWidth;
      var chunkStartY = 0;
      var data = ctx.getImageData(chunkStartX, chunkStartY,
                                  chunkWidth, chunkHeight).data;

      worker.postMessage({'type' : 'blur',
                          'imageData' : data,
                          'width' : chunkWidth,
                          'height' : chunkHeight,
                          'startX' : chunkStartX});
}
```

Canvas Image Data

Frank says: "postMessage is specified to allow efficient serialization of imageData objects for use with the canvas API. Some browsers that include the Worker and postMessage APIs may not support the extended serialization capabilities of postMessage yet.

Because of this, our image processing example presented in this chapter sends imageData.data (which serializes like a JavaScript Array) instead of sending the imageData object itself. As the Web Workers compute their tasks, they communicate their status and results back to the page. Listing 10-6 shows how data is sent from the worker(s) to the page after the blur filter has processed it. Again, the message contains a JavaScript object with fields for image data and coordinates marking the boundaries of the processed section."

On the HTML page side, a message handler consumes this data and uses it to update the canvas with the new pixel values. As processed image data comes in, the result is immediately visible. We now have a sample application that can process images while potentially taking advantage of multiple CPU cores. Moreover, we didn't lock up the UI and make it unresponsive while the Web Workers were active. Figure 10-7 shows the application in action.

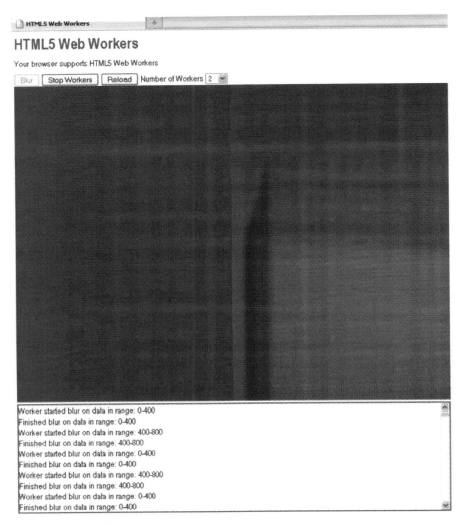

Figure 10-7. The blur application in action

The Application in Action

To see this example in action, the page blur.html has to be served up by a web server (for example, Apache or Python's SimpleHTTPServer). To following steps show how you can use Python SimpleHTTPServer to run the application:

1. Install Python.

2. Navigate to the directory that contains the example file (blur.html).

3. Start Python as follows:

```
python -m SimpleHTTPServer 9999
```

4. Open a browser and navigate to http://localhost:9999/blur.html. You should now see the page shown in Figure 10-7.

5. If you leave it running for a while, you will see the different quadrants of the image blur slowly. The number of quadrants that blur at the same time depends on the number of workers you started.

Example Code

For completeness, Listings 10-7, 10-8, and 10-9 contain the full code for the example application.

Listing 10-7. Content of the File blur.html

```
<!DOCTYPE html>
<title>Web Workers</title>
<link rel="stylesheet" href = "styles.css">

<h1>Web Workers</h1>

<p id="status">Your browser does not support Web Workers.</p>


<button id="startBlurButton" disabled>Blur</button>
<button id="stopButton" disabled>Stop Workers</button>
<button onclick="document.location = document.location;">Reload</button>

<label for="workerCount">Number of Workers</label>
<select id="workerCount">
    <option>1</option>
    <option selected>2</option>
    <option>4</option>
    <option>8</option>
    <option>16</option>
</select>

<div id="imageContainer"></div>
<div id="logOutput"></div>
<script>

var imageURL = "example2.png";
var image;
var ctx;
var workers = [];

function log(s) {
    var logOutput = document.getElementById("logOutput");
```

```
        logOutput.innerHTML = s + "<br>" + logOutput.innerHTML;
    }

    function setRunningState(p) {
        // while running, the stop button is enabled and the start button is not
        document.getElementById("startBlurButton").disabled = p;
        document.getElementById("stopButton").disabled = !p;
    }

    function initWorker(src) {
        var worker = new Worker(src);
        worker.addEventListener("message", messageHandler, true);
        worker.addEventListener("error", errorHandler, true);
        return worker;
    }

    function startBlur() {
        var workerCount = parseInt(document.getElementById("workerCount").value);
        var width = image.width/workerCount;

        for (var i=0; i<workerCount; i++) {
            var worker = initWorker("blurWorker.js");
            worker.index = i;
            worker.width = width;
            workers[i] = worker;

            sendBlurTask(worker, i, width);
        }
        setRunningState(true);
    }

    function sendBlurTask(worker, i, chunkWidth) {
            var chunkHeight = image.height;
            var chunkStartX = i * chunkWidth;
            var chunkStartY = 0;
            var data = ctx.getImageData(chunkStartX, chunkStartY,
                                        chunkWidth, chunkHeight).data;

            worker.postMessage({'type' : 'blur',
                                'imageData' : data,
                                'width' : chunkWidth,
                                'height' : chunkHeight,
                                'startX' : chunkStartX});
    }

    function stopBlur() {
        for (var i=0; i<workers.length; i++) {
            workers[i].terminate();
        }
        setRunningState(false);
    }
```

```javascript
function messageHandler(e) {
    var messageType = e.data.type;
    switch (messageType) {
        case ("status"):
            log(e.data.statusText);
            break;
        case ("progress"):
            var imageData = ctx.createImageData(e.data.width, e.data.height);

            for (var i = 0; i<imageData.data.length; i++) {
                var val = e.data.imageData[i];
                if (val === null || val > 255 || val < 0) {
                    log("illegal value: " + val + " at " + i);
                    return;
                }

                imageData.data[i] = val;
            }
            ctx.putImageData(imageData, e.data.startX, 0);

            // blur the same tile again
            sendBlurTask(e.target, e.target.index, e.target.width);
            break;
        default:
            break;
    }
}

function errorHandler(e) {
    log("error: " + e.message);
}

function loadImageData(url) {

    var canvas = document.createElement('canvas');
    ctx = canvas.getContext('2d');
    image = new Image();
    image.src = url;

    document.getElementById("imageContainer").appendChild(canvas);

    image.onload = function(){
        canvas.width = image.width;
        canvas.height = image.height;
        ctx.drawImage(image, 0, 0);
        window.imgdata = ctx.getImageData(0, 0, image.width, image.height);
        n = ctx.createImageData(image.width, image.height);
        setRunningState(false);
        log("Image loaded: " + image.width + "x" + image.height + " pixels");
    };
}
```

259

```
function loadDemo() {
    log("Loading image data");

    if (typeof(Worker) !== "undefined") {
        document.getElementById("status").innerHTML = "Your browser supports Web Workers";

        document.getElementById("stopButton").onclick = stopBlur;
        document.getElementById("startBlurButton").onclick = startBlur;

        loadImageData(imageURL);

        document.getElementById("startBlurButton").disabled = true;
        document.getElementById("stopButton").disabled = true;
    }

}

window.addEventListener("load", loadDemo, true);
</script>
```

Listing 10-8. *Content of the File blurWorker.js*

```
importScripts("blur.js");

function sendStatus(statusText) {
    postMessage({"type" : "status",
                "statusText" : statusText}
               );
}

function messageHandler(e) {
    var messageType = e.data.type;
    switch (messageType) {
        case ("blur"):
            sendStatus("Worker started blur on data in range: " +
                        e.data.startX + "-" + (e.data.startX+e.data.width));
            var imageData = e.data.imageData;
            imageData = boxBlur(imageData, e.data.width, e.data.height, e.data.startX);

            postMessage({"type" : "progress",
                        "imageData" : imageData,
                        "width" : e.data.width,
                        "height" : e.data.height,
                        "startX" : e.data.startX
                       });
            sendStatus("Finished blur on data in range: " +
                        e.data.startX + "-" + (e.data.width+e.data.startX));
            break;
        default:
            sendStatus("Worker got message: " + e.data);
    }
}
```

```
addEventListener("message", messageHandler, true);
```

Listing 10-9. *Content of the File blur.js*

```
function inRange(i, width, height) {
    return ((i>=0) && (i < width*height*4));
}

function averageNeighbors(imageData, width, height, i) {
    var v = imageData[i];

    // cardinal directions
    var north = inRange(i-width*4, width, height) ? imageData[i-width*4] : v;
    var south = inRange(i+width*4, width, height) ? imageData[i+width*4] : v;
    var west = inRange(i-4, width, height) ? imageData[i-4] : v;
    var east = inRange(i+4, width, height) ? imageData[i+4] : v;

    // diagonal neighbors
    var ne = inRange(i-width*4+4, width, height) ? imageData[i-width*4+4] : v;
    var nw = inRange(i-width*4-4, width, height) ? imageData[i-width*4-4] : v;
    var se = inRange(i+width*4+4, width, height) ? imageData[i+width*4+4] : v;
    var sw = inRange(i+width*4-4, width, height) ? imageData[i+width*4-4] : v;

    // average
    var newVal = Math.floor((north + south + east + west + se + sw + ne + nw + v)/9);

    if (isNaN(newVal)) {
        sendStatus("bad value " + i + " for height " + height);
        throw new Error("NaN");
    }
    return newVal;
}

function boxBlur(imageData, width, height) {
    var data = [];
    var val = 0;

    for (var i=0; i<width*height*4; i++) {
        val = averageNeighbors(imageData, width, height, i);
        data[i] = val;
    }

    return data;
}
```

Summary

In this chapter, you have seen how Web Workers can be used to create web applications with background processing. This chapter showed you how Web Workers (and inline and shared Web Workers) work. We discussed how you can use the APIs to create new workers and how you communicate between a worker and the context that spawned it. Finally, we showed you how you can build an application with Web Workers. In the next chapter, we'll demonstrate more ways that HTML5 lets you keep local copies of data and reduce the amount of network overhead in your applications.

CHAPTER 11

Using the Storage APIs

In this chapter, we will explore what you can do with HTML5 Web Storage—sometimes referred to as DOMStorage—an API that makes it easy to retain data across web requests. Before the Web Storage API, remote web servers needed to store any data that persisted by sending it back and forth from client to server. With the advent of the Web Storage API, developers can now store data directly on the client side in the browser for repeated access across requests or to be retrieved long after you completely close the browser, thus reducing network traffic.

We'll first look at how Web Storage differs from cookies and then explore how you can store and retrieve data. Next, we will look at the differences between localStorage and sessionStorage, the attributes and functions that the storage interface provides, and how you can handle Web Storage events. We wrap up with a look at Web SQL Database API and a few practical extras.

Overview of Web Storage

To explain the Web Storage API, it is best to review its predecessor, the intriguingly named cookie. Browser cookies—named after an age-old programming technique for passing small data values between programs—are a built-in way of sending text values back and forth from server to browser. Servers can use the values they put into these cookies to track user information across web pages. Cookie values are then transmitted back and forth every time a user visits a domain. For example, cookies can store a session identifier that allows a web server to know which shopping cart belongs to a user by storing a unique ID in a browser cookie that matches the server's own shopping cart database. Then, as a user moves from page to page, the shopping cart can be updated consistently. Another use for cookies is to store local values into an application so that these values can be used on subsequent page loads.

Cookie values can also be used for operations that are slightly less desirable to users, such as tracking which pages a user visits for the sake of targeted advertising. As such, some users have demanded that browsers include functionality to allow them to block or remove cookies either all of the time or for specific sites.

Love them or hate them, cookies have been supported by browsers since the earliest days of the Netscape browser, back in the mid-1990s. Cookies are also one of the few features that have been consistently supported across browser vendors since the early days of the Web. Cookies allow data to be tracked across multiple requests, as long as that data is carefully coordinated between the server and the browser code. Despite their ubiquity, cookies have some well-known drawbacks:

- Cookies are extremely limited in size. Generally, only about 4KB of data can be set in a cookie, meaning they are unacceptable for large values such as documents or mail.

- Cookies are transmitted back and forth from server to browser on every request scoped to that cookie. Not only does this mean that cookie data is visible on the network, making them a security risk when not encrypted, but also that any data persisted as cookies will be consuming network bandwidth every time a URL is loaded. As such, the relatively small size of cookies makes more sense.

In many cases, the same results could be achieved without involving a network or remote server. This is where the HTML5 Web Storage API comes in. By using this simple API, developers can store values in easily retrievable JavaScript objects that persist across page loads. By using either `sessionStorage` or `localStorage`, developers can choose to let those values survive either across page loads in a single window or tab or across browser restarts, respectively. Stored data is not transmitted across the network, and is easily accessed on return visits to a page. Furthermore, larger values can be persisted using the Web Storage API values as high as a few megabytes. This makes Web Storage suitable for document and file data that would quickly blow out the size limit of a cookie.

Browser Support for Web Storage

Web Storage is one of the most widely adopted features of HTML5. In fact, since the arrival of Internet Explorer 8 in 2009 all currently shipping browser versions support Web Storage in some capacity. At the time of this publication, the market share of browsers that do not support storage is dwindling down into single digit percentages.

Web Storage is one of the safest new APIs to use in your web applications today because of its widespread support. As usual, though, it is a good idea to first test if Web Storage is supported before you use it. The subsequent section "Checking for Browser Support" will show you how you can programmatically check if Web Storage is supported.

Using the Web Storage API

The Web Storage API is surprisingly simple to use. We'll start by covering basic storage and retrieval of values and then move on to the differences between `sessionStorage` and `localStorage`. Finally, we'll look at the more advanced aspects of the API, such as event notification when values change.

Checking for Browser Support

The storage database for a given domain is accessed directly from the `window` object. Therefore, determining if a user's browser supports the Web Storage API is as easy as checking for the existence of `window.sessionStorage` or `window.localStorage`. Listing 11-1 shows a routine that checks for storage support and displays a message about the browser's support for the Web Storage API. Instead of using this code, you can also use the JavaScript utility library Modernizr, which handles some cases that may result in a false positive.

Listing 11-1. *Checking for Web Storage Support*

```
function checkStorageSupport() {

  //sessionStorage
  if (window.sessionStorage) {
    alert('This browser supports sessionStorage');
  } else {
    alert('This browser does NOT support sessionStorage');
  }

  //localStorage
  if (window.localStorage) {
    alert('This browser supports localStorage');
  } else {
    alert('This browser does NOT support localStorage');
  }
}
```

Figure 11-1 shows this check for storage support in action.

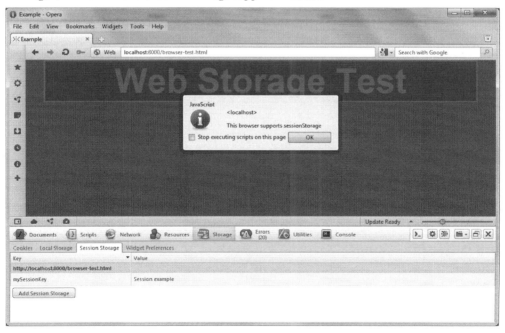

Figure 11-1. *Checking for browser support in Opera*

Some browsers do not support sessionStorage for files accessed directly from the file system. Make sure you serve up the pages from a web server when you run the examples in this chapter! For example, you can start Python's simple HTTP server in the code/storage directory as follows:

```
python -m SimpleHTTPServer 9999
```

After that, you can access the files at http://localhost:9999/. For example, http://localhost:9999/browser-test.html.

However, you are free to use any server or URL location to run the examples.

■ **Note** If a user is browsing with his browser set to "private" mode, then localStorage values will not actually persist once the browser is shut down. This is by design, as users of this mode have explicitly chosen to leave no traces behind. Nonetheless, your application should respond gracefully if storage values are not available in a later browsing session.

Setting and Retrieving Values

To begin, we'll focus on the session storage capability as you learn to set and retrieve simple values in a page. Setting a value can easily be done in a single statement, which we'll initially write using the long-hand notation:

```
sessionStorage.setItem('myFirstKey', 'myFirstValue');
```

There are a few important points to notice from this storage access statement:

- We can omit the reference to the window for a shorthand notation, as the storage objects are made available in the default page context.

- The function we are calling is setItem, which takes a key string and a value string. Although some browsers might support passing in nonstring values, the specification only allows strings as values.

- This particular call will set into the session storage the string myFirstValue, which can later be retrieved by the key myFirstKey.

To retrieve the value, the long-hand notation involves making a call to the getItem function. For example, if we augmented our previous example with the following statement

```
alert(sessionStorage.getItem('myFirstKey'));
```

The browser raises a JavaScript alert displaying the text myFirstValue. As you can see, setting and retrieving values from the Web Storage API is very straightforward.

However, there is an even simpler way to access the storage objects in your code. You are also able to use expando-properties to set values in storage. Using this approach, the setItem and getItem calls can be avoided entirely by simply setting and retrieving values corresponding to the key-value pair directly on the sessionStorage object. Using this approach, our value set call can be rewritten as follows:

```
sessionStorage.myFirstKey = 'myFirstValue';
```

Or even

```
sessionStorage['myFirstKey'] = 'myFirstValue';
```

Similarly, the value retrieval call can be rewritten as:

```
alert(sessionStorage.myFirstKey);
```

We'll use these formats interchangeably in the chapter for the sake of readability.

That's it for the basics. You now have all the knowledge you need to use session storage in your application. However, you might be wondering what's so special about this `sessionStorage` object. After all, JavaScript allows you to set and get properties on nearly any object. The difference is in the scope. What you may not have realized is that our example set and get calls do not need to occur in the same web page. As long as pages are served from the same origin—the combination of scheme, host, and port—then values set on `sessionStorage` can be retrieved from other pages using the same keys. This also applies to subsequent loads of the same page. As a developer, you are probably used to the idea that changes made in script will disappear whenever a page is reloaded. That is no longer true for values that are set in the Web Storage API; they will continue to exist across page loads.

Plugging Data Leaks

How long do the values persist? For objects set into `sessionStorage`, they will persist as long as the browser window (or tab) is not closed. As soon as a user closes the window—or browser, for that matter—the `sessionStorage` values are cleared out. It is useful to consider a `sessionStorage` value to be somewhat like a sticky note reminder. Values put into `sessionStorage` won't last long, and you should not put anything truly valuable into them, as the values are not guaranteed to be around whenever you are looking for them.

Why, then, would you choose to use the session storage area in your web application? Session storage is perfect for short-lived processes that would normally be represented in wizards or dialogs. If you have data to store over the course of a few pages, that you would not be keen to have resurface the next time a user visits your application, feel free to store them in the session storage area. In the past, these types of values might be submitted by forms and cookies and transmitted back and forth on every page load. Using storage eliminates that overhead.

The `sessionStorage` API has another very specific use that solves a problem that has plagued many web-applications: scoping of values. Take, for example, a shopping application that lets you purchase airline tickets. In such an application, preference data such as the ideal departure date and return date could be sent back and forth from browser to server using cookies. This allows the server to remember previous choices as the user moves through the application, picking seats and a choice of meals.

However, it is very common for users to open multiple windows as they shop for travel deals, comparing flights from different vendors for the same departure time. This causes problems in a cookie system, because if a user switches back and forth between browser windows while comparing prices and availability, they are likely to set cookie values in one window that will be unexpectedly applied to another window served from the same URL on its next operation. This is sometimes referred to as leaking data and is caused by the fact that cookies are shared based on the origin where they are stored. Figure 11-2 shows how this can play out.

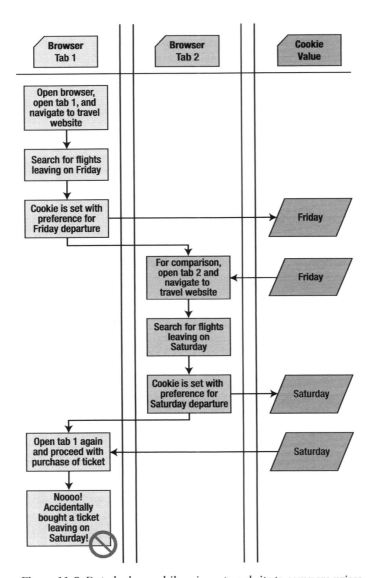

Figure 11-2. Data leakage while using a travel site to compare prices

Using sessionStorage, on the other hand, allows temporary values like a departure date to be saved across pages that access the application but not leak into other windows where the user is also browsing for flights. Therefore, those preferences will be isolated to each window where the corresponding flights are booked.

Local Versus Session Storage

Sometimes, an application needs values that persist beyond the life of a single tab or window or need to be shared across multiple views. In these cases, it is more appropriate to use a different Web Storage implementation: localStorage. The good news is that you already know how to use localStorage. The only programmatic difference between sessionStorage and localStorage is the name by which each is accessed—through the sessionStorage and localStorage objects, respectively. The primary behavioral differences are how long the values persist and how they are shared. Table 11-1 shows the differences between the two types of storage.

Table 11-1. Differences Between sessionStorage and localStorage

sessionStorage	localStorage
Values persist only as long as the window or tab in which they were stored (survives a browser refresh; not a browser restart).	Values persist beyond window and browser lifetimes.
Values are only visible within the window or tab that created them.	Values are shared across every window or tab running at the same origin.

Keep in mind that browsers sometimes redefine the lifespan of a tab or window. For example, some browsers will save and restore the current session when a browser crashes, or when a user shuts down the display with many open tabs. In these cases, the browser may choose to keep the sessionStorage around when the browser restarts or resumes. So, in effect, sessionStorage may live longer than you think!

Other Web Storage API Attributes and Functions

The Web Storage API is one of the simplest in the HTML5 set. We have already looked at both explicit and implicit ways to set and retrieve data from the session and local storage areas. Let's complete our survey of the API by looking at the full set of available attributes and function calls.

The sessionStorage and localStorage objects can be retrieved from the window object of the document in which they are being used. Other than their names and the duration of their values, they are identical in functionality. Both implement the Storage interface, which is shown in Listing 11-2.

Listing 11-2. The Storage Interface

```
interface Storage {
  readonly attribute unsigned long length;
  getter DOMString key(in unsigned long index);
  getter any getItem(in DOMString key);
  setter creator void setItem(in DOMString key, in any data);
  deleter void removeItem(in DOMString key);
  void clear();
};
```

Let's look at the attributes and functions here in more detail.

- The length attribute specifies how many key-value pairs are currently stored in the storage object. Remember that storage objects are specific to their origin, so that implies that the items (and length) of the storage object only reflect the items stored for the current origin.

- The key(index) function allows retrieval of a given key. Generally, this is most useful when you wish to iterate across all the keys in a particular storage object. Keys are zero-based, meaning that the first key is at index (0) and the last key is at index (length – 1). Once a key is retrieved, it can be used to fetch its corresponding value. Keys will retain their indices over the life of a given storage object unless a key or one of its predecessors is removed.

- As you've already seen, getItem(key) function is one way to retrieve the value based on a given key. The other is to reference the key as an array index to the storage object. In both cases, the value null will be returned if the key does not exist in storage.

- Similarly, setItem(key, value) function will put a value into storage under the specified key name, or replace an existing value if one already exists under that key name. Note that it is possible to receive an error when setting an item value; if the user has storage turned off for that site, or if the storage is already filled to its maximum amount, a QUOTA_EXCEEDED_ERR error will be thrown during the attempt. Make sure to handle such an error should your application depend on proper storage behavior.

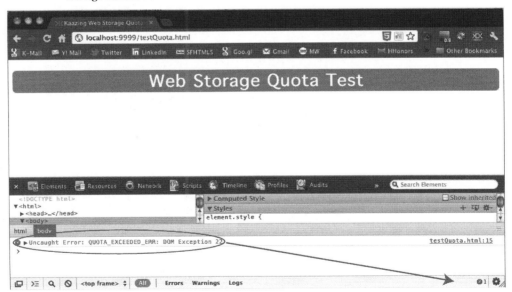

Figure 11-3. Quota Exceeded Error in Chrome

- The removeItem(key) function does exactly as you might expect. If a value is currently in storage under the specified key, this call will remove it. If no item was stored under that key, no action is taken.

■ **Note** Unlike some collection and data frameworks, removing an item does not return the old value as a result of the call to remove it. Make sure you've stored any copy you need independent of the removal.

- Finally, the clear() function removes all values from the storage list. It is safe to call this on an empty storage object; as such, a call will simply do nothing.

DISK SPACE QUOTA

Peter says: "The specification recommends that browsers allow five megabytes per origin. Browsers should prompt the user when the quota is reached in order to grant more space and may also provide ways for users to see how much space each origin is using.

In reality, the behavior is still a bit inconsistent. Some browsers silently allow a larger quota or prompt for a space increase, while others simply throw the QUOTA_EXCEEDED_ERR error shown in Figure 11-3, while others, like Opera, shown in Figure 11-4, implement a nice way to allocate more quota on the fly. The test file testQuota.html used in this example is located in the code/storage directory."

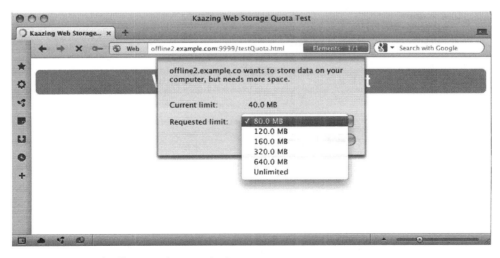

Figure 11-4. On-the-fly Quota increase in Opera

Communicating Web Storage Updates

Sometimes, things get a little more complicated, and storage needs to be accessed by more than one page, browser tab, or worker. Perhaps your application needs to trigger many operations in succession whenever a storage value is changed. For just these cases, the Web Storage API includes an event mechanism to allow notifications of data updates to be communicated to interested listeners. Web Storage events are fired on the window object for every window of the same origin as the storage operation, regardless of whether or not the listening window is doing any storage operations itself.

■ **Note** Web Storage events can be used to communicate between windows on the same origin. This will be explored a bit more thoroughly in the "Practical Extras" section.

To register to receive the storage events of a window's origin, simply register an event listener, for example:

```
window.addEventListener("storage", displayStorageEvent, true);
```

As you can see, the name storage is used to indicate interest in storage events. Any time a Storage event—either sessionStorage or localStorage—for that origin is raised any registered event listener will receive the storage event as the specified event handler. The storage event itself takes the form shown in Listing 11-3.

Listing 11-3. The StorageEvent Interface

```
interface StorageEvent : Event {
  readonly attribute DOMString key;
  readonly attribute any oldValue;
  readonly attribute any newValue;
  readonly attribute DOMString url;
  readonly attribute Storage storageArea;
};
```

The StorageEvent object will be the first object passed to the event handler, and it contains all the information necessary to understand the nature of the storage change.

- The key attribute contains the key value that was updated or removed in the storage.

- The oldValue contains the previous value corresponding to the key before it was updated, and the newValue contains the value after the change. If the value was newly added, the oldValue will be null, and if the value has been removed, the newValue will be null.

- The url will point to the origin where the storage event occurred.

- Finally, the storageArea provides a convenient reference to the sessionStorage or localStorage where the value was changed. This gives the handler an easy way to query the storage for current values or make changes based on other storage changes.

Listing 11-4 shows a simple event handler, which will raise an alert dialog with the contents of any storage event fired on the page's origin.

Listing 11-4. Event Handler that Displays Content of a Storage Event

```
// display the contents of a storage event
function displayStorageEvent(e) {
  var logged = "key:" + e.key + ", newValue:" + e.newValue + ", oldValue:" +
               e.oldValue +", url:" + e.url + ", storageArea:" + e.storageArea;

  alert(logged);
}

// add a storage event listener for this origin
window.addEventListener("storage", displayStorageEvent, true);
```

Exploring Web Storage

Since Web Storage is very similar in function to cookies, it is not too surprising that the most advanced browsers are treating them in a very similar manner. Values that are stored into localStorage or sessionStorage can be browsed similar to cookies in the latest browsers, as shown in Figure 11-5.

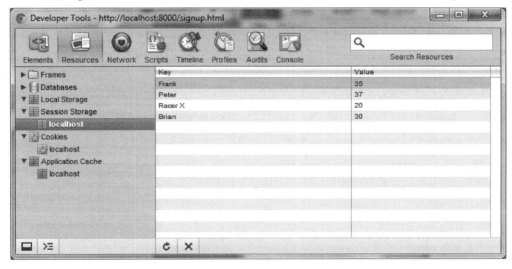

Figure 11-5. Storage values in Google Chrome's Resources Panel

This interface also grants users the ability to remove storage values as desired and easily see what values a given web site is recording while they visit the pages. Not surprisingly, the Safari browser has a similar, unified display for cookies and storage, as it is based on the same underlying WebKit rendering engine as Chrome is. Figure 11-6 shows the Safari Resources panel.

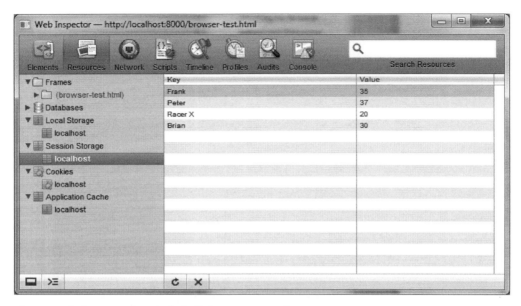

Figure 11-6. Storage values in Safari's Resources panel

Like the other browsers, the Opera Dragonfly storage display allows users to not only browse and delete storage values but also create them as shown in Figure 11-7.

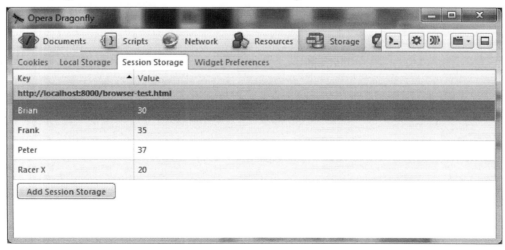

Figure 11-7. Storage values in Opera's Storage panel

As Web Storage becomes more widely implemented by the various browser vendors, expect both the capacity and tooling available to users and developers to expand rapidly.

Building an Application with Web Storage

Now, let's put together what you've learned by integrating storage into a web application. As applications grow more complex, it becomes increasingly important to manage as much data as possible without server interaction. Keeping data local to the client reduces network traffic and increases responsiveness by fetching data from a local machine instead of a remote location.

One common problem developers grapple with is how to manage data as users move from page to page within an application. Traditionally, web applications achieve this by storing data on a server and moving it back and forth while the user navigates pages. Alternatively, the application may attempt to keep the user in a single page and update everything dynamically. However, users are prone to wander, and getting data back into the display quickly when a user returns to your application's page is a great way to enhance the user experience.

In our sample application, we'll show how to store temporary application data locally while the user moves from page to page on a web site and quickly load it from storage on each page. To accomplish this, we'll build on the examples of previous chapters. In Chapter 5, we showed how easy it is to gather a user's current location. Then, in Chapter 7, we demonstrated how to take location data and send it to a remote server so that it can be viewed by any number of interested users. Here, we will go one step further: we will listen for broadcasted location data delivered via a WebSocket and store it in local storage so that it is immediately available as users move from page to page.

Imagine that our running club has live location information from its race participants being broadcast from their mobile devices and shared via a WebSocket server. It would be simple for a web application to display the current position of every racer live and in real time, as the racers upload new position information during the race. And a smart web site would cache those race positions to display them quickly as a user navigated among the pages of the site. That's exactly what we're going to build.

In order to achieve this, we'll need to introduce a demonstration web site that can save and restore our racer data. We've created a three-page example running race site and placed it in our online resources in the folder code/storage, but you can use any site of your choosing for your own demonstration. The key here is merely that you have multiple web pages that are easily traversed by a user. We will insert a bit of dynamic content into those pages to represent a live leader board, or a list of race participants and their current distance from the finish line. Figure 11-8 shows the three pages that make up the race site.

Figure 11-8. *The example race website*

Each of our web pages will contain a common section to display the leader board data. Each entry in the leader board will show the name of one of our racers and his or her current distance from the finish line. When any of our pages is loaded, it will make a WebSocket connection to a race broadcast server and listen for messages indicating the position of a racer. The racers, in turn, will be sending their current position to the same broadcast server, causing the position data to stream down to the page in real time.

All of this has been covered in previous chapters related to Geolocation and WebSocket. In fact, much of the demonstration code here is shared with the examples from earlier in this book. However, there is one key difference in this example: when the data arrives in the page, we will store it in the session storage area for later retrieval. Then, whenever a user navigates to a new page, the stored data will be retrieved and displayed before making a new WebSocket connection. In this way, the temporary data is transferred from page to page without using any cookies or web server communication.

To keep our data feed small, we'll send our racer location messages across the web in a simple format that is easy to read and parse. This format is a String that uses the semicolon character (;) as a delimiter separating the chunks of data: name, latitude, and longitude. For example, a racer named Racer X who is at latitude 37.20 and longitude –121.53 would be identified with the following string:

```
;Racer X;37.20;-121.53
```

■ **Note** A common technique is to use the JSON format to send object representations between client and server. We'll show you how to do that in the section "Practical Extras" later in this chapter.

Now, let's dig into the code itself. Each of our pages will contain identical JavaScript code to connect to the WebSocket server, process and display leader board messages, and save and restore the leader board using sessionStorage. As such, this code would be a prime candidate to include in a JavaScript library in a real application.

First, we'll establish a few utility methods that you've seen before. To calculate the distance of any particular racer from the finish line, we need routines to calculate distance between two geolocation positions as shown in Listing 11-5.

Listing 11-5. Distance Calculation Routine

```
// functions for determining the distance between two
// latitude and longitude positions
function toRadians(num) {
  return num * Math.PI / 180;
}

function distance(latitude1, longitude1, latitude2, longitude2) {
  // R is the radius of the earth in kilometers
  var R = 6371;

  var deltaLatitude = toRadians((latitude2-latitude1));
  var deltaLongitude = toRadians((longitude2-longitude1));
  latitude1 = toRadians(latitude1), latitude2 = toRadians(latitude2);

  var a = Math.sin(deltaLatitude/2) *
          Math.sin(deltaLatitude/2) +
          Math.cos(latitude1) *
```

```
            Math.cos(latitude2) *
            Math.sin(deltaLongitude/2) *
            Math.sin(deltaLongitude/2);

    var c = 2 * Math.atan2(Math.sqrt(a),
                           Math.sqrt(1-a));
    var d = R * c;
    return d;
}

// latitude and longitude for the finish line in the Lake Tahoe race
var finishLat = 39.17222;
var finishLong = -120.13778;
```

In this familiar set of functions—used earlier in Chapter 5—we calculate the distance between two points with a distance function. The details are not of particular importance, nor are they the most accurate representation of distance along a racetrack, but they'll do for our example.

In the final lines, we establish a latitude and longitude for the finish line location of the race. As you'll see, we will compare these coordinates with incoming racer positions to determine the racers' distance from the finish line, and thus, their ranks in the race.

Now, let's look at a tiny snippet of the HTML markup used to display the page.

```
<h2>Live T216 Leaderboard</h2>
<p id="leaderboardStatus">Leaderboard: Connecting...</p>
<div id="leaderboard"></div>
```

Although most of the page HTML is irrelevant to our demonstration, in these few lines, we declare some named elements with the IDs leaderboardStatus and leaderboard. The leaderboardStatus is where we will display the connection information for our WebSocket. And the leaderboard itself is where we will insert div elements to indicate the position information we are receiving from our WebSocket messages, using the utility function shown in Listing 11-6.

Listing 11-6. *Position Information Utility Function*

```
// display the name and distance in the page
function displayRacerLocation(name, distance) {
    // locate the HTML element for this ID
    // if one doesn't exist, create it
    var incomingRow = document.getElementById(name);
    if (!incomingRow) {
        incomingRow = document.createElement('div');
        incomingRow.setAttribute('id', name);
        incomingRow.userText = name;

        document.getElementById("leaderboard").appendChild(incomingRow);
    }

    incomingRow.innerHTML = incomingRow.userText + " is " +
                        Math.round(distance*10000)/10000 + " km from the finish line";
}
```

This utility is a simple display routine, which takes the racer's name and distance from the finish line. Figure 11-9 shows what the leader board section looks like on the index.html page.

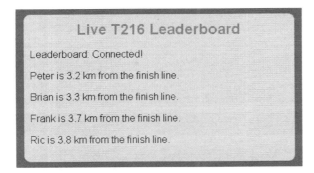

Figure 11-9. *The race leader board*

The name is used for two purposes; not only is it placed into the status message for that racer but it is also used to reference the unique div element where that racer's status is stored. If a div for our racer already exists, we will find it when we look it up using the standard document.getElementById() routine. If a div does not already exist in the page for that racer, we will create one and insert it into the leaderboard area. Either way, we update the div element corresponding to that racer with the latest distance from the finish line, which will immediately update it in the display of the page. If you have already read Chapter 7, this will be familiar to you from the example application we created there.

Our next function is the message processor that will be called whenever data is returned from the broadcasting race WebSocket server, as shown in Listing 11-7.

Listing 11-7. *WebSocket Message Processing Function*

```
// callback when new position data is retrieved from the websocket
function dataReturned(locationData) {
    // break the data into ID, latitude, and longitude
    var allData = locationData.split(";");
    var incomingId   = allData[1];
    var incomingLat  = allData[2];
    var incomingLong = allData[3];

    // update the row text with the new values
    var currentDistance = distance(incomingLat, incomingLong, finishLat, finishLong);

    // store the incoming user name and distance in storage
    window.sessionStorage[incomingId] = currentDistance;

    // display the new user data in the page
    displayRacerLocation(incomingId, currentDistance);
}
```

This function takes a string in the format described previously, a semicolon-separated message containing the name, latitude, and longitude of a racer. Our first step is to split it into its component parts using the JavaScript split() routine to produce the incomingId, incomingLat, and incomingLong, respectively.

Next, it passes the racer's latitude and longitude, as well as the latitude and longitude of the finish line, to the distance utility method we defined earlier, storing the resulting distance in the currentDistance variable.

Now that we actually have some data worth storing, we can look at the call which exercises Web Storage.

```
// store the incoming user name and distance in storage
window.sessionStorage[incomingId] = currentDistance;
```

In this line, we use the sessionStorage object on the window to store the current distance of the racer from the finish line as a value under the name and ID of the racer. In other words, we will set a value on the session storage with the key being the racer's name and the value being that racer's distance from the finish. As you will see momentarily, this data will be retrieved from storage as the user navigates from page to page on the web site. At the end of the function, we call the displayLocation() routine we previously defined to make sure that this most recent location update is displayed visually in the current page.

Now, on to our final function in our storage example—the load routine shown in Listing 11-8 that fires whenever visitors access the web page.

Listing 11-8. Initial Page Load Routine

```
// when the page loads, make a socket connection to the race broadcast server
function loadDemo() {
    // make sure the browser supports sessionStorage
    if (typeof(window.sessionStorage) === "undefined") {
        document.getElementById("leaderboardStatus").innerHTML = "Your browser does
                not support HTML5 Web Storage";
        return;
    }
    var storage = window.sessionStorage;
    // for each key in the storage database, display a new racer
    // location in the page
    for (var i=0; i < storage.length; i++) {
        var currRacer = storage.key(i);
        displayRacerLocation(currRacer, storage[currRacer]);
    }

    // test to make sure that Web Sockets are supported
    if (window.WebSocket) {

        // the location where our broadcast WebSocket server is located
        url = "ws://websockets.org:7999/broadcast";
        socket = new WebSocket(url);
        socket.onopen = function() {
            document.getElementById("leaderboardStatus").innerHTML = "Leaderboard:

                    Connected!";
        }
        socket.onmessage = function(e) {
            dataReturned(e.data);
        }
    }
}
```

This is a longer function than the others, and there is a lot going on. Let's take it step by step. First, as shown in Listing 11-9, we do a basic error check to make sure that the browser viewing the page supports sessionStorage by checking for its presence on the window object. If sessionStorage is not accessible, we simply update the leaderboardStatus area to indicate as much, and then return out of the loading routine. We won't be attempting to work around lack of browser storage in this example.

Listing 11-9. Checking for Browser Support

```
// make sure the browser supports sessionStorage
if (typeof(window.sessionStorage) === "undefined") {
    document.getElementById("leaderboardStatus").innerHTML = "Your browser does
            not support HTML5 Web Storage";
    return;
}
```

■ **Note** It is possible to rework this demonstration to simply forgo any persistence of data between page navigations and start each page load with a clean leader board if storage is not supported. However, our goal here is to show how storage optimizes the experience for both the user and the network.

The next thing we do on page load is to use the storage to retrieve any racer distance results that have already been served to this or other pages of our website. Recall that we are running an identical block of script code on every one of our site pages, so that the leader board follows the users as they browse around various locations. As such, the leader board may already have stored values into storage from other pages that will be retrieved and displayed here directly on load as shown in Listing 11-10. The previously saved values will follow the user during navigation, as long as the user does not close the window, tab, or browser, thus clearing out the session storage.

Listing 11-10. Displaying Stored Racer Data

```
var storage = window.sessionStorage;

// for each key in the storage database, display a new racer
// location in the page
for (var i=0; i < storage.length; i++) {
    var currRacer = storage.key(i);
    displayRacerLocation(currRacer, storage[currRacer]);
}
```

This is an important section of code. Here, we query the session for its length—in other words, the number of keys the storage contains. Then, we grab each key using storage.key() and store it into the currRacer variable, later using that variable to reference the key's corresponding value with storage[currRacer]. Together, the key and its value represent a racer and that racer's distance, which were stored on a visit to a previous page.

Once we have a previously stored racer name and distance, we display them using the displayRacerLocation() function. This all happens very quickly on page load, causing the page to instantaneously fill its leader board with previously transmitted values.

■ **Note** Our sample application relies on being the only application that stores values into the session storage area. If your application needs to share the storage object with other data, you will need to use a more nuanced key strategy than simply storing the keys at root level. We'll look at another storage strategy in the "Practical Extras" section.

Our last piece of load behavior is to hook up the page to the racer broadcast server using a simple WebSocket, as shown in Listing 11-11.

Listing 11-11. Connecting to the WebSocket Broadcast Service

```
// test to make sure that WebSocket is supported
if (window.WebSocket) {

    // the location where our broadcast WebSocket server is located
    // for the sake of example, we'll just show websockets.org
    url = "ws://websockets.org:7999/broadcast";
    socket = new WebSocket(url);
    socket.onopen = function() {
        document.getElementById("leaderboardStatus").innerHTML = "Leaderboard:◄
                Connected!";
    }
    socket.onmessage = function(e) {
        dataReturned(e.data);
    }
}
```

As we did before in our WebSocket chapter, we first check to make sure that the browser supports WebSocket by checking for the existence of the window.WebSocket object. Once we have verified that it exists, we connect to the URL where our WebSocket server is running. This server broadcasts racer location messages of the semicolon-separated format listed previously, and whenever we receive one of those messages via the socket.onmessage callback, we call our previously discussed dataReturned() function to process and display it. We also use the socket.onopen callback to update our leaderboardStatus area with a simple diagnostic message to indicate that the socket opened successfully.

That's it for our load routine. The final block of code we declare in our script block is the registration function, which requests that the loadDemo() function is called whenever page load is complete:

```
// add listeners on page load and unload
window.addEventListener("load", loadDemo, true);
```

As you have seen many times before, this event listener requests that our loadDemo() function will be called when the window has completed loading.

But how do we get racer data transmitted from the trails to the broadcast WebSocket server and into our pages? Well, we could actually use the tracker example previously declared in the WebSocket chapter by simply pointing its connect URL to the broadcast server listed previously. However, we have also created a very simple racer broadcast source page, shown in Listing 11-12, which serves a similar purpose. This page would theoretically be run on the mobile devices of the race participants. Although it does not include any Web Storage code itself, it is a convenient way to transmit the properly formatted

281

data when run in a browser with both WebSocket and Geolocation support. The file
racerBroadcast.html is available from the web site sample area provided for this book.

Listing 11-12. Contents of the File racerBroadcast.html

```
<!DOCTYPE html>

<html>

<head>
<title>Racer Broadcast</title>
<link rel="stylesheet" href="styles.css">
</head>

<body onload="loadDemo()">

<h1>Racer Broadcast</h1>

Racer name: <input type="text" id="racerName" value="Racer X"/>
<button onclick="startSendingLocation()">Start</button>

<div><strong>Geolocation</strong>: <p id="geoStatus">HTML5 Geolocation not↵
started.</p></div>
<div><strong>WebSocket</strong>: <p id="socketStatus">HTML5 Web Sockets are↵
<strong>not</strong> supported in your browser.</p></div>

<script type="text/javascript">

    // reference to the Web Socket
    var socket;

    var lastLocation;

    function updateSocketStatus(message) {
        document.getElementById("socketStatus").innerHTML = message;
    }

    function updateGeolocationStatus(message) {
        document.getElementById("geoStatus").innerHTML = message;
    }

    function handleLocationError(error) {
        switch(error.code)
        {
        case 0:
          updateGeolocationStatus("There was an error while retrieving your location: " +
                                 error.message);
          break;
        case 1:
          updateGeolocationStatus("The user prevented this page from retrieving a
                                 location.");
          break;
```

```
      case 2:
        updateGeolocationStatus("The browser was unable to determine your location: " +
                                    error.message);
        break;
      case 3:
        updateGeolocationStatus("The browser timed out before retrieving the location.");
        break;
    }
}

function loadDemo() {
    // test to make sure that Web Sockets are supported
    if (window.WebSocket) {

        // the location where our broadcast WebSocket server is located
        url = "ws://websockets.org:7999/broadcast";
        socket = new WebSocket(url);
        socket.onopen = function() {
            updateSocketStatus("Connected to WebSocket race broadcast server");
        }
    }
}

function updateLocation(position) {
    var latitude = position.coords.latitude;
    var longitude = position.coords.longitude;
    var timestamp = position.timestamp;

    updateGeolocationStatus("Location updated at " + timestamp);

    // Schedule a message to send my location via WebSocket
    var toSend =    ";" + document.getElementById("racerName").value
                    + ";" + latitude + ";" + longitude;
    setTimeout("sendMyLocation('" + toSend + "')", 1000);
}

function sendMyLocation(newLocation) {
    if (socket) {
        socket.send(newLocation);
        updateSocketStatus("Sent: " + newLocation);
    }
}

function startSendingLocation() {
    var geolocation;
    if(navigator.geolocation) {
        geolocation = navigator.geolocation;
        updateGeolocationStatus("HTML5 Geolocation is supported in your browser.");
    }
    else {
        geolocation = google.gears.factory.create('beta.geolocation');
        updateGeolocationStatus("Geolocation is supported via Google Gears");
```

```
        }

        // register for position updates using the Geolocation API
        geolocation.watchPosition(updateLocation,
                                  handleLocationError,
                                  {maximumAge:20000});
    }

</script>
</body>
</html>
```

We won't spend too much space covering this file in detail, as it is nearly identical to the tracker example in Chapter 7. The primary difference is that this file contains a text field for entering the racer's name:

```
Racer name: <input type="text" id="racerName" value="Racer X"/>
```

The racer's name is now sent to the broadcast server as part of the data string:

```
var toSend =    ";" + document.getElementById("racerName").value
                + ";" + latitude + ";" + longitude;
```

To try it out for yourself, open two windows in a browser that supports Web Storage, Geolocation, and WebSocket, such as Google Chrome. In the first, load the running club's index.html page. You will see it connect to the race broadcast site using WebSocket and then await any racer data notifications. In the second window, open the racerBroadcast.html file. After this page, too, has connected to the WebSocket broadcast site, enter a name for your racer, and click the Start button. You'll see that the racer broadcast has transmitted the location of your favorite racer, and it should show up in the leader board in your other browser window. Figure 11-10 shows what this looks like.

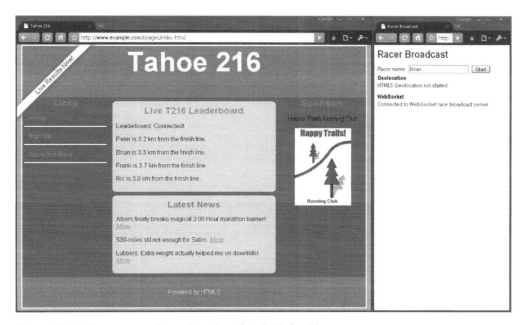

Figure 11-10. *Race page and racerBroadcast.html side by side*

Now, navigate to other racing club pages using the Signup and About the Race links on the left side of the page. Because all of these pages have been configured to load our script, they will immediately load and populate the leader board with the previous racer data, which was delivered while browsing other pages. Send more racer status notifications (from the broadcast page), and you'll see them propagate through the club site pages as you navigate, as well.

Now that we've finished our code, let's review what we've built. We've created a simple function block, suitable for inclusion in a shared JavaScript library, which connects to a WebSocket broadcast server and listens for racer updates. When an update is received, the script displays the position in the page *and* stores it using sessionStorage. When the page is loaded, it checks for any previously stored racer position values, thus maintaining the state as the user navigates the site. What are some of the benefits we gain from this approach?

- *Reduced network traffic:* Race information is stored locally in the browser. Once it arrives, it sticks around for every page load, rather than using cookies or server requests to fetch it again.

- *Immediate display of values:* The browser pages themselves can be cached rather than loaded from the network, because the dynamic parts of the page—the current leaderboard status—are local data. This data is rapidly displayed without any network load time.

- *Transient storage:* The race data isn't very useful after the race has completed. Consequently, we store it in session storage area, meaning it is discarded when the window or tab is shut down, and it no longer consumes any space.

```
┌─────────────────────────────────────────────────────────────────────┐
│                    A WORD ABOUT BULLETPROOFING                        │
└─────────────────────────────────────────────────────────────────────┘
```

Brian says: "We've accomplished a lot in this example using only a few lines of script code. But don't be lulled into thinking everything is this easy in a real, publicly accessible website. We took some shortcuts that simply are not acceptable for a production application.

For example, our message format does not support similarly named racers and would best be replaced by a unique identifier representing each racer. Our distance calculation is "as the crow flies" and not truly indicative of progress in an off-road race. Standard disclaimers apply—more localization, more error checking, and more attention to detail will make your site work for all participants."

This same technique we demonstrated in this example can be applied to any number of data types: chat, e-mail, and sports scores are other examples that can be cached and displayed from page to page using local or session storage just as we've shown here. If your application sends user-specific data back and forth from browser to server at regular intervals, consider using Web Storage to streamline your flow.

The Future of Browser Database Storage

The key-value Storage API is great for persisting data, but what about indexed storage that can be queried? HTML5 applications will eventually have access to indexed databases as well. The exact details of the database APIs are still solidifying, and there are two primary proposals.

The Web SQL Database

One of the proposals, Web SQL Database, has been implemented in Safari, Chrome, and Opera. Table 11-2 shows the browser support for Web SQL Database.

Table 11-2. Browser Support for HTML5 Web SQL Database

Browser	Details
Chrome	Supported in version 3.0 and greater
Firefox	Not supported
Internet Explorer	Not supported
Opera	Supported in version 10.5 and greater
Safari	Supported in version 3.2 and greater

Web SQL Database allows applications access to SQLite through an asynchronous JavaScript interface. Although it will not be part of the common Web platform nor the eventual recommended database API for HTML5 applications, the SQL API can be useful when targeting a specific platform such as mobile Safari. In any case, this API shows off the power of databases in the browser. Just like the other storage APIs, the browser can limit the amount of storage available to each origin and clear out the data when user data is cleared.

The Fate of Web SQL Database

Frank says: "Even though Web SQL DB is already in Safari, Chrome, and Opera, it will not be implemented in Firefox and it is listed as 'stalled' on the WHATWG wiki. The specification defines an API for executing SQL statements given as strings and defers to SQLite for the SQL dialect. Since it is undesirable for a standard to require a specific implementation of SQL, Web SQL Database has been surpassed by a newer specification, Indexed Database (formerly WebSimpleDB), which is simpler and not tied to a specific SQL database version. Browser implementations of Indexed Database are currently in progress, and we'll cover them in the next section."

Because Web SQL Database is already implemented in the wild, we are including a basic example but omiting the complete details of the API. This example demonstrates the basic use of the Web SQL Database API. It opens a database called mydb, creates a racers table if a table by that name does not already exist, and populates the table with a list of predefined names. Figure 11-11 shows this database with racers table in Safari's Web Inspector.

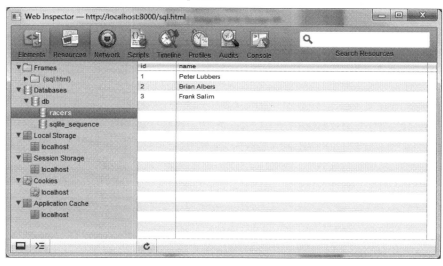

Figure 11-11. *Database with racers table in Safari's Web Inspector*

To begin, we open a database by name. The window.openDatabase() function returns a Database object through which database interaction takes place. The openDatabase() function takes a name as well as an optional version and description. With an open database, application code can now start transactions. SQL statements are executed in the context of a transaction using the transaction.executeSql() function. This simple example uses executeSql() to create a table, insert racer names into the table, and later query the database to create an HTML table. Figure 11-12 shows the output HTML file with the list of names retrieved from the table.

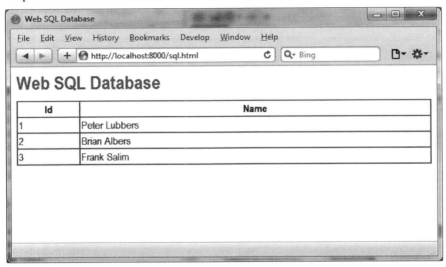

*Figure 11-12. sql.html displaying the results of SELECT * FROM racers*

Database operations can take some time to complete. Instead of blocking script execution until a result set is available, queries run in the background. When the results are available, a function given as the third argument to executeSQL() is called back with the transaction and the result set as arguments.

Listing 11-13 shows the complete code for the file sql.html; the sample code shown is also located in the code/storage folder.

Listing 11-13. Using the Web SQL Database API

```
<!DOCTYPE html>
<title>Web SQL Database</title>
<script>

    // open a database by name
    var db = openDatabase('db', '1.0', 'my first database', 2 * 1024 * 1024);

    function log(id, name) {
        var row = document.createElement("tr");
        var idCell = document.createElement("td");
        var nameCell = document.createElement("td");
        idCell.textContent = id;
        nameCell.textContent = name;
        row.appendChild(idCell);
        row.appendChild(nameCell);
```

```
            document.getElementById("racers").appendChild(row);
    }

    function doQuery() {
        db.transaction(function (tx) {
                tx.executeSql('SELECT * from racers', [], function(tx, result) {
                    // log SQL result set
                    for (var i=0; i<result.rows.length; i++) {
                        var item = result.rows.item(i);
                        log(item.id, item.name);
                    }
                });
            });
    }

    function initDatabase() {
        var names = ["Peter Lubbers", "Brian Albers", "Frank Salim"];

        db.transaction(function (tx) {
                tx.executeSql('CREATE TABLE IF NOT EXISTS racers (id integer primary key↵
autoincrement, name)');

                for (var i=0; i<names.length; i++) {
                    tx.executeSql('INSERT INTO racers (name) VALUES (?)', [names[i]]);
                }

                doQuery();
            });
    }

    initDatabase();
</script>

<h1>Web SQL Database</h1>

<table id="racers" border="1" cellspacing="0" style="width:100%">
    <th>Id</th>
    <th>Name</th>
</table>
```

The Indexed Database API

A second proposal for browser database storage gained prominence in 2010. The Indexed Database API is supported by Microsoft and Mozilla and is seen as a counter to the Web SQL Database. Where the Web SQL Database looks to bring the established SQL language into browsers, the Indexed Database aims to bring low-level indexed storage capabilities, with the hope that more developer-friendly libraries will be built on top of the indexed core.

While the Web SQL API supports using query languages to issue SQL statements against tables of data, the Indexed DB API issues synchronous or asynchronous function calls directly against a tree-like object storage engine. Unlike Web SQL, the Indexed DB does not work with tables and columns.

The support for the Indexed Database API is growing (see Table 11-3).

Table 11-3. Browser Support for the Indexed Database API

Browser	Details
Chrome	Supported in current versions
Firefox	Supported in current versions
Internet Explorer	Supported in version 10+
Opera	Not currently supported
Safari	Not currently supported

Microsoft and Mozilla have announced that they will not support the Web SQL Database and have thrown their weight behind the Indexed Database instead. Google's Chrome has joined in with support, and as such, it is likely that the Indexed Database is the future of standardized structured storage in the browser. Among their reasons are the fact that SQL is not a true standard and also that the only implementation of Web SQL was the SQLite project. With only one implementation and a loose standard, they could not support WebSQL in the HTML5 specification.

The Indexed Database API eschews query strings in favor of a low-level API that allows values to be stored directly in JavaScript objects. Values stored in the database can be retrieved by key or using indexes, and the API can be accessed in either synchronous or asynchronous manner. Like the WebSQL proposal, indexed databases are scoped by origin so that you can only access the storage created in your own web pages.

Creation or modification of Indexed Database storage is done under the context of transactions, which can be classified as either READ_ONLY, READ_WRITE, or VERSION_CHANGE. While the first two are probably self-explanatory, the VERSION_CHANGE transaction type is used whenever an operation will modify the structure of the database.

Retrieving records from an Indexed Database is done via a cursor object. A cursor object iterates over a range of records in either increasing or decreasing order. At any time a cursor either has a value or does not, due to the fact that it is either in the process of loading or has reached the end of its iteration.

A detailed description of the Indexed Database API is beyond the scope of this book. If you are intending to implement a query engine on top of the built-in API, you should consult the official specification at http://www.w3.org/TR/IndexedDB/. Otherwise, you would be wise to wait for one of the proposed engines layered on top of the standard to be made available to use a more developer-friendly database API. At this point, no third-party libraries have gained prominence or significant backing.

Why Use a Hammer...

Brian says: "...when you can instead use these ingots, that forge, and the mold of your choosing? On the Mozilla blog, Arun Ranganathan argued that he would welcome APIs like the Web SQL API being built on top of the Indexed Database standard. This attitude has perplexed many developers, as there is a widespread belief that, in order to make the Indexed Database usable, it will require third-party JavaScript

---

libraries built on top of the standard. The Indexed Database itself is simply too complex for most web developers to use it in its current form.

This begs the question: if developers end up needing third-party libraries to take advantage of the built-in storage API, wouldn't it be prudent to simply build that storage in native code rather than as a JavaScript library that must be downloaded and interpreted at runtime? Time will tell if the Indexed Database suits the needs of the majority."

Practical Extras

Sometimes, there are techniques that don't fit into our regular examples but nonetheless apply to many types of HTML5 applications. We present to you some short, but common, practical extras here.

JSON Object Storage

Although the specification for Web Storage allows for objects of any type to be stored as key-value pairs, in current implementations, some browsers limit values to be text string data types. There is a practical workaround, however, due to the fact that modern versions of browsers contain built-in support for JavaScript Object Notation (JSON).

JSON is a standard for data-interchange that can represent objects as strings and vice-versa. JSON has been used for over a decade to transmit objects from browser clients to servers over HTTP. Now, we can use it to serialize complex objects in and out of Web Storage in order to persist complex data types. Consider the script block in Listing 11-14.

Listing 11-14. *JSON Object Storage*

```
<script>

  var data;

  function loadData() {
    data = JSON.parse(sessionStorage["myStorageKey"])
  }

  function saveData() {
    sessionStorage["myStorageKey"] = JSON.stringify(data);
  }

  window.addEventListener("load", loadData, true);
  window.addEventListener("unload", saveData, true);

</script>
```

As you can see, the script contains event listeners to register handlers for load and unload events in the browser window. In this case, the handlers call the loadData() and saveData() functions, respectively.

In the loadData() function, the session storage area is queried for the value of a storage key, and that key is passed to the JSON.parse() function. The JSON.parse() routine will take a previously saved string representation of an object and reconstitute it into a copy of the original. This routine is called every time the page loads.

Similarly, the saveData() function takes a data value and calls JSON.stringify() on it to turn it into a string representation of the object. That string is, in turn, stored back into storage. By registering the saveData() function on the unload browser event, we ensure that it is called every time the user navigates away or shuts down the browser or window.

The practical result of these two functions is that any object we wish to track in storage, no matter if it is a complex object type, can be stored and reloaded as users navigate in and out of the application. This allows developers to extend the techniques we have already shown to nontext data.

A Window into Sharing

As alluded to in an earlier section, the ability for Web Storage events to fire in any window browsing the same origin has some powerful implications. It means that storage can be used to send messages from window to window, even if they are not all using the storage object itself. This, in turn implies that we can now share data across windows that have the same origin.

Let's see how this works using some code samples. To listen to cross-window messages, a simple script needs only to register a handler for storage events. Let's assume that a page running at http://www.example.com/storageLog.html contains the code shown in Listing 11-15 (the sample file storageLog.html for this example is also located in the code/storage folder).

Listing 11-15. Cross-Window Communication Using Storage

```
// display records of new storage events
function displayStorageEvent(e) {
  var incomingRow = document.createElement('div');
  document.getElementById("container").appendChild(incomingRow);

  var logged = "key:" + e.key + ", newValue:" + e.newValue + ", oldValue:" +
              e.oldValue + ", url:" + e.url + ", storageArea:" + e.storageArea;
              incomingRow.innerHTML = logged;
}

// add listeners on storage events
window.addEventListener("storage", displayStorageEvent, true);
```

After registering an event listener for the storage event type, this window will receive notification of storage changes in any pages. For example, if a browser window viewing http://www.example.com/browser-test.html that is currently browsing the same origin sets or changes a new storage value, the storageLog.html page will receive a notification. Therefore, to send a message to a receiving window, the sending window need only modify a storage object, and its old and new values will be sent as part of the notification. For example, if a storage value is updated using localStorage.setItem(), then the displayStorageEvent() handler in the storageLog.html page hosted at the same origin will receive an event. By carefully coordinating event names and values, the two pages can now communicate, a feat which has been difficult to accomplish before. Figure 11-13 shows the storageLog.html page in action, simply logging storage events it receives.

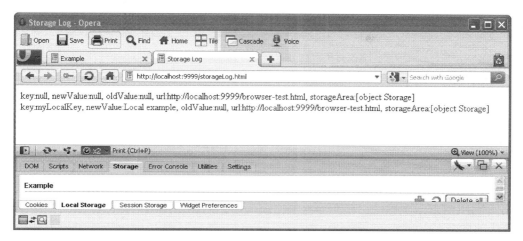

Figure 11-13. The storageLog.html page logging storage eventsSummary

Summary

In this chapter, we showed how Web Storage can be used as an alternative to browser cookies for keeping local copies of data across windows, tabs, and (with localStorage) even across browser restarts. You've seen that data can be appropriately segregated between windows by using sessionStorage, and shared—even across windows—by using storage events. In our full-fledged example, we showed a practical way to use storage to track data from page to page as users navigate a website, which could just as easily be applied to other data types. We even demonstrated how nontext data types can be stored when a page loads or unloads to save and restore the state of a page across visits.

In the next chapter, we'll show you how HTML5 lets you create offline applications.

CHAPTER 12

Creating Offline Web Applications

In this chapter, we will explore what you can do with offline HTML5 applications. HTML5 applications do not necessarily require constant access to the network, and loading cached resources can now be more flexibly controlled by developers.

Overview of HTML5 Offline Web Applications

The first, and most obvious, reason to use the application cache is offline support. In the age of universal connectivity, offline applications are still desirable. What do you do when you do not have a network connection? Before you say the days of intermittent connectivity are over, consider the following:

- Do all of the flights you take have onboard Wi-Fi?

- Do you have perfect signal coverage on your mobile Internet device (when was the last time you saw zero bars)?

- Can you count on having an Internet connection when you give presentations?

As more applications move to the Web, it is tempting to assume 24/7 uninterrupted connectivity for all users, but the reality of the Internet is that interruptions happen and, in situations like air travel, can happen predictably for several hours at a time.

Intermittent connectivity has been the Achilles' heel of network computing systems. If your applications depend on communication with remote hosts, and those hosts are unreachable, you're out of luck. However, when you do have an Internet connection, web applications can always be up-to-date, because the code loads from a remote location on each use.

If your applications require only occasional communication, they can still be useful as long as the application resources are stored locally. With the advent of browser-only devices, web applications that continue to function without continuous connectivity will only grow more important. Desktop applications that do not require continuous connectivity have historically held that advantage over web applications.

HTML5 exposes control over application caching to get the best of both worlds: applications built with web technology that run in the browser and update when they are online but can also be used offline. However, this new offline application feature must be used explicitly, because current web servers do not provide any default caching behavior for offline applications.

The HTML5 offline application cache makes it possible to augment an application to run without a network connection. You do not need a connection to the Internet just to draft an e-mail. HTML5 introduces the offline application cache that allows a Web application to run without network connectivity.

An application developer can specify specific additional resources comprising an HTML5 application (HTML, CSS, JavaScript, and images) to make an application available for offline use. There are many use cases for this, for example:

- Read and compose e-mail

- Edit documents

- Edit and display presentations

- Create to-do lists

Using offline storage can avoid the normal network requests needed to load an application. If the cache manifest is up to date, the browser knows it does not need to check if the other resources are also up to date, and most of the application can load very quickly out of the local application cache. Additionally, loading resources out of a cache (instead of making multiple HTTP requests to see if resources have been updated) saves bandwidth, which can be especially important for mobile web applications. Currently, slower loading is one way that web applications suffer in comparison with desktop applications. Caching can offset that.

The application cache gives developers explicit control over caching. The *cache manifest* file allows you to group related resources into a logical application. This is a powerful concept that can give web applications some of the characteristics of desktop applications. You can use this additional power in new, creative ways.

Resources identified in the cache manifest file create what is known as an *application cache*, which is the place where browsers store the resources persistently, typically on disk. Some browsers give users a way to view the data in the application cache. For example, the Offline cache device section in the internal about:cache page in Firefox shows you details about the application cache and a way to view individual files in the cache, as shown in Figure 12-1.

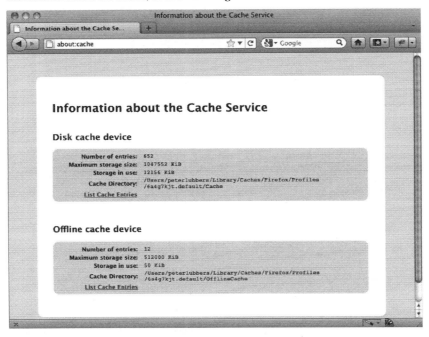

Figure 12-1. Viewing application cache entries in Firefox

Similarly, the internal page `chrome://appcache-internals/` provides details about the contents of the different application caches stored on your system. It also provides a way to view the contents and remove these caches entirely as shown in Figure 12-2.

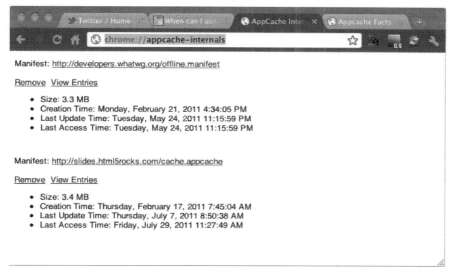

Figure 12-2. Viewing application cache entries in Chrome

Browser Support for HTML5 Offline Web Applications

For a complete overview of the current browser support, including mobile support, refer to `http://caniuse.com` and search for Offline Web Applications or Application Cache. If you have to support older browsers, it's always a good idea to first see whether Application Cache is supported before you use the API. The section "Checking for Browser Support" later in this chapter will show you how you can programmatically check for browser support.

Using the HTML5 Application Cache API

In this section, we will explore the specifics of how you can use the Offline Web Applications API.

Checking for Browser Support

Before you try to use the Offline Web Applications API, it is a good idea to check for browser support. Listing 12-1 shows how you can do that.

Listing 12-1. Checking Browser Support for the Offline Web Applications API

```
if(window.applicationCache) {
  // this browser supports offline applications
}
```

Creating a Simple Offline Application

Let's say that you want to create a one-page application that consists of an HTML document, a style sheet, and a JavaScript file. To add offline support to your HTML5 application, you include a manifest attribute on the html element as shown in the Listing 12-2.

Listing 12-2. The manifest Attribute on the HTML Element

```
<!DOCTYPE html>
<html manifest="application.appcache">
  .
  .
  .
</html>
```

Alongside the HTML document, provide a manifest file with the *.appcache extension) specifying which resources to cache. Listing 12-3 shows the contents of an example cache manifest file.

Listing 12-3. Contents of an Example Cache Manifest File

```
CACHE MANIFEST
example.html
example.js
example.css
example.gif
```

Going Offline

To make applications aware of intermittent connectivity, there are additional events exposed by HTML5 browsers. Your applications may have different modes for online and offline behavior. Some additions to the window.navigator object make that easier. First, navigator.onLine is a Boolean property that indicates whether the browser believes it is online. Of course, a true value of onLine is not a definite assurance that the servers that your web application must communicate with are reachable from the user's machine. On the other hand, a false value means the browser will not even attempt to connect out over the network. Listing 12-4 shows how you can check to see if your page is online or offline.

Listing 12-4. Checking Online Status

```
// When the page loads, set the status to online or offline
function loadDemo() {
  if (navigator.onLine) {
    log("Online");
  } else {
    log("Offline");
  }
}

// Now add event listeners to notify a change in online status
window.addEventListener("online", function(e) {
  log("Online");
}, true);
```

```
window.addEventListener("offline", function(e) {
  log("Offline");
}, true);
```

Manifest Files

Offline applications consist of a manifest listing one or more resources that browser will cache for offline use. Manifest files have the MIME type text/cache-manifest. The SimpleHTTPServer module in the Python standard library will serve files with the .manifest extension with the header Content-type: text/cache-manifest. To configure settings, open the file PYTHON_HOME/Lib/mimetypes.py, and add the following line:

```
'.appcache'    : 'text/cache-manifest manifest',
```

Other web servers may require additional configuration. For example, for Apache HTTP Server, you can update the mime.types file in the conf folder by adding the following line:

```
text/cache-manifest appcache
```

If you are using Microsoft IIS, in your website's home, double-click the MIME Types icon, then add the .appcache extension with MIME type text/cache-manifest in the Add MIME Type dialog.

The manifest syntax is simple line separated text that starts with CACHE MANIFEST (as the first line). Lines can end in CR, LF, or CRLF—the format is flexible—but the text must be UTF-8 encoded, which is the typical output for most text editors. Comments begin with the hash symbol and must be on their own lines; you cannot append a comment to other non-comment lines in the file.

Listing 12-5. Example Manifest File with All Possible Sections

```
CACHE MANIFEST
# files to cache
about.html
html5.css
index.html
happy-trails-rc.gif
lake-tahoe.JPG

#do not cache signup page
NETWORK
signup.html

FALLBACK
signup.html     offline.html
/app/ajax/      default.html
```

Let's look at the different sections.

If no CACHE: heading is specified, the files that are listed will be treated as files to be cached (caching is the default behavior). The following simple manifest specifies that three files (index.html, application.js, and style.css) must be cached:

```
CACHE MANIFEST
index.html
application.js
```

`style.css`

Similarly, the following section would do the same (you can use the same CACHE, NETWORK, and FALLBACK headers multiple times in a manifest file if you want to):

```
CACHE MANIFEST

# Cache section
CACHE:
Index.html
application.js
style.css
```

By listing a file in the CACHE section, you instruct the browser to serve the file from the application cache, even if the application is online. It is unnecessary to specify the application's main HTML resource. The HTML document that initially pointed to the manifest file is implicitly included (this is called a Master entry). However, if you want to cache multiple HTML documents or if you would like multiple HTML documents to act as possible entry points for the cacheable application, they should all be explicitly listed in the cache manifest file.

FALLBACK entries allow you to give alternate paths to replace resources that cannot be fetched. The manifest in Listing 12-5 would cause requests to /app/ajax/ or subpaths beginning with /app/ajax/ to fall back to default.html when /app/ajax/* is unreachable.

NETWORK specifies resources that are always fetched using the network. The difference with simply omitting these files from the manifest is that master entries are cached without being explicitly listed in the manifest file. To ensure that the application requests the file from the server even if the cached resource is cached in the application cache, you can place that file in the NETWORK: section.

The ApplicationCache API

The ApplicationCache API is an interface for working with the application cache. A new `window.applicationCache` object fires several events related to the state of the cache. The object has a numerical property, `window.applicationCache.status`, which indicates the state of the cache. The six states a cache can have are shown in Table 12-1.

Table 12-1. *The Six Cache States*

Numerical Property	Cache Status
0	UNCACHED
1	IDLE
2	CHECKING
3	DOWNLOADING
4	UPDATEREADY
5	OBSOLETE

Most pages on the Web today do not specify cache manifests and are uncached. Idle is the typical state for an application with a cache manifest. An application in the idle state has all its resources stored by the browser with no updates in progress. A cache enters the obsolete state if there was at one point a valid cache but the manifest is now missing. There are events (and callback attributes) in the API that correspond to some of these states. For instance, when the cache enters the idle state after an update, the cached event fires. At that time, an application might notify the user that they can disconnect from the network and still expect the application to be available in offline mode. Table 12-2 shows some common events and their associated caches states.

Table 12-2. *Common Events and Their Cache States*

Event	Associated Cache State
onchecking	CHECKING
ondownloading	DOWNLOADING
onupdateready	UPDATEREADY
onobsolete	OBSOLETE
oncached	IDLE

Additionally, there are events indicating update progress, when no update is available, or when an error has occurred:

- onerror
- onnoupdate
- onprogress

window.applicationCache has an update() method. Calling update() requests that the browser update the cache. This includes checking for a new version of the manifest file and downloading new resources if necessary. If there is no cache or if the cache is obsolete, an error will be thrown.

Application Cache in Action

Although creating the manifest file and using it in an application is relatively simple, what happens when you update pages on the server is not as intuitive as you might think. The main thing to keep in mind is that once the browser has successfully cached the application's resources in the application cache, it will *always* serve those pages from the cache first. After that, the browser will do only one more thing: check if the manifest file has been changed on the server.

To better understand how the process works, let's step through an example scenario, using the manifest file shown in Listing 12-5.

1. When you access the index.html page for the very first time (while online), say on http://www.example.com, the browser loads the page and its subresources (CSS, JavaScript, and image files).

2. While parsing the page, the browser comes across the manifest attribute in the html element and proceeds to load all the files listed in the CACHE (default)

and FALLBACK sections in the application cache for the example.com site (browsers allow about 5 MB of storage space).

3. From now on, when you navigate to http://www.example.com, the browser will always load the site from the application cache, and it will then attempt to check if the manifest file has been updated (it can only do the latter when you are online). This means that if you now go offline (voluntarily or otherwise) and point your browser at http://www.example.com, the browser will load the site from the application cache—yes, you can still use the site in its entirety in offline mode.

4. If you try to access a cached resource while you're offline, it will load from the application cache. When you try to access a NETWORK resource (signup.html), FALLBACK content (offline.html) will be served. NETWORK files will be available again only if you go back online.

5. So far so good. Everything works as expected. We will now try to step you through the digital minefield that you must cross when you change content on the server. When you change, for example, the about.html page on the server and access that page while you're in online mode by reloading the page in the browser, it would be reasonable to expect the updated page to show up. After all, you're online and have direct access to the server. However, you will just be looking at the same old page as before, possibly with a puzzled look on your face. The reason for this is that the browser will always load the page from the application cache, and after that it checks only one thing: whether the manifest file has been updated. Therefore, if you want updated resources to be downloaded you must make a change to the manifest file as well (do not just "touch" the file, because that will not be considered a change—it must be a byte-for-byte change). A common way to make this change is to add a version comment at the top of the file as shown in Listing 12.5. The browser does not actually understand the version comment, but it is a good best practice to follow. Because of this and because it is easy to overlook a new or removed file, it is recommended that you use some sort of build script to maintain the manifest file. HTML5 Boilerplate 2.0 (http://html5boilerplate.com) ships with a build file that can be used to automatically build and version the appcache file, a great addition to that already great resource.

6. When you make a change to both the about.html page and the manifest file and subsequently refresh the page in your browser while you're online you will, once again, be disappointed to see the same old page. What happened? Well, even though the browser has now found that the manifest has been updated and downloaded all of the files again into a new version of the cache, the page was already loaded from the application cache before the server check was performed, and the browser does not automatically reload the page for you in the browser. You can compare this process to how a new version of a software program (for example, the Firefox browser) can be downloaded in the background but require a restart of the program to take effect. If you can't wait for the next page refresh, you can programmatically add an event listener for the onupdateready event and prompt the user to refresh the page. A little confusing at first, but it all actually makes sense when you think about it.

Using Application Cache to Boost Performance

Peter says: "One nice side-effect of the application cache mechanism is that you can use it to prefetch resources. The regular browser cache stores pages that you have visited, but what is stored is dependent on both client and server configuration (browser settings and expires headers). Therefore, returning to specific pages by relying on regular browser caching is fickle to say the least—anyone who has ever attempted to rely on regular browser caching to navigate through the pages of a website while on an airplane will probably agree here.

Using application cache, however, allows you not only to cache pages as you visit them but also to cache pages *you have not even visited yet*; it can be used as an effective prefetching mechanism. When it is time to use one of those prefetched resources it will be loaded from the application cache on local disk and not from the server, speeding up the load time dramatically. Used wisely (don't prefetch Wikipedia), you can use application cache to dramatically improve performance. One important thing to remember is that regular browser caching is also still in effect, so watch for false positives, especially if you are trying to debug application cache behavior."

Building an Application with HTML5 Offline Web Applications

In this example application, we will track a runner's location while out on the trail (with intermittent or no connectivity). For example, Peter goes running, and he will have his new Geolocation–enabled phone and HTML5 web browser with him, but there is not always a great signal out in the woods around his house. He wants to use this application to track and record his location even when he cannot use the Internet.

When offline, the Geolocation API should continue to work on devices with hardware geolocation (such as GPS) but obviously not on devices that use IP geolocation. IP geolocation requires network connectivity to map the client's IP address to coordinates. In addition, offline applications can always access persistent storage on the local machine through APIs such as local storage or Indexed Database.

The example files for this application are located on the book's page at www.apress.com and at the book's website in the offline code folder, and you can start the demo by navigating to the code/offline folder and issuing the command:

```
Python —m SimpleHTTPServer 9999.
```

Prior to starting the web server, make sure you have configured Python to serve the manifest files (files with the *.appcache extension) with the correct mime type as described earlier. This is the most common cause of failure for offline web applications. If it does not work as expected, check the console in Chrome Developer tools for possible descriptive error messages.

This starts Python's HTTP server module on port 9999 (you can start it on any port, but you may need admin privileges to bind to ports lower than 1024. After starting the HTTP server, you can navigate to http://localhost :9999/tracker.html to see the application in action.

Figure 12-3 shows what happens in Firefox when you access the site for the first time: you are prompted to opt in to storing data on your computer (note, however, that not all browsers will prompt you before storing data).

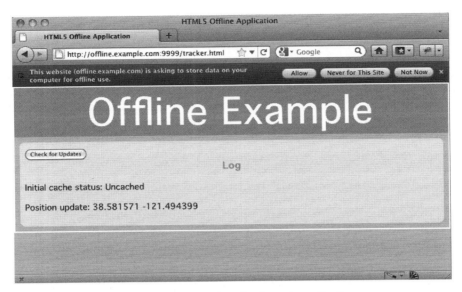

Figure 12-3. Firefox prompting to store data for the web application

After allowing the application to store data, the application cache process starts and the browser starts downloading the files referenced in the application cache manifest file (this happens after the page is loaded, and, therefore, it has minimal impact on the responsiveness of the page. Figure 12-4 shows how Chrome Developer Tools provide a detailed overview of what is cached for the localhost origin in the Resources pane. It also provides information in the console about the application cache events that fire while the page and the manifest were processed.

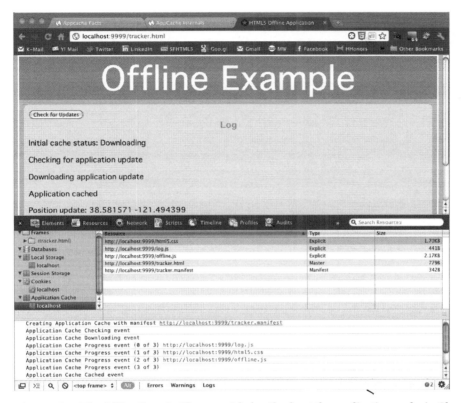

Figure 12-4. *The Offline Page in Chrome with details about the application cache in Chrome Developer Tools*

To run this application, you will need a web server serving these static resources. Remember that the manifest file must be served with the content type text/cache-manifest. If your browser supports the application cache, but the file is served with the incorrect content type, you will receive a cache error. An easy way to test this is to view the events that fire in the Chrome Developer Tools console as shown in Figure 12-4; it will tell you if the appcache file is served with the wrong mime type.

To run this application with complete functionality, you will need a server that can receive geolocation data. The server-side complement to this example would presumably store, analyze, and make available this data. It may or may not be served from the same origin as the static application.

Figure 12-5 shows the example application running in offline mode in Firefox. You can use File ➤ Work Offline to turn this mode on in Firefox and Opera. Other browsers do not have this convenience function, but you can disconnect from the network. Note, however, that disconnecting from the network does not interrupt the connection to a Python server running on localhost.

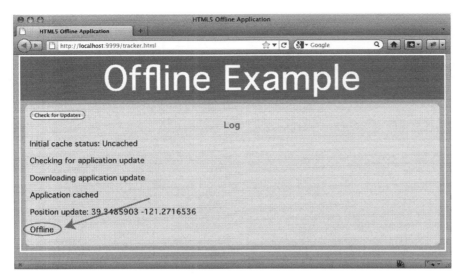

Figure 12-5. *The application in offline mode*

Creating a Manifest File for the Application Resources

First, in a text editor, create the tracker.appcache file as follows. This manifest file will list the files that are part of this application:

```
CACHE MANIFEST
# JavaScript
./offline.js
#./tracker.js
./log.js

# stylesheets
./html5.css

# images
```

Creating the HTML Structure and CSS for the UI

This is the basic UI structure of the example. Both tracker.html and html5.css will be cached, so the application will be served from the application cache.

```
<!DOCTYPE html>
<html lang="en" manifest="tracker.appcache">
<head>
    <title>HTML5 Offline Application</title>
    <script src="log.js"></script>
    <script src="offline.js"></script>
    <script src="tracker.js"></script>
```

```
    <link rel="stylesheet" href="html5.css">
</head>

<body>
    <header>
      <h1>Offline Example</h1>
    </header>

    <section>
      <article>
        <button id="installButton">Check for Updates</button>
        <h3>Log</h3>
        <div id="info">
        </div>
      </article>
    </section>
</body>
</html>
```

There are a couple of things to note in this HTML that pertain to this application's offline capabilities. The first is the manifest attribute on the HTML element. Most of the HTML examples in this book omit the <html> element because it is optional in HTML5. However, the ability to cache offline depends on specifying the manifest file there.

The second thing to note is the button. That will give the user control over configuring this application for offline use.

Creating the Offline JavaScript

For this example, the JavaScript is contained in multiple .js files included with <script> tags. These scripts are cached along with the HTML and CSS.

```
<offline.js>
/*
 * log each of the events fired by window.applicationCache
 */
window.applicationCache.onchecking = function(e) {
    log("Checking for application update");
}

window.applicationCache.onnoupdate = function(e) {
    log("No application update found");
}

window.applicationCache.onupdateready = function(e) {
    log("Application update ready");
}

window.applicationCache.onobsolete = function(e) {
    log("Application obsolete");
}

window.applicationCache.ondownloading = function(e) {
```

```
        log("Downloading application update");
    }

    window.applicationCache.oncached = function(e) {
        log("Application cached");
    }

    window.applicationCache.onerror = function(e) {
        log("Application cache error");
    }

    window.addEventListener("online", function(e) {
        log("Online");
    }, true);

    window.addEventListener("offline", function(e) {
        log("Offline");
    }, true);


    /*
     * Convert applicationCache status codes into messages
     */
    showCacheStatus = function(n) {
        statusMessages = ["Uncached","Idle","Checking","Downloading","Update Ready","Obsolete"];
        return statusMessages[n];
    }

    install = function() {
        log("Checking for updates");
        try {
            window.applicationCache.update();
        } catch (e) {
            applicationCache.onerror();
        }
    }

    onload = function(e) {
        // Check for required browser features
        if (!window.applicationCache) {
            log("HTML5 Offline Applications are not supported in your browser.");
            return;
        }

        if (!navigator.geolocation) {
            log("HTML5 Geolocation is not supported in your browser.");
            return;
        }

        if (!window.localStorage) {
            log("HTML5 Local Storage not supported in your browser.");
            return;
```

```
    }
    log("Initial cache status: " + showCacheStatus(window.applicationCache.status));
    document.getElementById("installButton").onclick = checkFor;
}

<log.js>
log = function() {
    var p = document.createElement("p");
    var message = Array.prototype.join.call(arguments, " ");
    p.innerHTML = message;
    document.getElementById("info").appendChild(p);
}
```

Check for ApplicationCache Support

In addition to the offline application cache, this example uses geolocation and local storage. We ensure that the browser supports all of these features when the page loads.

```
onload = function(e) {
    // Check for required browser features
    if (!window.applicationCache) {
        log("HTML5 Offline Applications are not supported in your browser.");
        return;
    }

    if (!navigator.geolocation) {
        log("HTML5 Geolocation is not supported in your browser.");
        return;
    }

    if (!window.localStorage) {
        log("HTML5 Local Storage is not supported in your browser.");
        return;
    }

    if (!window.WebSocket) {
        log("HTML5 WebSocket is not supported in your browser.");
        return;
    }
    log("Initial cache status: " + showCacheStatus(window.applicationCache.status));
    document.getElementById("installButton").onclick = install;
}
```

Adding the Update Button Handler

Next, add an update handler that updates the application cache as follows:

```
install = function() {
    log("Checking for updates");
    try {
        window.applicationCache.update();
```

```
    } catch (e) {
        applicationCache.onerror();
    }
}
```

Clicking this button will explicitly start the cache check that will cause all cache resources to be downloaded if necessary. When available updates have completely downloaded, a message is logged in the UI. At this point, the user knows that the application has successfully installed and can be run in offline mode.

Add Geolocation Tracking Code

This code is based on the geolocation code from Chapter 4. It is contained in the tracker.js JavaScript file.

```
/*
 * Track and report the current location
 */
var handlePositionUpdate = function(e) {
    var latitude = e.coords.latitude;
    var longitude = e.coords.longitude;
    log("Position update:", latitude, longitude);
    if(navigator.onLine) {
        uploadLocations(latitude, longitude);
    }
    storeLocation(latitude, longitude);
}

var handlePositionError = function(e) {
    log("Position error");
}

var uploadLocations = function(latitude, longitude) {
    var request = new XMLHttpRequest();
    request.open("POST", "http://geodata.example.net:8000/geoupload", true);
    request.send(localStorage.locations);
}

var geolocationConfig = {"maximumAge":20000};

navigator.geolocation.watchPosition(handlePositionUpdate,
                                    handlePositionError,
                                    geolocationConfig);
```

Adding Storage Code

Next, add the code that writes updates to localStorage when the application is in offline mode.

```
var storeLocation = function(latitude, longitude) {
    // load stored location list
    var locations = JSON.parse(localStorage.locations || "[]");
    // add location
```

```
    locations.push({"latitude" : latitude, "longitude" : longitude});
    // save new location list
    localStorage.locations = JSON.stringify(locations);
}
```

This application stores coordinates using HTML5 local storage as described in Chapter 9. Local storage is a natural fit for offline-capable applications, because it provides a way to persist data locally in the browser. The data will be available in future sessions. When network connectivity is restored, the application can synchronize with a remote server.

Using storage here has the added benefit of allowing recovery from failed upload requests. If the application experiences a network error for any reason, or if the application is closed (by user action, browser or operating system crash, or page navigation) the data is stored for future transmission.

Adding Offline Event Handling

Every time the location update handler runs, it checks the connectivity status. If the application is online, it will store and upload the coordinates. If the application is offline, it will merely store the coordinates. When the application comes back online, it can update the UI to show the online status and upload any data is stored while online.

```
window.addEventListener("online", function(e) {
    log("Online");
}, true);

window.addEventListener("offline", function(e) {
    log("Offline");
}, true);
```

The connectivity status may change while the application is not actively running. For instance, the user may have closed the browser, refreshed, or navigated to a different site. To handle these cases, our offline application checks to see if it has come back online on each page load. If it has, it will attempt to synchronize with the remote server.

```
// Synchronize with the server if the browser is now online
if(navigator.onLine) {
    uploadLocations();
}
```

Summary

In this chapter, you have seen how HTML5 Offline Web Applications can be used to create compelling applications that can be used even when there is no Internet connection. You can ensure that all your files are cached by specifying the files that are part of the web application in the cache manifest file and then referencing the files from the main HTML page of the application. Then, by adding event listeners for online and offline status changes, you can make your site behave differently based on whether an Internet connection is available or not.

In the final chapter, we will discuss the future of HTML5 programming.

CHAPTER 13

The Future of HTML5

As you have already seen in this book, HTML5 provides powerful programming features. We also discussed the history behind HTML5's development and HTML5's new plugin-free paradigm. In this chapter, we will look at where things are going. We will discuss some of the features that are not fully baked yet but hold tremendous promise.

Browser Support for HTML5

Adoption of HTML5 features is accelerating with each new browser update. Several of the features we covered have actually shipped in browsers while we wrote this book. HTML5 development in browsers is undeniably gaining tremendous momentum.

Today, many developers still struggle to develop consistent web applications that work with older browsers. Internet Explorer 6 represents the harshest of the legacy browsers in common use on the Internet today But even IE6 has a limited lifetime, as it becomes harder and harder to procure any operating system that supports it. In time, there will be close to zero users browsing the Web with IE6. More and more users of Internet Explorer are being upgraded to the latest versions. There will always be an oldest browser to contend with, but that bar rises as time passes; at the time of this writing, the market share of Internet Explorer 6 is under 10% and falling. Most users who upgrade go straight to a modern replacement. In time, the lowest common denominator will include HTML5 Video, Canvas, WebSocket, and whatever other features you may have to emulate today to reach a wider audience.

In this book, we covered features that are largely stable and shipping in multiple browsers. There are additional extensions to HTML and APIs currently in earlier stages of development. In this chapter, we will look at some of the upcoming features. Some are in early experimental stages, while others may see eventual standardization and wide availability with only minor changes from their current state.

HTML Evolves

In this section, we'll explore several exciting features that may appear in browsers in the near future. You probably won't need to wait until 2022 for these, either. There will probably not be a formalized HTML6; the WHATWG has hinted that future development will simply be referred to as "HTML." Development will be incremental, with specific features and their specifications evolving individually, rather than as a consolidated effort. Browsers will take up features as they gain consensus, and the upcoming features might even be widely available in browsers well before HTML5 is set in stone. The community responsible for driving the Web forward is committed to evolving the platform to meet the needs of users and developers.

WebGL

WebGL is an API for 3D graphics on the Web. Historically, several browser vendors including Mozilla, Opera, and Google have worked on separate experimental 3D APIs for JavaScript. Today, WebGL is progressing along a path toward standardization and wide availability across HTML5 browsers. The standardization process is taking place with browser vendors and The Khronos Group, the body responsible for OpenGL, a cross-platform 3D drawing standard created in 1992. OpenGL, currently at specification version 4.0, is widely used in gaming and computer-aided design applications as a counterpart and competitor to Microsoft's Direct3D.

As you saw in Chapter 2, you get a 2D drawing context from a canvas element by calling getContext("2d") on the element. Unsurprisingly, this leaves the door open for additional types of drawing contexts. WebGL also uses the canvas element, but through a 3D context. Current implementations use experimental vendor prefixes (moz-webgl, webkit-3d, etc.) as the arguments to the getContext() call. In a WebGL-enabled build of Firefox, for example, you can get a 3D context by calling getContext("moz-webgl") on a canvas element. The API of the object returned by such a call to getContext() is different from the 2D canvas equivalent, as this one provides OpenGL bindings instead of drawing operations. Rather than making calls to draw lines and fill shapes, the WebGL version of the canvas context manages textures and vertex buffers.

HTML in Three Dimensions

WebGL, like the rest of HTML5, will be an integral part of the web platform. Because WebGL renders to a canvas element, it is part of the document. You can position and transform 3D canvas elements, just as you can place images or 2D canvases on a page. In fact, you can do anything you can do with any other canvas element, including overlaying text and video and performing animations. Combining other document elements and a 3D canvas will make heads-up displays (HUDs) and mixed 2D and 3D interfaces much simpler to develop when compared to pure 3D display technologies. Imagine taking a 3D scene and using HTML markup to overlay a simple web user interface on it. Quite unlike the nonnative menus and controls found in many OpenGL applications, WebGL software will incorporate nicely styled HTML5 form elements with ease.

The existing network architecture of the Web will also complement WebGL. WebGL applications will be able to fetch resources such as textures and models from URLs. Multiplayer games can communicate with WebSocket. For example, Figure 13-1 shows an example of this in action. Google recently ported the classic 3D game Quake II to the Web using HTML5 WebSocket, Audio, and WebGL, complete with multiplayer competition. Game logic and graphics were implemented in JavaScript, making calls to a WebGL canvas for rendering. Communication to the server to coordinate player movement was achieved using a persistent WebSocket connection.

Figure 13-1. Quake II

3D Shaders

WebGL is a binding for OpenGL ES 2 in JavaScript, so it uses the programmable graphics pipeline that is standardized in OpenGL, including shaders. Shaders allow highly flexible rendering effects to be applied to a 3D scene, increasing the realism of the display. WebGL shaders are written in GL Shading Language (GLSL). This adds yet another single-purpose language to the web stack. An HTML5 application with WebGL consists of HTML for structure, CSS for style, JavaScript for logic, and GLSL for shaders. Developers can transfer their knowledge of OpenGL shaders to a similar API in a web environment.

WebGL is likely to be a foundational layer for 3D graphics on the Web. Just as JavaScript libraries have abstracted over DOM and provided powerful high-level constructs, there are libraries providing additional functionality on top of WebGL. Libraries are currently under development for scene graphs, 3D file formats such as COLLADA, and complete engines for game development. Figure 13-2 shows Shader Toy—a WebGL shader workbench built by Inigo Quilez that comes with shaders by nine other demoscene artists. This particular screenshot shows Leizex by Rgba. We can expect an explosion of high-level rendering libraries that bring 3D scene creation power to novice Web programmers in the near future.

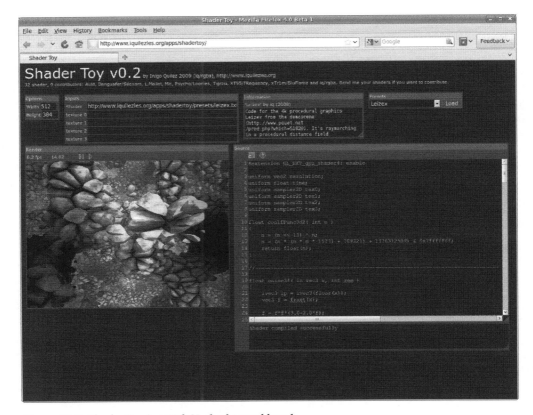

Figure 13-2. Shader Toy is a WebGL shader workbench

Devices

Web applications will need access to multimedia hardware such as webcams, microphones, or attached storage devices. For this, there is already a proposed device element to give web applications access to data streams from attached hardware. Of course, there are serious privacy implications, so not every script will be able to use your webcam at will. We will probably see a UI pattern of prompting for user permission as seen in the Geolocation and Storage APIs when an application requests elevated privileges. The obvious application for webcams is video conferencing, but there are many other amazing possibilities for computer vision in web applications including augmented reality and head tracking.

Audio Data API

Programmable audio APIs will do for <audio> what <canvas> did for <img>. Prior to the canvas tag, images on the Web were largely opaque to scripts. Image creation and manipulation had to occur on the sidelines—namely, on the server. Now, there are tools for creating and manipulating visual media based on the canvas element. Similarly, audio data APIs will enable music creation in HTML5 applications. This will help round out the content-creation capabilities available to web applications and move us closer to a self-hosting world of tools to create media on and for the Web. Imagine editing audio on the Web without having to leave the browser.

Simple playback of sounds can be done with the <audio> element. However, any application that manipulates, analyzes, or generates sound on the fly needs a lower-level API. Text-to-speech, speech-to-speech translation, synthesizers, and music visualization aren't possible without access to audio data.

We can expect the standard audio API to work well with microphone input from the data element as well as files included with audio tags. With <device> and an audio data API, you may be able to make an HTML5 application that allows users to record and edit sound from within a page. Audio clips will be able to be stored in local browser storage and reused and combined with canvas-based editing tools.

Presently, Mozilla has an experimental implementation available in nightly builds. The Mozilla audio data API could act as a starting point for standard cross-browser audio programming capabilities.

Touchscreen Device Events

As Web access shifts ever more from desktops and laptops to mobile phones and tablets, HTML5 is also continuing to adapt with changes in interaction handling. When Apple introduced the iPhone, it also introduced into its browser a set of special events that could be used to handle multitouch inputs and device rotation. Although these events have not yet been standardized, they are being picked up by other vendors of mobile devices. Learning them today will allow you to optimize your web applications for the most popular devices now.

Orientation

The simplest event to handle on a mobile device is the orientation event. The orientation event can be added to the document body:

```
<body onorientationchange="rotateDisplay();">
```

In the event handler for the orientation change, your code can reference the window.orientation property. This property will give one of the rotation values shown in Table 13-1, which is relative to the orientation the device was in when the page was initially loaded.

Table 13-1. Orientation Values and Their Meanings

Orientation Value	Meaning
0	The page is being held in the same orientation as its original load.
-90	The device has been rotated 90 degrees clockwise (right) since the original load.
180	The device has been rotated upside-down since the original page load.
90	The device has been rotated 90 degrees counter-clockwise (left) since the page was originally loaded.

Once the orientation is known, you can choose to adjust the content accordingly.

Gestures

The next type of event supported by mobile devices is a high-level event known as the *gesture*. Consider gesture events as representing a multitouch change in size or rotation. This is usually performed when the user places two or more fingers on the screen simultaneously and pinches or twists. A twist represents a rotation, while a pinch in or out represents a zoom out or in, respectively. To receive gesture events, your code needs to register one of the handlers shown in Table 13-2.

Table 13-2. Event Handlers for Gestures

Event Handler	Description
ongesturestart	A user has placed multiple fingers on the screen and has begun a movement.
ongesturechange	The user is in the process of moving multiple fingers in a scale or rotation.
ongestureend	The user has completed the scale or rotation by removing fingers.

During the gesture, the event handler is free to check the rotation and scale properties of the corresponding event and update the display accordingly. Listing 13-1 shows an example usage of the gesture handlers.

Listing 13-1. Example Gesture Handler

```
function gestureChange(event) {
  // Retrieve the amount of change in scale caused by the user gesture
  // Consider a value of 1.0 to represent the original size, while smaller
  //  numbers represent a zoom in and larger numbers represent a zoom
  //  out, based on the ratio of the scale value
var scale = event.scale;

  // Retrieve the amount of change in rotation caused by the user gesture
  // The rotation value is in degrees from 0 to 360, where positive values
  //  indicate a rotation clockwise and negative values indicate a counter-
  //  clockwise rotation
var rotation = event.rotation;

  // Update the display based on the rotation.
}

// register our gesture change listener on a document node
node.addEventListener("gesturechange", gestureChange, false);
```

Gesture events are particularly appropriate in applications that need to manipulate objects or displays, such as in diagramming tools or navigation tools.

Touches

For those cases where you need low-level control over device events, the touch events provide as much information as you will likely need. Table 13-3 shows the different touch events.

Table 13-3. Touch Events

Event Handler	Description
ontouchstart	A finger has been placed on the surface of the touch device. Multitouch events will occur as more fingers are placed on the device.
ontouchmove	One or more of the fingers on the device has moved its location in a drag operation.
ontouchend	One or more fingers have been lifted away from the device screen.
ontouchcancel	An unexpected interruption has stopped the touch operations.

Unlike the other mobile device events, the touch events need to represent that there are multiple points of data—the many potential fingers—present at the same time. As such, the API for touch handling is a little bit more complex as shown in Listing 13-2.

Listing 13-2. Touch API

```
function touchMove(event) {
// the touches list contains an entry for every finger currently touching the screen
var touches = event.touches;

  // the changedTouches list contains only those finger touches modified at this
  // moment in time, either by being added, removed, or repositioned
varchangedTouches = event.changedTouches;

  // targetTouches contains only those touches which are placed in the node
  // where this listener is registered
vartargetTouches = event.targetTouches;

  // once you have the touches you'd like to track, you can reference
  // most attributes you would normally get from other event objects
varfirstTouch = touches[0];
varfirstTouchX = firstTouch.pageX;
varfirstTouchY = firstTouch.pageY;
}

// register one of the touch listeners for our example
node.addEventListener("touchmove", touchMove, false);
```

You may find that the device's native event handling interferes with your handling of the touch and gesture events. In those cases, you should make the following call:

```
event.preventDefault();
```

319

This overrides the behavior of the default browser interface and handles the event yourself. Until the mobile events are standardized, it is recommended that you consult the documentation of the devices you are targeting with your application.

Peer-to-Peer Networking

We haven't seen the end of advanced networking in web applications either. With both HTTP and WebSocket, there is a client (the browser or other user agent) and a server (the host of the URL). Peer-to-peer (P2P) networking allows clients to communicate directly. This is often more efficient than sending all data through a server. Efficiency, of course, reduces hosting costs and improves application performance. P2P should make for faster multiplayer games and collaboration software.

Another immediate application for P2P combined with the device element is efficient video chat in HTML5. In peer-to-peer video chat, conversation partners would be able to send data directly to each other without routing through a central server. Outside of HTML5, P2P video chat has been wildly popular in applications like Skype. Because of the high bandwidth required by streaming video, it is likely that neither of those applications would have been possible without peer-to-peer communication.

Browser vendors are already experimenting with P2P networking, such as Opera's Unite technology, which hosts a simplified web server directly in the browser. Opera Unite lets users create and expose services to their peers for chatting, file sharing, and document collaboration.

Of course, P2P networking for the web will require a protocol that takes security and network intermediaries into consideration as well as an API for developers to program against.

Ultimate Direction

So far, we have focused on empowering developers to build powerful HTML5 applications. A different perspective is to consider how HTML5 empowers users of web applications. Many HTML5 features allow you to remove or reduce the complexity of scripts and perform feats that previously required plugins. HTML5 video, for example, lets you specify controls, autoplay, buffering behavior, and a placeholder image without any JavaScript. With CSS3, you can move animation and effects from scripts to styles. This declarative code makes applications more amenable to user styles and ultimately returns power to the people who use your creations every day.

You've seen how the development tools in all the modern browsers are exposing information about HTML5 features like storage, as well as critically important JavaScript debugging, profiling, and command-line evaluation. HTML5 development will trend toward simplicity, declarative code, and lightweight tools within the browsers or web applications themselves.

Google feels confident enough about the continuing evolution of HTML that it has released the Google Chrome operating system, a streamlined operating system built around a browser and media player. Google's operating system aims to include enough functionality using HTML APIs to provide a compelling user experience where applications are delivered using the standardized web infrastructure. Similarly, Microsoft has announced that Windows 8 will not support any plugins in the new Metro mode, including the company's own Silverlight plugin.

Summary

In this book, you have learned how to use powerful HTML5 APIs. Use them wisely!

In this final chapter, we have given you a glimpse of some of the things that are coming, such as 3D graphics, the new device element, touch events, and P2P networking. Development of HTML5 shows no sign of slowing down and will be very exciting to watch.

Think back for a minute. For those of you who have been surfing the Web, or perhaps even developing for it for ten years or more, consider how far HTML technology has come in just the last few years. Ten years ago, "professional HTML programming" meant learning to use the new features of HTML 4. Cutting edge developers at the time were just discovering dynamic page updates and XMLHttpRequests. The term "Ajax" was still years from introduction, even if the techniques Ajax described were starting to gain traction. Much of the professional programming in browsers was written to wrangle frames and manipulate image maps.

Today, functions that took pages of script can be performed with just markup. Multiple new methods for communication and interaction are now available to all those willing to download one of the many free HTML5 browsers, crack open their favorite text editors, and try their hands at professional HTML5 programming.

We hope you have enjoyed this exploration of web development, and we hope it has inspired your creativity. We look forward to writing about the innovations you create using HTML5 a decade from now.

Index